KOREA

One POW's Story

Lloyd L. Roberts

HUNTINGTON BEACH, CALIFORNIA

Lloyd L. Roberts
16312 Woodstock Lane
Huntington Beach, CA 92647
USA
Email: koreapowbook@gmail.com
Website: koreapow.wordpress.com
Facebook: www.facebook.com/KoreaOnePowsStory

Publisher's Note: This book is a work of non-fiction which has been self-published by the author.

Front Cover Photo (Modified): Aftermath of the May 18th Ambush of US Army 2nd Infantry Division along the Hongchon-Inje Road. (US Army Photo by Cpl R.T. Turner in the National Archives.)

Book and Cover Design: Susan Roberts

Book Layout © 2014 BookDesignTemplates.com

Korea: One POW's Story / Lloyd L. Roberts. -- 1st Edition (BW Interior)
ISBN-10:0996106316
ISBN-13:978-0-9961063-1-3

For Dorothy

CONTENTS

FORWARD

This book is being written 40 years after the events described. Many details have been forgotten, especially names. I seem to have a particular problem in remembering people's names. Days and weeks during which nothing significant happened have been lost in a haze. A day spent waiting for chow, washing your bowl and spoon and sleeping fitfully in lice infested clothing usually turned out to be just like the day before and the day after.

However, other events such as getting strafed or napalmed by F80's remain like a somewhat blurred series of color snapshots, but just as clear as something which happened last week. After forty years I can still close my eyes and look down at one of our buddies, his feet nearly severed, begging us to kill him. I remember the weather on memorable days, where the sun was and which way was north. This may be a legacy from my days as a kid when I would go hunting several times each week and at that time I always made a point of keeping track of where north was when walking through woods until it became a subconscious habit.

The chronology of events is also sometimes difficult. I may have trouble remembering whether we had attacked a certain hill before or after we had relieved the Marines for example, but the relative occurrence of an event is generally much less important than the event itself. Wherever I could, I attempted to use independent sources to date events which I remember. For example, we learned of the death of the King of England sometime in the winter of 1952 but it required a search of the library to determine the precise date.

As stated before, I have trouble remembering names. Even today, I have often been introduced to five or six new people at some engineering meeting at work and then one minute later I could not remember any of their names. However, I do remember the names of at least some of those I encountered in Korea, maybe 1% or thereabouts. In this book I have given the full name of an acquaintance the first time if is used in the text when known or remembered and thereafter I will use whatever name we used for him at the time. In other cases, I may remember a name, usually a last name such as Shepard, but I do not remember his first name. In this case Shepard will be used without any qualifications. Lastly, there are many I remember clearly, but for whom I cannot recall a name. For these I will invent a name, such as Joe or Mike and clearly indicate, the first time, that it is a fictitious name by enclosing it in single quotation marks.

And finally, let me add a word on "Truth and Fiction". There is no fiction in this account, other than the few pseudonyms used to indicate real people whose names I have forgotten or to protect the privacy of those I haven't. On a heroism scale of one to 10, 10 being equivalent to John Wayne in "The Sands of Iwo Jima," I would rate myself about a one. About all that means is that at least I never dropped my rifle and ran. I only used my rifle when I had no other choice and even then I'm quite certain that I never killed anyone because the enemy was just too far away. I have no need to inflate the facts with macho-bullshit; the plain facts themselves are sufficiently depressing, frightening, enlightening or boring as the case may be.

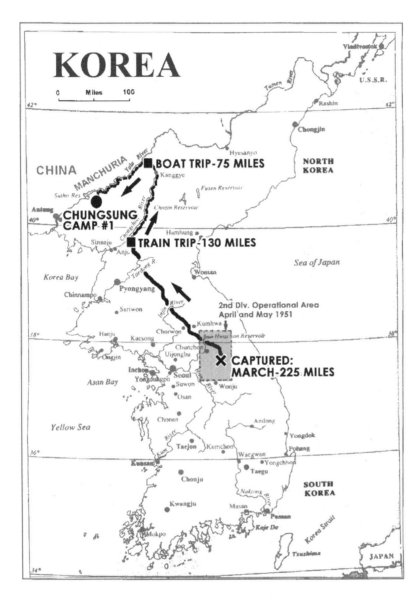

Figure 1: Korea and my estimated route to the POW Camp

PART ONE

BACK TO KOREA

CHAPTER 1

Greetings

"Greetings: *You are to report for induction . . .* " I had guessed what the letter was going to say as soon as I saw the envelope. It was late December 1950 and I had just returned to my apartment from work. Work wasn't really "work" most of the time because I enjoyed it. I was employed by the Admiral TV distributor in Minneapolis making house calls. I would service eight to 12 TV sets per day and received $3 for each call; although sometimes I had to come back several times for free until the customer was satisfied. Often I didn't get back until nine or 10 o'clock at night. This night was no exception. As I opened the letter, I was stunned. I felt sick. This wasn't supposed to happen. I thought I had done my time in the service. Another stint in the Army was the last thing I wanted.

Figure 2: M1 Carbine .30 Cal

Four years earlier it had been different; then, I had really wanted to join the Army. After I turned 18 on Sept. 30, 1946, I tried to enlist in the Army, mainly for the GI Bill, but also to get away from home or to be more accurate, away from my stepfather, who I didn't get along with. When I arrived in Fort Snelling (in St. Paul), the World War II build-up was rapidly winding down. Hundreds of veterans leaving the Army were processing through Snelling and the doctors were apparently getting very choosey about whom they accepted, so I was rejected due to poor eyesight. I still wanted to get in so they allowed me to "volunteer for the draft," as the procedure was then called. It seemed that the draft had less stringent physical requirements.

Figure 3: 105mm Howitzer

Then it was off to Fort Knox, Kentucky for eight weeks of Field Artillery Basic Training. We learned to handle the 105mm Howitzer, the 6x6 truck and the Ml Carbine. The M1 Garand was the Army's primary weapon, but we never even saw one during Basic Training. I was young and naive and usually tried to do my best at every job I was given but I also sometimes "talked back" to the Sergeant and questioned orders if I thought they didn't make sense. Needless to say, this did not endear me to either my Platoon Sergeant or my company Commander. So you can imagine the chagrin of the Captain when I qualified as best shot in the battalion on the rifle range and he had to call me into his office and present me with the award. He said I "was the last person he expected to win it." Four years later I would live to regret that award.

January 4, 1947 I left Camp Stoneman, California and shipped out of San Francisco. We sailed direct to Korea and landed in Inchon about three weeks later. I was soon settled into occupation duty at Kwangju, southwest Korea, getting more training and pulling guard duty on railroad yards, warehouses and ammunition dumps.

In Basic Training I had trained with the Carbine, but on arrival in Korea I was issued an M1 Garand. After a month we were not given any opportunity to fire the Garand, so one day while guarding an ammunition dump several miles from camp, I decided to try out my rifle anyway.

The dump contained tons of old Japanese ammunition, grenades and artillery shells leftover from WWII, as well as rifle ammo for my Garand. I borrowed a few rounds from one of the open cases, and then began looking for a likely target. I noticed several crows in a field about 200 yards away, so I got down into the prone position, sighted carefully, and fired.

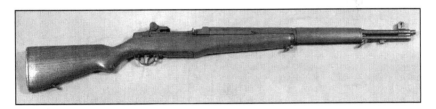

Figure 4: M1 Garand 30.06

The report was deafening and seemed to echo all over the valley, and I didn't even hit the crow. I then realized that I might be in trouble with my Sergeant, so I quickly cleaned the barrel of my rifle and replaced the shell I had fired. When we got back from guard duty, the Sergeant fell us all out and then went down the line, sniffing the barrel of each man's rifle, and counting to verify that we each had the eight shells we had been issued. We all had the proper number of bullets and he was unable to detect the odor of gunpowder, so the Sarge couldn't pin it on any of us. I was the Number One screw-up in his squad, so he was quite sure I had been the culprit, and he told me so. But I didn't care; I had gotten away with another one.

We often interacted with the local civilians (especially the kids) while guarding facilities and I thought they were interesting and basically not much different from us. But to some of the GI's, they were just "Gooks." I remember one day as we drove along the highway in a convoy of trucks, we were passing an old Korean man with a long white beard, a tall black hat and dressed in a traditional white blouse and baggy pants, riding his bicycle into town. A soldier on the truck ahead leaned over the side, grabbed the old Korean and sent him flying end over end into the ditch. The guys in the truck ahead seemed to find this highly amusing. I didn't see anything funny as I watched the old man pick himself up from the ditch behind us. Incidents like this undoubtedly left a legacy of hatred among the Korean population. Three years later when North Korea invaded the south and pushed us into the Pusan Perimeter, some of these civilians may have welcomed the opportunity to get even.

It was April 1947, and it seemed as if I had only just arrived in Korea, when they said I was shipping out. It seems that Congress had decided to end the World War II draft law and that was what I had volunteered into. I was going home whether I wanted to or not. On May 28, 1947, I was discharged and on my way home. I wasn't too disappointed because I now was eligible for the GI Bill. I soon enrolled at Dunwoody Institute in Minneapolis studying electronics and put Korea completely out of my mind.

In June 1950 I graduated from Dunwoody and started my first job as a TV repairman. TV was still very new. Minneapolis only had two or three stations and some of them were still broadcasting test patterns until 10 o'clock in the morning. At night you could tune in Kukla, Fran and Ollie, Milton Berle and Jackie Gleason. I serviced TV sets all day long, but I couldn't afford to buy one; so I built one from scratch. I bought and scrounged parts wherever I could and finally got it working but I still didn't watch much TV. I was working long hours, six days a week, and most of my spare time was spent building HAM radio equipment and reading electronics books.

On June 25th, 1950, North Korea invaded South Korea. By all accounts I have read later this was a momentous occasion. Truman cut short his trip home to Missouri, rushed back to the White House and called numerous late night sessions to review the situation. I remember almost none of this. I went about my job and leisure activities only dimly aware that there was a small "Police Action" going on in the Far East. And here I was one of the very few who had actually been to this country. The average person had no idea where Korea was and could care less. I really didn't care either. I was not an avid reader of newspapers or magazines and didn't follow the war news closely on the radio or TV. Korea was not my problem.

The letter of "Greetings" had been a rude shock. Suddenly I was exquisitely aware of Korea. Thousands of guys were dying over there. I could be one of them. I wondered what I could do to avoid this. Someone suggested I write to the Draft Board and state that Mankato (not Minneapolis) was my hometown. If nothing else, this might buy me a little time. It did, but only two weeks. I got another letter of greetings, this time from the Mankato Draft Board. I was now resigned to my fate, so I wrapped-up my affairs, stored my electronics equipment, tools and clothes and got ready to leave. All I could do now was keep my fingers crossed and hope I got a job somewhere in electronics or communications.

CHAPTER TWO

Drafted Again

I was to report to Fort Riley, Kansas on January 15th, 1951 for induction, medical tests and processing. We got off the train at Manhattan, Kansas, the closest town to Fort Riley and were bused into camp. It was like all other army camps: rows and rows of two-story barracks left over from WW II.

One of the first things we did was get tetanus, typhoid and smallpox shots. Then we began the paper work processing. The processing was like all the previous times in the army. You would start in the morning with your papers and be herded from one building to the next, and from one clerk-typist to the next, each with the responsibility for filling out some small portion of your papers. This would continue all day.

One of these clerk-typists noted my TV experience, my HAM radio license with Morse-Code qualification at 20 words per minute, and my First Class Radiotelephone license and said I was a cinch to get into military communications. He then looked down a list of job specialties called Military Operations Specialties (MOS) and assigned me a 4-digit number corresponding to "Radio Station Operator." I felt greatly relieved, at least, I wasn't going into the infantry. It never occurred to me to question that this MOS had been assigned to me by a lowly Corporal who made his decision after less than one minute of consideration.

Every day, shipping orders were posted on the wall in one of the buildings. Some were going to Europe, a few were being posted stateside but most were going to Korea or Japan. I finally spotted my name on the board. I was to return home for about a week leave and then report to Pier 91, a Navy embarkation point in Seattle. From there, I would ship to Japan. Well, that didn't sound too bad. In fact, I thought I had it made and felt a little sorry for the guys who I knew were going to be sent straight to the front line.

The furlough home went too fast and when that last day arrived, I packed my duffle bag and we drove to the train depot in Mankato. It was a February night, late, dark and cold. My mother was the only one seeing me off. As the train pulled out, I glanced back just once. She was still standing under the dim platform light. She had seemed worried about my leaving and I sensed that she felt she might never see me again, but I wasn't as concerned as I should have been. At worst, I thought it would just be a couple of years out of my life wasted in some uninteresting job in the Army.

The train ride across North Dakota and Montana was as monotonous as the view out the window despite the occasional stops for passengers. I began to notice that now almost half the passengers were in uniform. It was beginning to look more like a troop train than a passenger train. In the afternoon, the mind numbing view out the window was interrupted by a small procession of soldiers swaying down the aisle, some of them obviously very drunk and one carrying a half full fifth of bourbon. The parade was led by a young, plump and very homely girl, probably in her twenties. She disappeared into a small compartment at the back end of the car with one of the soldiers, the others waited patiently as lap dogs in line outside the compartment door. It took me a moment to realize what was going on, and then I felt a little embarrassed. I glanced around furtively at some of the nearby civilians. A few had silly grins on their faces but most were trying very hard to make believe that they didn't see a thing.

We pulled into Seattle and were bused to Pier 91. I didn't know what I was doing at a Navy base. It was right on the "Sound" with Navy ships docked nearby. I didn't wonder very long because somebody hollered "Chow!" and I was hungry. It was a small mess hall with a big sign - "Take all you want, eat all you take." They were having big thick steaks, mashed potatoes, gravy and apple pie a-la-mode, the works. I ate everything, and then went back for seconds, another steak and more apple pie. I wondered why in hell I hadn't enlisted in the Navy.

That only lasted one day and then we were trucked to Fort Lawton. It was Feb. 15th and I had now been in the Army for one month. We went through more processing but mostly it was just waiting around and pulling KP (Kitchen Police). I filled out a $40 allotment to my mother so she could make the car payments on my '50 Chevy, and then got some more shots, Typhus and Cholera in addition to the ones I had received at Ft. Riley.

> If I hadn't been so dumb and trusting I might have figured out that maybe they were sending me to a country more primitive than Japan. In fact, I had now received the same series of shots that I had received before shipping out to Korea in 1947.

Around February 27, we finally found out what we had all been waiting around for, enough guys to fill up a ship. It was one of the "Liberty" ships left over from WW II and named for some general we've never heard of. Trucks shuttled men all day by the hundreds. When our turn came, we grabbed our duffle bags and lined up at the gangplank. When the sergeant called your name, you would sing-out, "YO" and stagger up the gangplank into the side of the ship. We then struggled down two levels to the bowels of the ship. Our room was immense and seemed to extend from one side of the ship to the other. Hundreds of poles extended from floor to ceiling. Each pair of poles supported four bunks which could be swung up when not being used. When the bunks were down, the aisles between them were only about

2 feet wide. These rooms extended almost from bow to stern and from the main deck, four decks down into the belly of the ship, except for some areas occupied by the engine rooms, etc. They said it held 5000 troops, and I didn't doubt it. As we eased out of the berth, it seemed like all 5000 guys were topside for a last look at the USA.

For about 34,000 men, it would truly be their last look. This was the number killed in the three years of war. (**Blair**, *The Forgotten War*, p. ix)

Not many were smiling. I, however, I was feeling quite buoyant, after all they had told me I was going to Japan to be a Radio Station Operator. This could be a fun adventure. I might even learn something useful. I glanced again at some of the faces gazing at the receding shoreline and felt a twinge of guilt. I was probably going to end up in some cushy job in Japan, while most of these guys were headed for the front line and some would be coming home in a box.

We covered 300 to 500 miles a day. The North Pacific in winter was cold, wet and windy. We seemed to hit a storm every few days, and I don't remember ever seeing the sun. The first night we hit one helluva storm. Guys started getting sick right away. Many tried to tough-it-out and act macho. Only sissies got sick! Soon guys were running to the head or heading topside, but many didn't make it. They were vomiting all over the floor, in their bunks, and in the hallways. As the ship rolled from side to side, vomit began running across the floor in little slimy streams and dripping down the stairs in the gangways on the way topside. I headed for the "head" about the 6th time, but when I opened the steel hatch, I changed my mind. A toilet had become plugged and was overflowing. The floor was covered with about 4 inches of seawater, vomit, paper, etc. and each time the ship rolled, a wave about 2 feet deep would crash against first one wall, then the other.

I headed topside. The ocean was pitch-black. The wind roared in the rigging, and rain and sleet beat against my face. I headed for the rail, then slipped and slid head first into the scupper. I caught the edge and stopped with my head all the way through the hole. I momentarily glimpsed the black ocean and white foam along the bow as I pulled myself back. I looked at the scupper; it wasn't big enough for a man to pass through; though if I had gone overboard, no one would have known I was gone until roll call the next morning.

After a miserable twelve days, we landed in Japan around March 12 and were trucked to a nearby base. We started processing again immediately, but this time it went much faster. I entered a large room with many desks and a PFC or corporal at each desk typing away. I sat down at the next available desk and some PFC glanced at my papers. He said there weren't any openings for "radio station operators," so he gave me a new MOS: another four digit number which this time signified, "Field Radio Repairman." I began to have a sinking feeling. What did the "Field" in Field Radio Repairman mean? He said that would probably be radio repair somewhere behind the front lines. I was beginning to see how the Army worked. Everything depended on some PFC sitting at a typewriter who probably didn't give a damn if you got into the right job or not. I was also beginning to regret that excellent score I had made on the rifle range back in Basic Training four years previously.

We left about Mar 19th on a Japanese passenger train headed south. Many of the passengers were soldiers headed for Korea. We clattered along through the countryside of low hills and rice paddies. At the larger towns, we would stop for a few minutes. Vendors crowded around at each stop trying to sell us food and junk trinkets. About midday we pulled into a large city. The sign said Hiroshima. It had been just a little more than five years since "the bomb" had been dropped and yet the place was teeming with people. The city seemed to consist of thousands of small one story tin shacks, many of them obviously made out of salvaged material. They didn't seem to resent us; they were just interested in trying to sell us something. A few hours later, we arrived at a seaport and loaded on a large ocean going ferry for the short trip across the Sea of Japan to Pusan, Korea.

CHAPTER THREE

Korea Again

We sailed northwest all night. The sea was surprisingly calm. In the morning we arrived at Pusan. It was the busiest, most chaotic port I had ever been in. It was filthy dirty with ships being unloaded on all sides by equally filthy Korean stevedores. Ammunition, C Rations and everything else needed for a war was piled on the docks, sometimes two or three stories high. Trucks were hauling it off as fast as they could.

We filed into a large empty warehouse. A few men were sorted out for various destinations, but most of us were again herded onto a nearby train. The cars were ancient and dilapidated, the seats hard and straight backed. Heat was provided by a small wood burning stove in the middle of each car. We headed north. It grew dark and cold, the cars swayed and rattled. The only light was from a few kerosene lanterns and the fire in the wood stove. Some heated C Rations on the stove or boiled coffee, others played cards, most just talked or tried to sleep.

A rumor rustled through the car. Two guys had shot themselves in another car. One had shot himself in the leg with a 45 automatic. No one doubted it. It got a little quieter and the cars rattled on. I found it impossible to sleep.

The next day we arrived in a "place." It was always that way. You were moved from one "place" to another "place." I guess someone knew the names of these places but somehow it never filtered down to me. This particular place was somewhere in the mountains of central

Korea, well below the front lines. It was cold, with patches of snow still on the ground. We were marched up a hill to an old Japanese army barracks left over from their 40 years occupation of Korea. It was amazing that the buildings were still standing, since the war must have come through there at least twice in the previous six months.

We had been issued fatigues and combat boots in the 'states', but I had continued to wear my low-cut oxford dress shoes until I arrived in Korea because they were more comfortable. This was another one of my many mistakes. I should have been wearing my combat boots every day to break them in and get my feet used to them. But then, of course, I was going to be operating a radio transmitter at some cushy post. What would I need combat boots for? So far they hadn't really bothered me very much. We hardly walked anyplace except between ship, train and truck. I was wearing my combat boots as we hiked the few hundred yards up to the old barracks but my feet still hadn't had a real workout.

We found bunks for the night and someone got the wood stove in our room going. It felt like about 20 degrees F outside and the pungent odor of pine smoke filled the building. I always liked the smell of burning pine from a campfire or stove. It was almost cozy. We hit the sack.

The old barracks must have been a replacement staging area, because the following morning men started moving out to different units. Some of us were loaded on a 6x6 for a long bone jarring ride to the 2nd Division rear area. The weather was warming up because now we were getting a cold rain mixed with sleet. After several hours the truck stopped, overlooking a small valley full of tents, equipment and soldiers. Three of us, a young Mexican kid, another white soldier and myself, were told to grab our duffle bags and climb down. The driver pointed to a large Khaki windowless van parked about a half mile away.

This was the longest walk I had attempted since I had entered the Army and I now became painfully aware of just how out of shape I was. The other two guys were no better off. We stopped several times and set our 60 lb. duffel bags down for a rest. When we arrived at the van we could see that it was some type of mobile radio maintenance unit. About this time, the three of us discovered that we all had the same MOS, Field Radio Repair. Maybe this was where we were going to be working. The area looked fairly safe and we couldn't hear any big guns. I guessed I could put up with that, as long as no one was shooting at me.

A canvas flap over the door to the van parted and a short, wiry, young Spanish-looking tech sergeant stepped out. He was neatly dressed in wool dress khakis and a field jacket. He looked sharp compared to our fatigues. He asked the other white kid to come inside. In about two minutes the sergeant ushered the white kid out again and told me to come inside.

The flap closed behind me and my eyes adjusted to the dimmer light in a few seconds. Both walls of the van were lined with work benches and test equipment. Each bench seemed to have specialized test equipment for servicing certain types of radios. There was only one other person in the van, a Spanish/Mexican looking technician working on a transceiver. The sergeant said they were looking for only one technician and asked what experience I had. I told him about the TV repair as well as the HAM radio experience. After a couple of minutes, he told me to wait outside as he called the young Mexican kid in.

When the sergeant disappeared inside, I mentioned to the other white kid with me that I didn't think we had a hope in hell of getting the job. That would be one "chip on my shoulder." After a few very brief moments, the sergeant stepped back outside and told us we should report to E Company, 23rd regiment, which was camped in reserve up in the hills not too far away. I asked what we would be doing and he answered with no trace of apology in his voice, "you're going to be infantry riflemen, I guess." I was angry. I felt betrayed. I realized that they had lied to me or at least had been "kidding me along" ever since I had been drafted.

Why couldn't they just have told me that there was damn little chance of getting a job working on radios? Why couldn't they have just told me that I most likely would be going into an infantry unit? I could have done things differently. I would have better prepared myself. We climbed into the back of a jeep and the driver headed up toward the hills. Now I was starting out with two chips on my shoulder.

CHAPTER FOUR

Rifleman

The 2nd Infantry Division consisted of three regiments: the 9th, 23rd, (the one I was in) and the 38th. Each regiment had 3 to 4000 men made up from 3 battalions of about 900 men each. Each battalion, in turn, consisted of 4 companies and finally, the company was made up of about 200 men. The company was broken down into 3 platoons. Each platoon was led by a lieutenant. The company commander was a Captain. The platoon was further broken down into squads of anywhere from five to 15 men, depending on how many got shot that day and whether or not replacements were available. The companies in a battalion were designated by the letters A through L and these were supplemented by headquarters companies and often other units. The 2nd Division also had two extra battalions attached; these were the Dutch attached to the 38th regiment and the French attached to our 23rd Regiment. (**Blair**, *The Forgotten War,* p. 611)

I was in "Easy" Company; this meant that we were the first of four Companies in the 2nd battalion of the 23rd regiment of the 2nd Division. Anytime the 2nd Division was active on the front, usually only two regiments would be fighting, while the third would be held in ready reserve a few miles back.

Our driver stopped the jeep by a broad ravine and said, "*This is it.*" We got out, hoisting our duffle bags after us. He pointed up the hill and indicated that "E" Company was up there. We trudged up a muddy track till the broad slope leveled out a couple of hundred yards from the road. Many small "pup tents" were visible all along the ravine under the trees. A few larger tents probably indicated Company Headquarters. We were directed to the First Sergeants tent.

A First Sergeant is sort of a general manager for the infantry Company. He handles personnel problems, sees that the troops are fed and generally takes care of all the mundane duties of a combat unit.

This First Sergeant was a middle aged, unremarkable man. He didn't seem interested in seeing us. I was sent to 2nd Platoon and told to ask for my new squad leader, 'Emil Erdman'. He, in turn, assigned me to share a pup tent with Albert DeSmet, a kid from Michigan. A few of the guys asked me where I was from but most just kept to themselves or sat in their tents writing letters or cleaning their rifles. I unpacked some things and got my mess kit ready; we were having hot chow. We got in line and the servers dumped several spoonful's of stew, potatoes and canned peaches in my mess kit. I saw why they called it a "mess kit." Everything ended up in one mess in the middle. Oh well, it still tasted good because I hadn't eaten since breakfast. It was starting to drizzle. I sat on a box and shoveled my chow down as fast as I could, rinsed my canteen in the tub of hot water and headed back to my tent.

It was getting dark and a light rain was falling. Al showed me where to roll out my sleeping bag and said we'd better hit the sack because things always got started early in a line unit. I tried to sleep but couldn't and instead lay awake tossing and turning, wondering where I had gone wrong. I felt like a trapped animal, but finally dozed-off.

The 23rd Regiment of the 2nd Division had gone into reserve on March 13, 1951 near Saemal, Central Korea, 50 miles east of Seoul and about 10 miles NE of Wonju. **Figure 5** shows the operational area of the 2nd Division during April/May and this is also shown by the dotted rectangle on **Figure 1**. The 2nd Division was reorganizing and refilling their ranks after the slaughter of February 12th and 13th near Hoengsong where two battalions had been surrounded by the Chinese Communist Forces (CCF). They had lost most of their big guns and trucks and had sustained 100 killed, 500 wounded and almost 1000 missing and presumed captured. But the CCF winter offensive had been halted and UN Forces had begun tentative moves northward to regain some of the lost territory. (**Blair**; *pp. 491,755)*

I didn't realize it at the time, but I had joined a discouraged and defeated unit. This was the second defeat, having been similarly cut off and savaged on November 29 at Kunuri. This probably explained the somber disinterested reception I had been given.

The Company was in reserve, but that didn't mean that we would just lie around shooting the breeze. This was a time to train, clean weapons, repair equipment and patrol. You might think a patrol while in reserve would be a "walk in the park," but there were estimates of as many as 14,000 North Korean gorillas and CCF stragglers in the mountains to the east of us. (**Blair**, *The Forgotten War*, p. 776) A simple training patrol could quickly turn into a nasty situation if you ran into only a small fraction of those guys.

They got right down to business with me. I was issued an M1 rifle first thing. Someone noted the serial number. It was clean and well-oiled but also obviously well used. I noted that the stock had several notches cut in it, along with innumerable scratches and dings. I had no desire to add any more notches.

I was also outfitted with all the other paraphernalia of an infantry soldier. This consisted of: (1) a shelter half, and pole which when combined with your buddy's half, formed a small pup tent, (2) blanket, (3) backpack, (4) belt with canteen, (5) ammo, (6) shovel, (7) first-aid pack and bayonet, and (8) sleeping bag.

When going on patrol we would break down our tent and each guy would spread his shelter-half out on the ground then lay the blanket on top. Next you would roll the whole thing up into a tight roll with the tent pole and pegs inside. This roll would then be bent over the top of the backpack and tied down in the shape of an upside down "U." The rolled-up sleeping bag was then tied below the pack. Inside the pack you would carry extra socks, shirts, pants, a few C rations you may have squirreled away, or anything else you wanted to pack around.

The next morning after chow we were told to pack-up. We were going on patrol. The lieutenant, our platoon leader, called me over to inform me that I was going to be his telephone runner. Whenever dug-in on a defensive position, it would be my job to string wire from my platoon to the company commander's bunker and set-up the telephones so all the platoons could be tied in together. I grunted an "ok," then found out that I also had to carry one or two rolls of telephone wire and a hand-crank telephone in addition to my pack, M1, a couple of grenades and maybe a couple of bandoliers of ammo. I guessed that this whole pile of equipment would weigh from 60 to 80 pounds.

We headed out for the hills and started climbing. The Lieutenant insisted I keep up with him. I did, until the hill got really steep. I was in no shape for this and gradually fell behind. Some of the other new guys were in no better shape and also fell behind but at least they weren't carrying rolls of wire and a telephone. My new boots started to really pinch in the back of the ankle. I now remembered some sergeant telling me, years before in boot camp, that new boots should be soaked in water overnight and then worn until they were dry. This was one of the things I could have done if I had been told I was going into the infantry.

All morning we struggled up the muddy, rocky trail through a heavy pine forest. I had to rest about every 100 feet and was now bringing up the rear of the entire company. The lieutenant would lope back to the rear every once in a while to chew me out for not keeping up, then he would head back up the hill almost at a trot. He never once asked what I had been doing for the last four years.

After climbing about 2000 feet, the trail began to level-off. I began to move a little faster but so did everyone else. I was still bringing up the rear. Up ahead, "E" Company had apparently stopped and spread out along the ridge line. They were digging fox holes when I arrived. The lieutenant wanted the telephone wire strung out immediately. I set up the phones and checked them out then looked around for my buddy Al. He had by then finished our foxhole and it was about chow time. I was almost too tired to eat. I opened a can of cold C rations anyway and along with hard biscuits and chocolate made a meal, of sorts.

The squad leader came around to our foxholes as dusk was falling. He said each foxhole had to keep one guy on guard duty throughout the night. This meant two hours on and 2 hours off. I didn't think I could stay awake any longer so Al took the first shift. It seemed only minutes later when someone was shaking me. It was Al. It was pitch black and my radium dial watch said ten o'clock. Somehow I had to keep awake two more hours. I sat up and peered out over the edge of the hole. I couldn't see anything but occasionally I heard faint rustling from nearby foxholes. We somehow made it through the night without falling asleep on guard duty. In the morning I was told to see the captain. He was very irritated with me for not keeping up and said they were getting someone else to be runner. From then on I was going to be just an ordinary grunt rifleman. I was almost relieved.

We picked up and headed out once again. It was somewhat easier to keep up now without the telephone wire. Near dusk we camped in a small wooded valley. It was eerily quiet. The low wooded hills around were equally silent. Not even the rumble of distant guns. We dug in around the perimeter and heated our C ration cans and hot chocolate. It began to feel like all of those supposed 14,000 guerrillas loose in the hills were peering down at us. But the officers didn't seem concerned at all. I hoped they knew what they were doing.

One of the guys was carrying a small portable broadcast receiver in his pack. We tried to get some music or news but only got a lot of static and some Korean stations. Armed Forces Radio Station (AFRS) in Japan was barely audible through the static. When I had arrived in Japan, this was the station I thought I was going to be working at. I didn't care to be reminded. I decided we needed a better antenna. Wire for an antenna was never a problem in Korea. Wherever the US Army traveled they just reeled out telephone wire by the mile from the back of a jeep. If a wire broke someplace and they lost the telephone connection, instead of looking for the break, they would often just run another wire along the ditch. Some ditches along well traveled roads appeared to have hundreds of wires lying in them. Even the trail through our remote wooded valley had numerous old telephone wires lying around, so I grabbed a few and pulled on them till I found a broken one. I then dragged about a thousand feet of wire up a low 200 foot hill north of camp and tied it to a tree. I then came back down and stretched the wire to another tree next to the radio and hooked it up. AFRS now came in clear as a bell.

The lieutenant picked me and three other greenhorns and sent us up on the hill near where the other end of my antenna was tied. This hill was really a ridge line heading north. We were supposed to dig in and post guards 2 on and 2 off all night. He hinted that if anyone tried to sneak up on us during the night, they might come that way. I suspect he picked me because, if I had time to screw around with the radio antenna, then maybe I deserved a little extra duty. It was getting quite dark by the time we got to the top of the hill. Luckily we found several old fox holes still in good shape and settled in for the night. This was only a training patrol and I figured the lieutenant was just trying to scare us with all the talk of guerrillas. He did a damn good job. We knew the woods must be full of little animals, but how much noise would a big two legged animal make. Every so often one would hear the rustle of leaves. You could swear some of the shadows moved. I didn't sleep much that night. I don't think anybody did.

Morning! I was bushed but relieved to see daylight. All of the previous nights' sinister shadows revealed themselves to be just bushes. I felt a little foolish, but reminded myself that one of these nights the shadows really would move.

The day was cold and cloudy. Light rain was falling. We dug out our ponchos and slipped them over our heads. The poncho was one of the better inventions of the Army. It was just a simple 6-foot square waterproof tarp with a hole in the middle. The hole had a drawstring so you could pull it tight around your neck. You then put your helmet back on. No matter how hard it rained, you stayed snug and dry underneath. It was just like walking along with a small tent draped over you, your pack and your rifle. If you needed to get to your rifle in a hurry, it was easy to just flip the poncho up out of the way and unsling the rifle.

"E" Company moved on, winding its way up into some low pine-covered hills. We dug in for the night just below a ridge line overlooking a valley. Our ponchos now served to keep most of the rain out of our foxhole. We just stretched them over the top and weighed the sides down with rocks, leaving a small opening to peer out of.

I woke up. Something cold was in my face. Sometime in the night about a foot of heavy wet snow had fallen and collapsed our ponchos' on top of us. It was still coming down but it was not cold. After breakfast we slipped and slid down the mountain to a gravel road winding along the hill sides. The snow turned to rain and we set up camp in the valley near some rice paddies. Everyone dug foxholes although we didn't seem to be near any action. I supposed it was just part of the training. After dark, the rain was coming down in sheets. Everything was soaked. We threw up small dikes around our foxholes to keep the rain out. No one was going to attack in this weather, so we both just crawled into our hole and went to sleep. It didn't last long. I was violently awakened by a roar as about 10 gallons of ice water dumped on my head. We quickly stretched the ponchos back again and weighed them down with bigger rocks, then bailed most of the water out of the bottom of our hole. By now we were both thoroughly soaked, cold and completely miserable. I wondered if any army has solved the problem of living in foxholes during heavy rain without getting wet.

Daylight was never more welcome. The rain had stopped but everything was still soaked. After a few miles of walking along the road we began to dry out a little. We headed back into the hills on a narrow path along the bottom of a steep wooded ravine. I hadn't gotten much sleep for several nights and was feeling a little light-headed. I also had a general go-to-hell attitude about damn near everything concerned with the army. I started thinking that I had only fired the M1 rifle, which I had been carrying all over those hills, one time and that was about three years before. The M1 fires a 30.06 caliber high velocity bullet. The cartridge is about two and 1/4 inch long compared to about one and 1/2 inch for the cartridge of the M1 Carbine which I trained with in 1946. Since this was a training exercise, I thought, in my "don't give a damn way," why not try out my rifle on some harmless target. With no further thought I paused, raised my M1, aimed at a tree up on the side of the hill and fired. The report was almost deafening as it echoed up and down the ravine. I have never seen 250 men so instantly galvanized into action. Most either hit the ground or dived for cover while frantically readying their weapons. Two hundred and forty-nine pairs of eyes raked the hillsides for the enemy, then finding none, they turned on me.

As soon as the shot rang-out, I knew it was a mistake. It was an impulsive and stupid thing to do. Most of those guys had survived at least two massacres and numerous firefights and skirmishes. That's how you survive, by reacting instantly and instinctively. I got chewed out by everyone from my squad leader up to the company commander for the next half hour. I deserved every bit of it, but secretly a little Devil on my shoulder was smirking and enjoying himself the rest of the day.

After supper, we got word that we were going on a night training patrol. Our platoon leader, a lieutenant, started out after dark and we followed in single file. It was a very dark, overcast night and each step was an act of faith; faith in the guy ahead who was supposed to whisper a warning each time he had to avoid some obstacle. It didn't always work; sometimes you fell in an abandoned foxhole or tripped over a rice paddy dike. I didn't know how the lieutenant knew where he was going. We had been stumbling along for over an hour when suddenly there was a muffled pop high overhead and the entire valley was bathed in white light. The word was quickly passed down to drop to the ground and freeze. We lay motionless as more flares illuminated the valley to our left and right. I expected any moment to hear machine guns open up on us, but all was quiet. After an eternity, the last flare winked out and we cautiously moved on. I wondered if these were Chinese flares or some from our own side and just part of the training. Our night vision didn't return for several more minutes, but soon we didn't need night vision as distant search lights, several miles away, were switched on and played their beams on the low cloud layers. These lights were "friendlies" and they provided just enough light in our area to permit us to rapidly retrace our steps back to our foxholes. After I got back, I concluded that everything had just been part of a training exercise.

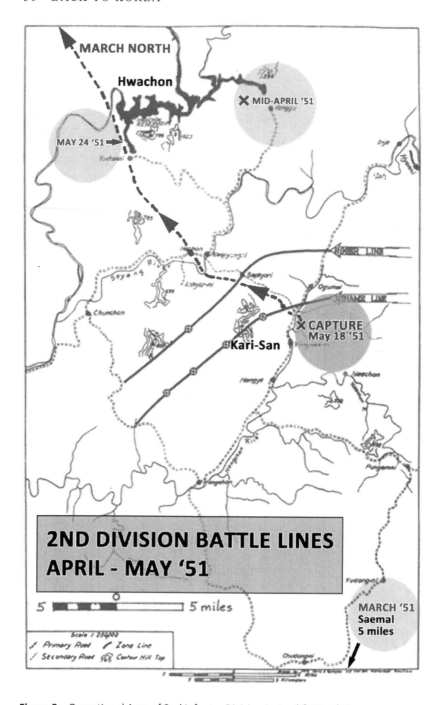

Figure 5: Operational Area of 2nd Infantry Division in April & May '51

CHAPTER FIVE

Into The Line

The 23rd was coming out of reserve. We were to assemble at Hongchon, about 20 miles north of Saemal where we had spent the last two weeks in reserve, mostly in training patrols (see **Figure 5** and **Figure 11**). It was April 1, 1951 and we were scheduled to relieve the 5th Marine regiment on April 3 on the Soyang river, just north of Chunchon. The goal for this drive was to push the Chinese north to line Kansas. Objectives defined by lines across the terrain were often given names such as, Arizona, Reno or Fish. In this case, Kansas was a line running across Korea from the Imjin River north of Seoul, then south of the Hwachon reservoir to Yang Yang on the east coast. The 2nd Division would be moving up the mountainous central region toward Hwachon Reservoir. (**Munroe**, p. 121)

The Company loaded up on 6x6's and we headed out. I didn't know where. No one ever bothered to tell us where we were or where we were going. Often we only had a few minutes' notice. It was just; "Fall out with all your gear in 10 minutes. We're moving out." You would pile into the back of the truck on hard wooden seats along both sides. The canvas top would be rolled back in good weather. In cold or rainy weather, the top would be covered. If you sat close to the front you could see virtually nothing as you bounced and jolted along rutted narrow roads. Sitting near the back at least you could see where you had been while getting a face full of dust and exhaust fumes.

We passed through what was left of a large Korean city, (probably Wonju.) It was totally flattened, just piles of rubble with the remains of a chimney sticking up here and there along with a few shattered tree trunks. I don't recall ever seeing any Korean city that was not flattened, other than those in the Pusan perimeter. We crossed a large river on a temporary bridge. All the bridges were temporary. Some had been blown up three or four times.

Figure 6: GMC 6x6 Cargo Truck

After hours of bone jarring, monotonous miles we stopped at what was left of a small town. A few houses were actually still standing. They had no windows or doors, but at least they kept the rain off. We moved in to stay the night. With nothing better to do, we nosed around the neighborhood. Someone noticed what appeared to be a trap door leading to a root cellar behind one of the houses. We pried it open and peered inside. It was piled from floor to ceiling with silk goods. Some of the guys started pulling them out and scattering them around on the ground. There were beautiful silk dresses, blouses and pants along with big soft, white comforters. Those were obviously somebody's most prized possessions which they had hoped to save, and they had belonged to people we were supposed to be helping. I thought this was senseless destruction and would only make more enemies for us.

In the morning I got up, heated some C rations, and then wandered around some more to check out the area. Some tanks had pulled into our front yard during the night. They seemed to be just sitting there, waiting around like we were. I was walking along not paying attention, when the nearest tank, about 100 feet away, fired his 90-mm gun. I must have jumped a foot. Now I knew how the guys must have felt when I had fired my M1 without warning them.

We were told to be ready to move out in an hour or so, but first we had to be deloused. Some medic had checked the Korean houses we were sleeping in and found them full of lice. We lined up and the guy squirted DDT down our shirts and pants and in our hair. We piled back into the trucks and headed north again.

Our company had been dropped off close to the front lines. We moved up into the nearby low hills by the road and dug in from force of habit. The front was still well to the north. We seemed to be waiting for other units to catch up. Some more new replacements joined the company. By now I was a veteran of more than two weeks. 'Dick', one of the new guys, was told to buddy-up with me. I showed him how to dig a foxhole. It was a warm sunny spring day. The ground wasn't too bad. After an hour or so we had a nice hole, about 4 feet deep just over the ridge line and looking down on a broad rice paddy about 400 yards below.

Dick seemed to be excited and gung ho about the prospect of going into action. He said he couldn't wait to shoot an enemy soldier. I didn't point out that they often shot back. As we were tidying up our foxhole, we noticed a Korean civilian dressed in white walking across the field below. Dick raised his M1 and took aim. I said, "Wait a minute!" and pushed the muzzle of the rifle up a few inches and asked him what the hell he was doing. He said, "I just want to get myself a Gook." I explained that it was probably the farmer that owned the land there and he was most likely on our side. This was just another example of the attitude of a few of the guys. As long as there was a war going on, apparently they thought all the laws had been suspended, and they could do pretty much whatever they damn well felt like.

The next morning Easy Company moved out along with the entire 2nd battalion. The column wound single file up into the mountains. It was warm and sunny. We snaked up along a wooded ridge line to the north. It looked like we would be ready for anything. We had no Korean bearers so everybody had to carry something extra. In addition to my usual pack and rifle, I was lugging several bandoliers of M1 ammo, half a dozen grenades, a BAR (Browning Automatic Rifle) and some BAR ammo. The BAR was a 30-caliber machine gun with a tripod which could be fired as a hand-held weapon if you were in a hurry. It used large bottom loading clips of ammo and it was heavy. Its 16 pounds felt like 30 pounds by the time I had climbed a thousand feet.

Figure 7: Browning Automatic Rifle (BAR)

I didn't dare complain too much though, because some of the men were packing 98 pound cases of 30 caliber ammo. My feet were getting worse all the time. Starting out in the morning was the worst. The backs of both ankles were rubbed raw. Tape didn't seem to help much either, in spite of two pairs of socks. But after an hour or so of walking, the ankles became a little numb and just bearable. However, I knew that the next morning it would be the same all over again, or worse.

Everybody was having a tough time. We would climb a hundred feet, rest a minute, and then climb another hundred. Some of the guys in the heavy weapons platoon were pooping-out. The sergeant had me swap my BAR for the 75mm recoilless rifle they were carrying. It was about 7 feet long and fired a 3-inch shell. I don't know how much it weighed, but it felt like a ton. It mounted on a heavy tripod which some other poor bastard had to carry. The shells were about 3 inches in diameter and maybe 2 ½ feet long. The casing holding the shell and powder was full of small holes to let the gases escape out the back of the gun as the shell was propelled forward down the barrel. The object was to fire a large high explosive shell from a relatively light weight gun without generating any recoil. As you can imagine, you didn't want to stand behind when it fired. I didn't last more than 500 feet before I had enough. I traded for some 75mm shells which didn't feel much lighter.

As we neared the top of our mountain, the Marines started coming down past us. We just pulled off to the side and sat down to let them pass. They looked tough and confident. Compared to them, we were mostly a bunch of sad sacks. Of course, we were on our way up and totally pooped while they were well rested and headed down into reserve. They didn't miss the chance to make the usual derogatory remarks about our appearance or poke fun at the army in general. What I found difficult to understand, however, was that most of them seemed to be enjoying what they were doing.

Since we were taking over the Marine positions, we at least didn't have to dig foxholes. We were told to expect an attack that night. Mines and booby traps had been set up down the hill in front of our holes. This was not training anymore. This was for real. No one complained when the squad leader told us it was 2 hours on and 2 hours off. Everything was okay until I went on the Midnight to 2:00 A.M. watch. They said this was the hour the Chinese liked best for attack. The night dragged on forever. Somebody got jumpy and a few shots were fired. It got quiet again. It was probably just a shadow, or maybe a deer or skunk.

Figure 8: 75mm Recoilless Rifle

CHAPTER SIX

First Firefight

The next morning we moved down off the mountain and along a road to the base of a small hill about 500 feet high. Somebody spotted enemy soldiers on the top. We were ordered to take the hill immediately. We dropped our packs and were told to take only rifle, ammo, shovel, canteen and grenades. We spread out along the base of the hill and started cautiously up. Some guys were not so cautious and moved well ahead of others like me. I was scared and certainly didn't intend to lead the way up. About half way up, I heard shots fired in front of me. Everyone dropped to the ground and it seemed like most of the guys around me were shooting up toward the top of the hill. I didn't fire because I didn't see anything to shoot at. The lieutenant came up behind me and asked why I was not firing. I said, "Because I don't see anyone to shoot at." He looked disgusted and told me to fire anyway but I still didn't. Some of our guys were further up ahead with brush and trees all over the area. Men all around me were shooting over the heads of the guys in front and others below were shooting over my head. I thought it was crazy and stupid to waste all that ammo and also risk hitting one of our men up ahead.

The shooting died down somewhat and we scurried up to the ridge line. As we came up on the ridge, heavy firing erupted on a parallel ridge line about 300 to 400 yards away. Either North Koreans or Chinese were shooting at as from the other hill. I was scared stiff and dropped to the ground with my face in the dirt below the line of fire from the other hill. The din all around me was terrific but I could still hear bullets zipping over my head and whacking into trees behind me. Most of our guys were lying on their bellies on the ridge line and firing at the opposite ridge. However, our captain was stalking back and forth on the ridge as if he were bulletproof, all the while waving his arms and giving orders.

The captain noticed that I was cowering down out of harm's way and not firing so he strode over and yelled," Get your ass up here and start firing." I immediately crawled up a few feet and peered over at the opposite ridge while keeping my head low. Our side continued to pour a tremendous volume of fire at the other ridge and bullets from the Chinese continued to thud into the dirt and trees around us. I scoured the trees and rocks ahead and slightly below but could see no movement or anything that looked like a person. After a few minutes I tried to compensate for the range, then aimed for the tree line and fired. I fired a few more times before the shooting gradually diminished and then stopped. I never did see anyone on the other side and others I talked to didn't see anyone either.

As a kid living on a farm in Southern Minnesota, I grew up with guns. I learned to shoot under supervision probably at about 6 or seven years of age and was allowed to use a single shot bolt action 22 when I was only eight years old. Later I was given a Winchester multiple shot pump action 22 and a 410-gauge shotgun. I earned some of the money for my ammunition by trapping skunks, muskrats, weasels, etc. I think that anyone who skins a skunk for money to buy bullets necessarily develops a higher appreciation for the value of those bullets. I did not believe in wasting ammunition and generally would not shoot until I saw my intended target and also believed I had a reasonable chance of hitting it. I thought that most of the shooting on the ridge that day was wasted. A few marksmen with scope sights could have accomplished as much or more. Instead, we continued to lug great amounts of ammunition up large mountains and then blow it away with little effect.

We moved on along the ridge and on up to a higher intersecting ridge. We spread out for the night on a gentle, very rocky slope under sparse pines. I started digging a foxhole with a lot more enthusiasm than I had ever done before, but finally gave up. No one else was able to dig any holes either, even with pick axes. It was early April and our hill was somewhere around 4000 feet elevation. The night turned very cold and the wind came up. Since we had dropped our packs several miles back in the valley, we knew it was going to be a bad night. All we had were fatigues over summer underwear, plus a field jacket. We weren't allowed fires because we didn't know where the CCF was. I tried to curl up in a ball to conserve body heat without much success. Also no matter what position I assumed, it seemed at least one sharp rock would prod me in an unacceptable place. I ended up being awake all night, shivering and my teeth chattering. Altogether, this was an even more miserable night then the one I had spent in a waterlogged foxhole.

By 4:00 A.M. I'm sure everyone was ready to move on. As we plodded slowly along the ridges, the warmth of the sun and the exertion finally overcame the chills. Late that afternoon we settled around a very rocky, rounded and almost barren hilltop which we shared with two or three scraggly pine trees. I started to dig my foxhole but I was odd man out. If you have an odd number of men in the squad and you are too spread out to share with an adjoining squad, then you can end up with only one guy in a foxhole. That was just my luck that evening. After two hours of steady digging in what looked like a promising spot, I was only down about 12 inches and my shovel was getting pretty beat up. A few guys had been able to get hold of one of the company picks and thereby got their holes down to a reasonable 3 or 4 feet. It was another miserable cold night and we still had no sleeping bags, but by now I was so tired I managed to doze a little anyway.

First light revealed a heavy fog covering the mountain. Visibility was about 200 yards. The men were just beginning to stir and I sat on the edge of my hole and wondered if I could scrounge up some hot C rations. Suddenly there was a rustling whoosh ending abruptly in a very loud but seemingly muffled "crump." There was a flash and explosion about a hundred feet away, disappearing in a small cloud of dust and rocks. Incoming mortars! I dove into my hole and now regretted that I hadn't spent the night digging instead of trying to sleep. A second, then a third mortar dropped in our area. Every minute or two another dropped on our hilltop.

I've often heard it said that "there no atheists in fox holes." This is not true in my case. I'm sure that many want to, after the fact, give their religion credit for surviving when regaling members of their congregation, but I saw no evidence that a Supreme Being or a belief in religion provided any protection for anyone. Few situations can engender a more helpless feeling than to have mortars dropping in randomly from above. At no time did it ever cross my mind to ask God for protection, any more than it would have occurred to me to ask Santa Claus.

In between shells I glanced around to see where they had landed and if anyone had been hit. Then I noticed the strangest sight about 100 feet away. One of the guys had climbed out of his foxhole and dropped his pants. He then proceeded to relieve himself about 10 feet from his own foxhole. He was either very nonchalant or else he thought he could get the job done before the next mortar round. He had squatted down facing to my left when there was a brief flash of orange immediately behind and apparently almost underneath him. He disappeared in a small cloud of dust and rocks. There was a short silence, followed by cries for, "Medic!" The mortars continued for a few more minutes, and then there was silence.

We got orders to move down off the mountain immediately. There was a scramble as we picked up our gear and headed down the steep path. Sometime later while taking a break on the way down, several litter cases were carried past us. Four men on each litter were struggling with their loads on the steep slope. One of the wounded was the guy hit in the rear by the mortar. Surprisingly, he was still alive; at least his eyes were open and looking around.

Figure 9: 60mm Mortar

The French battalion had been set-up in defensive positions on a certain sector when it was decided, for whatever reason, that our 2nd battalion would replace them. The French had already cleared the hill by the time we arrived and it was already dark as we began filing up the narrow path. There was a small explosion somewhere up ahead, then a while later, another. Word was quickly passed down to halt where we were and remain on the path. It seems the French had strung booby traps and mines all over the hill just off the path. Apparently they pulled out without telling us. We moved on, gingerly staying close to the guy ahead and making sure we didn't stray off the path at any time. We located their abandoned foxholes and settled in carefully for the night. Next day we checked the area to locate all the booby traps. I heard later that several guys were wounded by the French booby traps. I didn't know if anyone had been killed. In the light of day we could also see that the ground was littered with small empty liquor bottles, the type given out on airline flights. From the number of bottles, they must have been half-smashed while they were on the hill. Everybody was thoroughly pissed-off at the French.

The 2nd Division had two extra foreign battalions attached. A Dutch battalion was attached to the 38th regiment of the 2nd Division and a French battalion was attached to our 23rd. This beefed-up the regiment when needed or otherwise it allowed one of our three battalions to take a short break.

CHAPTER SEVEN

Dumb Luck

My feet were getting worse every day. It was particularly difficult to get my boots on in the morning. The first hour or so of walking was especially painful. I hadn't gone far this particular morning when I stopped and gingerly pulled one boot off. The sock was damp and a little bloody as usual. As I carefully peeled the sock off, a large hunk of skin came off with it. The entire back of my ankle was raw and red. It also looked like it may have been infected. The squad leader called the platoon leader over. He looked at it and said that I had better walk back to the temporary aid station about a mile back. I limped into the aid station later that morning. It was nothing more than a group of 20x30 foot tents set up in the valley next to the road. Things were quiet at the moment so one of the doctors looked at my ankle right away. He was not concerned at all, and taped both ankles up, then said I was okay to go back to my unit. I guess it was no big deal compared to some of the cases he must have seen. They pointed out a heavily wooded mountain about 3 or 4 miles away as the present location of Easy Company. The shortest way was to cut straight across the valley. The valley was very woodsy with small hills and several creeks. There appeared to be no houses or farms anywhere in the direction I had to go. I headed out on a foot path in the general direction of the mountain.

Heavy fighting seemed to have broken out on the mountain. Artillery shells were bursting on the upper slopes. It looked like I might have been missing some action. It was mid-April and a beautiful spring day. It always seemed so especially wrong to shoot at people and get shot at on such a nice day. The trees and bushes were almost fully leaved and the grass and weeds were beginning to form a green carpet along the path. It reminded me of a typical spring day in Minnesota.

I limped steadily along the path with my M1 slung over my shoulder. I was totally alone. There wasn't another person or habitat in sight anywhere. I felt almost carefree. For the first time since I had joined the army, no one was telling me where to go or how fast to walk. With a little imagination, I could have been a kid again and just out hunting with my 22 rifle and my dog.

The path ahead dipped down into a deeply wooded, dark glade and then crossed a shallow rocky stream. I stepped lightly on the protruding rocks, keeping my gaze downward to avoid slipping. As I reached the other bank, I became aware of a movement in my peripheral vision. I quickly looked up to my right and stared into the eyes of a North Korean Soldier about 50 feet away. There were two others behind him. They wore dark green uniforms and were carrying burp guns. The closest one had a dark brown belt and I briefly glimpsed some kind of insignia. We both froze for half second. He seemed as startled as I, and then they spun around and disappeared back into the bushes. I unslung my rifle as I ducked down and sprinted forward along the path through some bushes on the far bank. I ran up the path and out the far side of the glen while looking around for any sign of the three or their buddies. The pain in my feet was totally forgotten. I wondered why they hadn't shot me. I could only guess that they were a small reconnaissance patrol and they didn't want to draw attention to themselves so far behind our lines.

I covered the last couple of miles to the mountain at a fast jog with only a few short stops to check the area behind me. Finally I spotted a column of GI's winding down a path from the mountain and located Easy company. Some of them were bitter. They said I had missed a "good fight." Several guys were wounded and some killed trying to take the mountain. They Thought I had been just goofing off at the aid station. I told the lieutenant about the 3 North Koreans and he didn't seem interested or else he didn't believe me. Maybe he had bigger problems. Anyway, he didn't even send a patrol out to investigate. The North Koreans had made the right decision, and they got away with it. They had been lucky, but so had I.

As the Division moved north, the Chinese and North Koreans were trapped south of Hwachon Reservoir which stretched for about 30 miles in a more or less East-West direction. Operation SWING was intended to envelope and mop-up these enemy troops. (**Munroe**, p.122)

We had gathered along a winding gravel road which twisted through a narrow valley. Steep, heavily wooded hills rose abruptly above the road. Our trucks dropped us off near a number of tanks parked along the road. The tanks fired-up their engines. The rumble of the many engines made it difficult to converse. The exhaust smoke was stifling at times. By hand signals we were told to climb on the tanks as they got ready to move. We hung on wherever we could as they moved slowly out. I hoped they didn't have to fire the big gun while we were hanging on the outside. The tanks pulled off a few miles up the road, we dismounted and spread out. As night fell, we dug foxholes all around the tanks. We were on alert all night. The guys in the tanks were not sleeping either. Morning was another cloudy, drizzly day. We moved single file along the road. Suddenly I heard the sound of an aircraft engine. He sounded low. Then we spotted him. It was an AT-6, a low wing, single engine plane used for observation and spotting enemy troop movements behind their lines. He roared low over us dragging about 300 feet of wire snagged on his tail wheel. The wire was whipping about violently as it snapped through the treetop. We expected him to crash any second, but he disappeared over the hills and the sound of his engine faded into silence. We were supposed to be near Hwachon Reservoir and I guessed that he must have hooked one of the many high voltage power lines from the Hwachon dam generating station. That was one lucky guy. He was way too low to bail out. Once again, "dumb luck" had saved somebodies bacon.

Figure 10: Sherman Tank

CHAPTER EIGHT

A Walk in the Sun

The weather seemed to be getting warmer every day and we were moving north again. It was a beautiful, warm, spring day with a few white puffy clouds in the sky. Everything was fresh and green as only young, new green leaves can make it. Easy company puffed its way slowly, single file up the mountain. Fox, George, and Hotel companies were somewhere off to our left or right.

As we reached the top of the hill, we paused to rest and a long, wooded ridge line stretched north for at least a couple of miles. I thought the captain was pissed-off at me. In fact, he'd been ticked off at me ever since I had joined the company. I had been bugging him, trying to get a transfer to a radio operator job in Division rear and he seemed to resent it.

Most of the officers I had met seemed to be intelligent and well educated, but their life and career were based on interests and goals quite different from mine and from the other guys in the company. To become an officer, they must have studied the arts of battle, tactics, maneuver, and offensive and defensive strategies. It's difficult to imagine someone studying all of these subjects without the intention and hope of putting them to use some day.

And now they were in Korea. This was the chance to show the "stuff of which they were made." I'm sure most of these officers had also studied history, especially the history of great battles such as the Civil War. For example, there was Pickett's charge at Gettysburg where the Confederate General Armistead led his men all the way up

Cemetery Ridge, then died with his hand on a Union cannon. Or on the Union side during the same battle, General Hancock rode up and down in the open on the Union line during the heaviest artillery barrage to calm the fears of his men. History is replete with such stories and such men are always portrayed as heroes, even though they may have been on the wrong side. If they lived, they were promoted; if they died, they were heroes. They couldn't lose, as long as they didn't shirk their duty.

This was my only explanation for the actions of our captain, who strode up and down the ridge line during my first fire fight, oblivious to the whine and zip of bullets, some of which must have missed him by mere inches. I didn't disparage his courage or deny the importance of his actions but for myself, I wasn't convinced yet that anything in Korea was worth risking my life for. Contrary to the captain, dying a hero was just about the last thing on my agenda.

Well anyway, on this beautiful spring day, the Captain would fix me! As we prepared to move out along the ridge, he said, "Roberts! Take the point." Now, "the Point," was the leader. He's the guy at the head of the column and the first guy into enemy territory. If shooting starts, often the first one hit was the guy on the point. If there were mines or booby traps, the point man was often the one who stepped on it or tripped the wire.

I headed out slowly along the ridge line. The path ahead wound through trees, brush, and rocks and up and down small hillocks. I was nervous. I felt like a duck in a shooting gallery. Most point men volunteered and they volunteered because they liked it. I guessed it gave them a high, like skydiving or Russian roulette. I scanned all the trees and rocks ahead, looking for some sign of movement. I also glanced down every few steps looking for trip wires. It was slow going. I could hear the shuffle and clank of the rest of the company coming along behind. This could have been fun if it weren't so damned dangerous; something like when we were kids playing follow the leader.

A small reconnaissance plane was droning low over the hills a couple of miles ahead. He must have spotted something because soon artillery shells went rustling by high overhead, then landed with a distant "crump" on the hills ahead. The shells had proximity fuses because a few of them burst overhead as they were passing through the small cumulus clouds. Apparently some of the clouds were dense enough to reflect enough radio energy back to trip the fuse or maybe some of them were overly sensitive. It was nothing to worry about because they were bursting about 3 to 5000 feet overhead.

One shell landed about a half mile off to our right. It exploded in a great burst of white with thousands of white phosphorous streamers arcing over to strike the ground in a circular pattern like a giant inverted bowl. We heard later that it was a "short round" and that it had landed in one of the other companies. It hit their CP and several guys were hurt. A short round wasn't all that unusual. It seemed to happen every time there was a heavy amount of artillery laid down.

The artillery stopped and soon we saw why. We heard the deep rumbling growl of aircraft engines somewhere. Four Marine Corsairs appeared low over the hills ahead. Small black specks separated from their bellies and fell in tumbling arcs toward the green hillside. Napalm! Bright orange slashes blossomed along the ridge ahead, then quickly transformed into billowing, oily black clouds. We moved on ahead.

The path cut through a small clump of pines and brush. I stopped. Up ahead, about 200 yards, was another slightly higher ridge line, crossing our ridge line at right angles. It looked like the perfect place for an ambush. I peered at the slope ahead for a few seconds. Small rocks and bushes began to look like soldiers. I was sure I saw one of them move. I think I had one or two other guys behind me convinced that they too saw something. The captain came up and scanned the area with field glasses. He didn't see anything. The captain had had enough. I was too jumpy and moving too slow. He had one of the "gung ho" guys take over the point. It was okay with me. We moved off again.

About midday we reached the area that had been napalmed by the Corsairs that morning. The hill on both sides of the path was charred a grayish black. No blade of grass was visible for hundreds of yards ahead. The blackened trunks of trees with scraggly remnants of branches stood quietly in every direction. The soot covered rocks were the only survivors. Along the path, on the hillside and among the rocks lay small naked, blackened figures, their arms legs and bodies still frozen in strange improbable positions as if time had stopped in the midst of their agony. One lay, his arm stretched rigidly out, fist clenched as if clutching at that last glimpse of blue sky. Another was huddled by a rock, curled in a fetal position, with his arms covering his head. There were no traces of clothing on most and no way to distinguish officer from peasant. Some of our guys joked about "fried gooks," the rest just seemed a little quieter than usual.

The captain decided to take a break at this time, right on the edge of the desolation. We all fell out, some to rest and others to grab a bite of whatever we had brought along. I opened a can of C rations and started to eat it cold, and then I had a sudden juvenile notion. I walked over the nearest body, sat down on it and continued to eat my C rations. It was a dumb adolescent stunt, intended to show my buddies - "Hey guys, this doesn't bother me," even though it did. After about 10 seconds, I thought better of it and got up and sat with my squad, to finish my cold spaghetti and meatballs.

We moved on through the area, found some good defensive positions and dug in for the night. It had been a beautiful, warm spring day. The woods and mountains were the equal of any in the Smokies or the foothills of the Sierra Madre. I thought it rather ironic that I could still find the time to steal a few brief moments of pleasure from the wilderness around me.

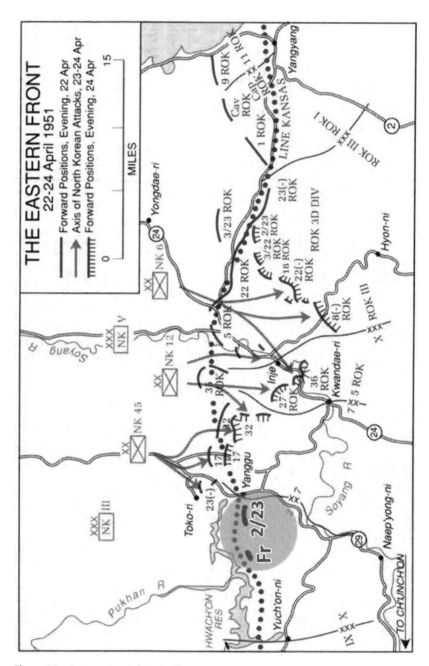

Figure 11: Eastern Front, late April

CHAPTER NINE

Mopping Up

The 23rd regiment continued to mop up south of Hwachon reservoir and then moved east along the south side of the reservoir to clear the area. The area was relatively quiet, with little action other than a few small skirmishes. (**Munroe**, p.122)

On **Figure 11**, our position below Hwachon is indicated by 2/23, the second battalion of the 23rd. The French battalion on our left is indicated as "Fr".

It was another beautiful warm day. Easy company was camped on a grassy plateau with only very low hills in the distance. There were a few low trees along the small creek that wandered through our meadow. We seemed to be marking time waiting for somebody or something, but as usual nobody told me anything. They didn't tell anybody else anything either. It was just a lazy afternoon and some of the guys were taking advantage of it by pulling off their shirts and washing up in the creek or just trying to get a little tan.

I noticed one of our guys about 50 yards away suddenly drop. I watched curiously as one of his buddies went over to investigate, then there was a small commotion and someone hollered for the medic. It was no use though; he had been shot and instantly killed. No one had heard the shot. The only sounds were those of a normal spring day; the quiet sounds of our camp, the low murmur of the creek and a few meadowlarks. We speculated on the source of the bullet. Some thought it was a sniper very far away who connected with a "lucky" shot. I thought it was probably just a stray round fired at a high angle into the air by someone maybe 3 miles away. It could even have been one of our own people. After a while, everyone resumed their previous activities but with one ear cocked for any distant sounds.

The next day we got an early start and headed northeast into the mountains. The mountain ahead was covered in fires and numerous fires burned on other nearby mountains. Most of the mountains around us were 3000 to 5000 feet high and densely covered with pine trees. They were separated by narrow valleys, each with a small stream meandering through them. We plodded up the trail until about half way up; our way was blocked by dense smoke. I liked the smell of burning pine, but this was too much. We headed off the trail and made our way up the slope through hot blackened regions still smoldering and even burning here and there. We stepped rapidly through a few small areas where the dry pines were burning fiercely and showering us with ash and incandescent pine needles. No one seemed the least bit concerned about getting cut -off and trapped by the fires. Maybe it was because the wind was calm and the fires were not spreading rapidly; on the other hand, maybe it was because the Chinese posed a much greater threat. The smoke was spreading throughout the hills and drifting low over the valleys. It burned our eyes and made breathing difficult.

This was about April 21 and the Chinese had set numerous large forest fires all over the central Korean area to hide the gathering of their troops for the big spring offensive. (**Blair**, *The Forgotten War*, p.821)

Later intelligence estimates ranged as high as 300,000 CCF massing on the central front. If we average GI's had heard these estimates, we probably would have been totally demoralized.

We finally reached the top about midday and dug-in. It had been a clear, hot day and the fires certainly didn't help. The Korean bearers carrying 5 gallon water cans were nowhere in sight and almost everybody's canteen was empty. I felt a little twinge of panic. I couldn't wait till the next day for water. When I was about eight or 10, I had suffered a heat stroke while picking potatoes on a hot, late summer day in Minnesota. My mother told me the temperature that day had been more than 110 degrees F. Ever since that day, I seem to get overheated very easily. I got a little dizzy and sick, then stopped sweating and began to have intermittent chills. I knew heat exhaustion could be fatal if not taken care of.

They asked for volunteers to go down to a stream in the valley and bring back water. I jumped at the chance along with four others. We each carried two strings of five canteens hooked together with a belt through their chains. We headed down the hill at a fast clip, at times sliding on our heels or rumps. At the base of the hill we found a nice cool spring which emptied into the creek. The water looked beautiful, cold and clear. I forgot all the warnings about not drinking the water and scooped up big handfuls, then dipped my helmet in and poured it over my head. When we were all sated and the canteens were filled and capped, we headed back.

Now I suddenly became conscious of how alone we were. Just the five of us all weighted down with canteens. We'd be sitting ducks. We lucked out again though and after about an hour we were welcomed-back into Easy company by one bunch of thirsty guys. We told everyone that it was spring water and shouldn't require Halozone tablets. Normally when we filled our canteens in a stream or rice paddy, we would drop a Halazone tablet in the canteen and let it sit for half an hour to give it time to kill all the bugs. Later that night, a few five gallon cans of water were brought up and we were out of trouble for a while.

We had been lucky, the Chinese or North Koreans seemed to be evacuating the terrain ahead of us without much fighting, although units on our flanks were seeing a little more action. We filed down into a deep heavily wooded ravine with a creek winding through it and a clearing at one end. We were going to be there a while so the platoon leader told us to fall out and wash up in the creek.

It was another warm day, so we stripped our shirts off and broke out the soap and towels. Some guys even took the time to shave. I set my glasses down on a large flat rock beside me and soaped up my arms and face, then scooped up handfuls of the icy water and splashed it over me. It felt good after our long hike. As I dried my eyes with a towel, I felt someone brush past me and heard a crunch. I looked down. Some klutz had stepped on my glasses. Now I was really in trouble. Without glasses, my best vision in my "good" eye was 20/240. The platoon leader said I should just make the best of it until I could have a new pair made in division rear.

At the first opportunity, I asked the captain about getting new glasses. He was very unsympathetic and made it clear that he suspected that I had broken my glasses on purpose as a ploy to avoid combat. He didn't give a damn about my problem.

We were interrupted by a small MedEvac helicopter. It roared in low over our heads and landed in the clearing. Four men emerged from the trees carrying a stretcher over to the chopper. A soldier was wrapped in a blanket and strapped into one of the wire baskets slung on the side of the helicopter above the landing skids. It lifted off amid a blizzard of dirt and leaves and climbed out to the east into the sun, and then it was gone.

After a while we found out it was some guy in our company who had apparently blundered into a booby trap or something. One or two guys seemed a little envious of the one in the wire basket. He probably had his ticket home, if he didn't die. I definitely didn't want to go home that way, if I could help it.

My platoon leader asked how well I could see without my glasses. I explained that I could see the sights of my rifle, although they were blurred, but the worst part was that at 200 yards I didn't think I could tell the difference between a Chinese and one of our guys. That settled it; he said I would be transferred to Headquarters Company until they could arrange to send me to the rear for new glasses. The army could have avoided all this hassle if they had abided by their own rules. They told me when I was first inducted, back in Fort Riley, that I was required to carry two pairs of glasses. But they were always in such a hurry to get me over to Korea, that they would never take the time to have an extra pair of glasses made.

CHAPTER TEN

Headquarters Company

Easy company was still up in the hills but I was now down in Headquarters Company temporarily until I could get new glasses. Headquarters Company was where some of the officers hung out when they were not up on the line with the men. When the other companies were on the line, headquarters would not be very far away - that usually meant less than 5 miles. Headquarters also saw to it that the men were fed, supplied with ammo and in general performed all the other chores required of a combat battalion.

At Headquarters I met Don Heim, who had also broken his glasses. He had come out of a machine gun squad. They put us to work at whatever needed to be done; such as helping move equipment, loading and unloading trucks and jeeps and escorting Korean laborers hauling food and ammo up on the mountains.

On this particular night Headquarters Company was located on the south side of low hills with the battalion spread out in higher hills just to the north and maybe a couple of miles away. A broad valley stretched away to the south. Several trucks and jeeps were parked around the base of the hill. Some of the officers were staying in a couple of windowless Korean houses and the rest of us had our pup tents set-up wherever we felt like. A jeep with an ammunition trailer attached was parked next to an embankment. The trailer was loaded with mortar rounds, bazooka shells and 75mm recoilless shells, all in cardboard or metal canisters. I pitched my tent just behind the trailer without paying any attention to what was in it, crawled into my sleeping bag and promptly went to sleep.

Sometime in the night there was a terrific explosion. For an instant I was half awake and half conscious of flying dirt and rocks along with the pungent odor of something like gunpowder. I tore myself out of my sleeping bag and dove into a nearby foxhole with my ears still ringing. It was pitch-black and I was now wide awake and checking to see if I had all my parts. Someone came around with a flashlight after a few minutes to see what had happened. Something had hit the jeep trailer next to my tent and there appeared to be a small crater underneath the trailer, which was still sitting more or less where it had been before. A few more rounds came thudding in during the night but none came as close as the first. I spent the remainder of the night in my foxhole.

In the morning we could better see what had happened. Apparently a Chinese 76mm armor piercing shell (this was about 3 inches in diameter) must have arced down just clearing the slope of the hill and cut through the middle of the trailer, then buried itself in the ground under the trailer before exploding. Armor piercing shells are intended to penetrate tank armor, and then explode inside. They only require enough explosive to kill the crew inside the tank. The shell had left a jagged hole a few inches in diameter as it tore through the ammunition canisters and then had only made a small 3 foot crater in the ground underneath the trailer. Amazingly, the shell had passed through several shells of some type without detonating them. My tent was no more than 6 feet from the impact point. If the Chinese had used a high explosive shell, I would have been blown into little pieces.

That day I began looking around for a little safer place to sleep. I found a small opening in the side of the hill about 100 yards away. I crawled in and started digging with my small foxhole shovel. The hill was very soft sandstone and it was easy to gouge-out with a sharp shovel. In a couple of hours of spare time I now had a nice, snug horizontal hole about 8 feet deep and 3 feet around inside. Just when I thought I had it made, we had to move out again and I never got to use the best foxhole I ever had.

Figure 12: Russian 76mm Howitzer

CHAPTER ELEVEN

Reserve Again

It was about April 28th and the central area of Korea was still relatively quiet, but the CCF had started their big spring offensive in Western Korea. The British units among many others had been heavily hit. The 2nd division had pulled back south of Hwachon to protect our left flank, since units to the west of us had been hit and were falling back. The 23rd regiment pulled back to the NE. end of the "No Name Line" while the 2nd battalion went into reserve. The "No Name Line" ran NE through the mountains parallel to the Hongchon-Inje road (see **Figure 5**). The 23rd occupied its NE end just south of Ogumal. (**Munroe**, p. 124)

We were back in reserve again. We had settled in a small valley surrounded by pine covered low hills and we had set-up our pup tents under the trees in a ravine leading up into the hills. Now we could relax for a few days, maybe. That hope didn't last long. The company commander decided to keep everybody busy with busy work. We were maybe five to 10 miles behind the lines and the captain had us working all day hauling sand from the river bed to make little paths between the company areas. When that was done, we hauled little rocks to outline all the paths. This was sheer idiocy. There must have been something better to do with our time. They even put up a company bulletin board. I read a notice on the board stating that the Division rear was looking for someone who could send and receive Morse code at 20 WPM. It seemed that some radio traffic went by Morse, probably to keep it secure from enemy eavesdropping.

I immediately requested to talk to the captain and told him that I had been a HAM radio operator and that I knew Morse code at 20 WPM. I knew he hated my guts but I didn't see how he could refuse to let me apply for this job. He was still convinced that I was trying to dodge front line duty. He was absolutely right; who wouldn't? Well maybe there were a few guys who genuinely seemed to enjoy the excitement and danger. But most of us, I thought, would jump at most any chance to get into a less dangerous area.

The captain refused to take my application. He said I was in a rifle company now and by God I was going to stay there. He also refused to send me back to the rear to get glasses. Now it was my turn to get pissed-off. I was becoming thoroughly disgusted with the army. They pulled a bunch of guys off the street with little or no recent training and shoved them directly into combat. In my case I had eight weeks of Basic Training, marching, target practice, dry run practice on a 105 Howitzer, making my bunk, KP and scrubbing floors. After this I had three months in Korea in 1947, mostly pulling guard duty.

Four years later I was drafted back into the army with absolutely no refresher training. I was soft from civilian life and could not do even one proper pushup or chin-up. I was then shipped immediately over to Korea and handed an M1 rifle, a gun I had never even fired on the range. It should be noted that in 1946, I had qualified with the Carbine, which is a smaller and lighter weapon.

Next, I was given a little more than one week of training patrols, and then I was shoved into combat climbing 2000 to 5000 foot hills with a pack, rifle, ammo and other equipment which in some cases weighed as much as 80 pounds.

I wasn't trained to pull my weight as a member of my squad, in fact it was all I could do to just keep up with the other guys, much less figure out what was going on.

And finally I did not really know what we were over there fighting for. Sure, we had a couple of lectures on the "communist menace," but it mostly went in one ear and out the other. I liked electronics, science, girls and classical music, in about that order. I seldom read newspapers or paid any attention to politics. I had never bothered to vote. I couldn't see dying in a dirty little war, in a dirty little country on the opposite side of the globe. I had too many other things I wanted to do.

I would guess that over half the men in our company were not much better off than I was. We were ill-trained, unmotivated and poorly led. It's no wonder our units often collapsed into a fleeing mob, abandoning vehicles and equipment, as soon as they got into real trouble.

Until then we had always had to put our sleeping bags on the hard ground whether in our foxholes or in our pup tents. This time in reserve, someone started spreading pine boughs on the floor of their tent, and then everybody started doing it. A couple of days later everyone was issued an inflatable rubber air mattress, (made in Japan). The first night it was heaven, and my best night's sleep in Korea. The second night, my pup tent buddy set our tent on fire while trying to make coffee on a sterno can. It burned a large hole in our tent and many small holes in our air mattresses. So much for that.

On November 30, 1950, the 2nd division retreat from Kunuri was blocked by one division of Chinese troops, about 10,000 men. Most of the men panicked and abandoned the greater part of their vehicles and heavy weapons as they ran the 10-mile gauntlet through the roadblock. They suffered 3000 casualties, mostly killed and captured, out of the 10,000 men in the division.

In contrast, the Marine division at the Chosin reservoir on December 10, 1950 was surrounded by three Chinese armies which later was determined to be 120,000 men. (**Blair**, *The Forgotten War*, p.543) The Marines were all volunteers, well trained and motivated. They stuck together and fought their way out 70 miles to the sea, in 20 to 30 below weather, bringing their dead and wounded and almost all their equipment. They did suffer heavy casualties, 4400 dead and wounded, with another 6000 frostbite cases. If this had been an army division, I'm sure not one person would have made it out.

I had a little spare time one afternoon and wandered over to an adjoining ravine. The ground was littered with unused 155 artillery shell radio proximity fuses. Each had a miniature radar transmitter and receiver built into the nose of the fuse, which was designed to screw into the nose of the artillery shell. The purpose was to detonate the shell just above the ground so that shrapnel would spray down into the enemy foxholes. I was intrigued by the sophisticated electronics in such a small device so I took one back to my tent and spent about an hour trying to take it apart. I was not having any luck, and then I suddenly thought, "What the hell am I doing this for?" It had enough high explosive to blow my head off. I put the fuse back where I had got it and began looking for something safer to do.

We were having rice and fish one night (maybe the cook new something we didn't know). I never did care for fish; nevertheless I took one taste, and then dumped it into the garbage can. I was not the only one; the garbage can was full of rice and fish. I went back to my tent and heated a can of C ration pork and beans, but I was still hungry. My buddies were in the same boat and we started wondering where we could get some more food. We had been eyeing the cases of C rations stacked up in front of the company tent. The sergeant had placed them in the open where he could keep an eye on them. We devised a plan. At dark, I crawled toward the stack, keeping the stack between me and the sergeant's open tent flap. When I had reached the stack I grabbed one, then I crawled back, about 100 yards to our tent. We sliced open the case and divided up the spoils. I made sure I got a can of my favorite - fruit cocktail. Some of the other guys decided that they too would try it so they crawled down and grabbed a couple more cases. Everybody got some of the booty and we stuffed it into our backpacks for later use. The next morning the sergeant was madder than hell. He had counted the cases and knew that several were missing. If he had fallen-us out for a shakedown, we would have all been in trouble.

One of our last days in reserve, we were marched down to a battalion tent for a lecture. The subject was what to do if you were captured by the enemy. We were told that, if captured, we should try to escape as soon as possible because after a week in captivity, there wasn't much chance of making it back. In that case, we should just make the best of it. They said we should give name, rank and serial number and nothing else. And then they taught us one Chinese word- "TOWSHUNG". They said it meant "I surrender." But I didn't pay much attention because I thought it was never going happen to me.

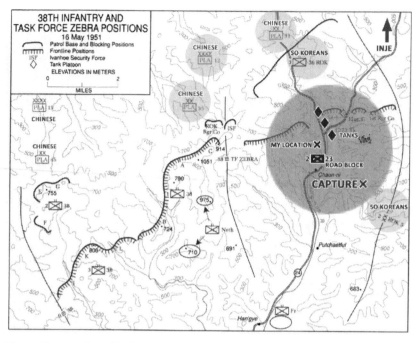

Figure 13: Location of 2nd Division on May 16-18, 1951

CHAPTER TWELVE

On the No Name Line

The 2nd battalion of the 23rd had moved up to the NNL on May 14, 1951 after about two weeks in reserve. We were on the Hongchon-Inje road about 5 miles north east of Hangye. We were part of what was called Task Force Zebra composed of our 2nd battalion, a company of rangers, the 72nd Tank battalion and a battalion of ROKs (see **Figure 13**). (**Blair**, *The Forgotten War,* p. 873)

General Van Fleet's intelligence predicted a massive CCF attack on May 16. Air observers also reported large numbers of troops heading our way. Top level officers were given this information but the troops were kept totally in the dark. Later intelligence showed that three CCF armies were to attack the ROKs on our right flank and two CCF armies would simultaneously attack the 2nd Division. The Chinese knew they could always rely on the ROKs to abandon their weapons and bug out. After this, they planned on using all five armies (about 150,000 men) to surround the 2nd Division and annihilate it. (**Ibid.** p.871)

We got orders to move out in a hurry. It was a warm sunny day. Everyone was scrambling around stuffing things into their duffle bags and back packs. I had a small portable tube type radio that one of the guys gave me when it had quit working. I found out that it used the same types of tubes as in our walkie-talkies. By scrounging tubes from damaged W-T, I got it working again. I stowed this in my pack but it didn't leave room for much else. Some of the guys who had stolen C ration cases were now desperately trying to get rid of the evidence. Even soldiers were able to accumulate a surprising amount of junk during two weeks in reserve.

I was still in Headquarters Company, so I threw my stuff on the Headquarters truck and the column started north in great clouds of dust and noise. Later in the day Headquarters Company pulled off the main road into what looked like a Korean farmyard about 5 miles north of Hangye. It reminded me, somewhat, of a small Midwestern farm. A small road cut up through a sloping apple orchard to clumps of cottonwoods surrounding a farmyard. A typical, mud-walled, thatched roof, three room Korean house was situated on the north side of the yard. A couple of small barns or sheds sat under trees on the west side up against the hill side. A large root cellar next to the sheds was probably used for storage of turnips, apples and such. This would make a great foxhole, I thought.

Our trucks quickly filled up the yard and spilled over into the adjacent fields. We took over the place. The original owner was nowhere in sight, in fact, it appeared to have been abandoned for some time. Don Heim and I helped unload equipment. We set up our pup tents, and then I checked out the area. We didn't stay in the Korean house because it was probably full of lice. One of our Patton tanks was parked in the apple orchard. No one seemed to be around so I climbed up and crawled inside. Everything looked okay, so it must have just been a mechanical problem. I shut the hatch as I left.

No luck on the root cellar for my foxhole, the first sergeant had commandeered that. We heard that he had been with the unit since it came to Korea about eight months previously and he had a major case of the nerves. I didn't blame him. He also drank. He would work in one of the Headquarters Company tents but at the first sound of gunfire or mortars he would almost jump out of his skin. He would then dive into his hole and wouldn't come out again until the danger was long past. He didn't like me and I didn't like him.

Don and I hit the sack in our pup tent. I heard the ever present artillery rumbling somewhere maybe five or 15 miles away. After a while you didn't even notice it, like traffic in the street.

On May 14th, the 2nd Division was dispersed as follows in the mountains west of the Hongchon - Inje road: The 9th NW of Hangye; the 3/38 on hill 800; the l/38 on hill 1051, Mt.Kari-San; the 2/38 NW of 1051 and the 2/23 (our unit) NE of 1051 but west of the road. There were supposed to be four divisions of ROKs stretching from our right flank several miles into the mountains to the east. The 38th had turned hills 800 and 1051 into veritable fortresses. Hills were designated by a number such as 1051 (3150 feet) which indicated its height in meters above sea level. (See **Figure 13**)

The following day, May 15th, the front was still relatively quiet. The CCF were still getting their forces into position for the May 16 attack. (**Blair**, *The Forgotten War*, p. 871)

The day was bright and sunny. Trucks had moved in down the road a way and set up large portable hot showers. These consisted of tents with wood deck floors erected next to the creek. Shower heads were strung overhead in the tent and a big heater and pump provided lots of high pressure hot water. It was great! I could have stayed there all day but they kicked you out after 10 minutes. For most of us, it was our first shower in more than two months. Lots of guys from different units were being run through but the men of Easy Company, up on the hill in their foxholes, were missing out on this.

There seemed to be little action anywhere other than the usual artillery. Don and I kept busy helping around the kitchen, unloading supplies, etc. We had a new guy join us in Headquarters Company;

I'll call him 'Peter'. Like me, Peter had been recalled back into the Army after a few years as a civilian. He was about 5'-8" and must have weighed at least 250 pounds. They had shoved him right into the line and quickly discovered that he couldn't even make it to the top of the first hill to join his company. Rather than have a couple of guys carry him up the mountain, the captain decided to just send him to join Don and me at Headquarters Company. The Sergeant assigned him to help the cooks, which was like putting me in charge of the candy rations.

The next day (May 16) started as an overcast rainy day otherwise not much was happening. Peter seemed to be enjoying his new job helping the cooks and sampling all the food. Routine chores filled the day and by dark I was bushed and hit the sack in my pup tent. Rain pattered on the canvas as I fell asleep.

I awoke suddenly. Something was not right. It was about midnight and I heard a low rumble intermixed with hundreds of voices. The distant sounds of artillery seemed closer and more frequent. I crawled out of my tent and looked down toward the road about a hundred yards away. I made out a dark, moving mass of people coming down the road from the NE and shuffling past at a jog or fast walk. A few had flashlights and some were calling-out, but most were just quietly hurrying along. Some of the other guys were already up and I asked what was going on. They said they had heard that the ROKs to our NE had been hit and were bugging out, as usual. Nobody seemed very concerned so I went back to sleep.

It was later determined that hundreds of CCF and NK soldiers had infiltrated the ranks of the ROKs and civilians during the night, and thus were able to get behind our lines and set-up road blocks.

I was awakened early the next day (May 17th) and the camp was buzzing. The sergeant confirmed that the ROKs had been hit. He said our guys up on the hill in front of us had also been hit by thousands of Chinese and they were still coming. He said the men up on the hill needed ammo right away. About 50 Korean civilian bearers were loaded up with cases of 30 caliber machine gun and M1 ammo. They all had the standard Korean "A Frame" back pack which is, as you might guess, shaped like a capital "A." Sticks protruding out at the crossbar on the "A" hold whatever load is being carried. The bearer's arms are slipped through large straps attached to the frame.

> It was May 16th early evening, and after dark. Three CCF armies (nine divisions) hit the five divisions of ROKs on our right flank who then collapsed. At least 40,000 of them abandoned all their equipment, even their rifles, and bugged-out. Many came down the road past our camp and many tried to escape back through the 2nd division lines. Two CCF armies (six divisions) hit the 2nd division head-on. The 2/23, 1/38 and 2/38 were the hardest hit. Our artillery fired 17,000 rounds into the advancing Chinese. (**Blair**, *The Forgotten War*, p. 876) Our men on the hills could not tell the difference between escaping South Koreans and attacking Chinese and 100's of South Koreans were machine gunned to death.

Each case of 30 caliber ammo weighed 98 pounds. That was a number I'll never forget. Most of the Koreans carried one 98-pound case on their A Frame but a few of the big husky guys carried two, for a total weight of 196 pounds. Four of us GI's escorted the 50 Koreans onto the trail and up the hill. It was about a 1500 foot vertical ascent. It had been raining and the path was slippery. In some places the path rose at almost a 45-degree angle. But these Koreans were tough. They just kept plodding upward, one step with a two-second pause, followed by another step. Every hundred feet, they would rest their A Frame against the hill and take a couple minutes break, and then they would start up again. We were getting pooped just keeping up with them.

About halfway up the hill at a particularly steep part, a couple of smaller Koreans, (they probably didn't weigh over 120 pounds.) were having an extremely tough time. I got behind and lifted up on the A Frame to help along. In spite of this one of them looked like he was about to collapse physically. He was trembling and staggering under the load. I told him to set it down, and then I slipped into the shoulder straps and started up the hill with his A Frame. It was brutal. After a couple of hundred feet I had to set it down and give it back to the little guy. This went on the rest of the way to the top. We spelled the smaller guys who were having the toughest time.

At the top, our guys were very glad to see us. They had burned up a lot of ammo during the night. The Chinese had backed-off for the time being because of daylight. One of the machine gunners said that he knew he had killed many South Korean ROKs who were trying to bug out through his position. In the dark he couldn't tell the difference between ROKs and CCF. Our bearers distributed their ammo and we headed down the hill at a very fast pace. The sergeant said we would probably be shepherding some more stuff up the mountain the next day.

May 17th - The 3rd battalion had been rushed up to join our 2/23. The French had also been brought up to an area about 2 miles south of us and the 1/23 was placed 2 miles south of the French. Chiles, the 23rd commander, requested permission to pull us back to Hangye. But General Almond "didn't think the situation was precarious." He probably reached this conclusion while sitting in a tent well behind the lines. During the night and day of the 17th, 38,000 artillery rounds from 300 guns were fired. B26 bombers were also bombing the Chinese where they had broken through our lines on the left. The 2/23 and the 3/23 were ordered to send all their nonessential vehicles to the rear. They ran into a roadblock set up by the infiltrators from the previous night. All the trucks were lost. The one exception was the jeep driven by Chiles' executive officer, James Stacy. Chiles stated that "It should have been sent to the Smithsonian Institution. All five tires were flat. The hood had been blown off. The gas tank was riddled with holes, and otherwise the vehicle was like Swiss cheese. Stacy was unscathed - a true miracle." The 23rd was hit hard again the night of May 17-18 but they held onto their hill positions. (**Blair**, *The Forgotten War*, p. 877)

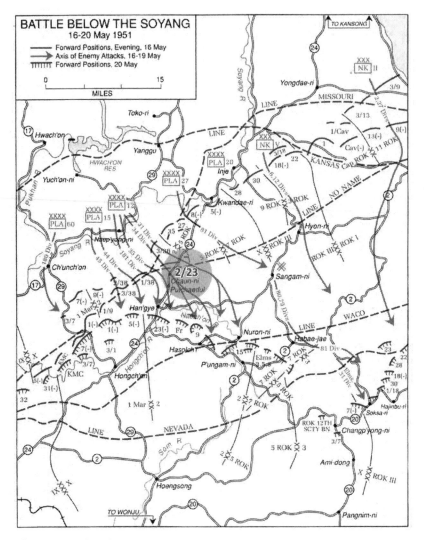

Figure 14: Below the Soyang, Mid May

CHAPTER THIRTEEN

The Last Day

May 18th dawned clear and sunny but the atmosphere was tense. Our GI's up on the hill had been hit hard again, but the CCF had again backed-off at daylight. Our camp at the bottom of the hill was relatively quiet except for an occasional mortar round dropping nearby. Every time this happened, our first sergeant would dive into his hole. If you wanted to talk to him, you had to poke your head down the hole - he wouldn't come out.

We got orders to pack-up and be ready to move out at any moment. About 10AM some of the trucks were starting to move out. The Headquarters Company trucks were going to bring up the tail end. Just at this moment, our Sergeant, grabbed Don and me and gave us a direct order. The men on the hill had pulled out of the line and were withdrawing to new positions a few miles to the south. They were unable to carry all their ammunition, so they had tried to bury it on the mountain but were unable to finish the job. He ordered Don and me to take Koreans and go back up the hill and either finish the job or destroy the ammo.

We knew the sergeant disliked us but we thought it was just plain vindictive to send us on a mission like this. By the time we got back (if we got back), we could expect our trucks to be long gone. We had the Koreans grab picks and shovels then we took off at a fast jog up the hill. We were traveling light and the hill was only about 800 feet high, so we made it in about an hour. We were totally alone. There was no sign of any of our guys and fortunately there was no sign of

Chinese either. We found the ammo in a large hole about five by 8 feet and 4 feet deep. It was about half full of mortar rounds, machine gun ammo, grenades, etc. If we threw dirt on it, it would only be about one foot under the surface; which didn't sound too good, so we decided to burn it?

I grabbed some white phosphorous grenades, pulled the pins on two of them and flipped them into the hole, then ran like hell. As we ducked, they went off with a "Whump, Whump." I then walked part way back to peer gingerly into the hole. The cartons and boxes were starting to burn, so we thought we better get the hell out of there before the mortar rounds started going off.

Figure 15: Marine Corsair

As we started back, a tank on the road below started his engine and pulled out on the Inje road facing north, and then fired a burst of 50 caliber. We looked north to see what he was firing at. Thousands of tan uniformed Chinese were swarming down the slope of the hill about a mile north of our hill. We realized that we were now closer to the Chinese than we were to our own lines.

Don and I started to run. After a few minutes we stopped to catch our breath and see how far the Chinese had come. They seemed to be running too, because they were spreading rapidly across the valley and heading for the Inje road. A gull-wing Navy Corsair was just pulling out of a dive after apparently strafing the Chinese. We noticed that smoke was starting to stream behind as he headed south toward us, level at our altitude of about 1500 feet. He continued to fly straight and level as the smoke changed to bright orange flame. For a few brief moments I completely forgot about the Chinese as I wondered why he didn't get out. The Corsair whined past our hill at high speed, the engine sounding perfectly normal despite the streamers of flame shooting from its cowling. Just after passing us, the tiny figure of what appeared to be a man separated from the Corsair and fell toward the valley below. As he fell, he seemed to be kicking his legs and thrashing his arms about. When he disappeared from view behind a low hill south east of me, his chute still had not appeared. It was unlikely that there was enough altitude left for his chute to open. We remembered the Chinese and continued running down the ridge line.

As we ran down the path to our farmhouse, we were relieved to see that the trucks had not left us behind. We told the sergeant that we had burned the ammo and that there were thousands of Chinese about a mile north of us coming down the road. He said we should first destroy all the buildings, and then get the hell out. I still had one white phosphorous grenade, so I walked around behind the three room Korean house and looked in each room to make sure no one was in it, and then I pulled the pin and tossed the grenade into the center room. It went "ping, snap," as the handle flew off and the spring loaded firing pin ignited the fuse. I knew I had three and ½ seconds from the "snap" as I ran quickly around the end of the house. Less than 10 feet from the front of the house there was the expected muffled "whump" and then all four outside mud walls collapsed outward amid a big white cloud.

The sergeant hollered "Mortars!" as he dove into his foxhole. I sauntered across the yard to the trucks, trying to keep a straight face. I hadn't intended to scare hell out of the Sarge, but now that I had and had also gotten away with it, I was pleased as punch.

I recently heard from a woman (Janis Garrison Curran) who said that her father, Lt. Charles Garrison, had bailed of a Corsair on May 18, 1951 near Chaun-ni, Korea; this is almost exactly where I was captured on May 18th. Four Corsairs were strafing when Lt. Garrison's plane was hit in the region of the engine and caught fire. He immediately turned south followed by his wing man Ensign Marion Dragastin who kept telling him to bail out because he was on fire. Finally Dragastin saw him bail out but hang up on the horizontal stabilizer. He finally broke free and his chute opened but then his wing man reported that he had fallen out of his chute harness. Shortly after, he corrected himself by

that it was his emergency pack which was falling free. This must have been what I saw and mistook for a person falling. In my panic to get out of there, I never did see a parachute or the following Consair.

Dragastin followed Garrison's chute down and reported that the Lieutenant had landed okay but had pointed to his stomach, meaning that he had injured his mid-section either by hitting the horizontal stabilizer or due to ground fire. While flying cover, Dragastin was hit and crashed into a mountain and was killed. Garrison was seen three weeks later in a POW camp near Wonson, but he never came home from the war. The above details are from an article in Stag magazine, Volume 6, No 1, Jan 1955.

The 38th on our left flank had been surrounded and told to fight their way out and withdraw south to the 9th position. The Chinese had set up a roadblock about 2 miles south of our position, at Yongnae-ri, but I was unaware of it. They had also infiltrated into the rear on our left and right flanks. About noon, the 23rd was ordered to "readjust your position." That's the army's way of saying, "get the hell out of there." Later estimates placed the total numbers of Chinese and N. Korean troops at 175,000. (Munroe, p. 133)

The 2nd battalion was supposed to move down the west side of the road while the 3rd battalion took the east side. This was intended to clear the road block. I was supposed to move down the road with the vehicles. Two tanks led the mile long column of vehicles. When the tanks crossed a small bridge, it collapsed; effectively blocking the road for any following vehicles. As the tanks continued, they both hit mines and were disabled. As the 23rd tried to move south, they were attacked from the rear and both flanks. Since I was in the very tail end of the column, I had to run the entire gauntlet. As usual, I was totally unaware of most of this big picture going on within one or two miles, the little picture within a few hundred yards was more than enough to keep me occupied. (Blair, The Forgotten War, .881)

The Sarge quickly emerged from his hole and ran to his jeep. Don Heim, me and another guy jumped in and we sped down the driveway to the road, then headed south behind our Headquarters trucks. We immediately saw that this was not going to be easy. We hadn't gone over a quarter mile and already the road ahead for at least a mile was solid vehicles. Heavy firing was coming from the head of the column and from the hills above the west side of the road. Bullets began slamming into the vehicles around us and zinging off the road. Some jeeps and even trucks had managed to drive off the left side of the road, down the embankment and across the shallow Hongchon River which paralleled the road on the east side. The road beside us was too steep even for our jeep so we jumped out and scrambled down to the river and splashed across the inches deep water to the other side. I was right behind the sergeant as we ran up the gravel slope on the opposite bank. The firing was an almost continuous rattle, mostly from the Chinese in the hills above us but I didn't look up there. I didn't want to look up there because almost every second I could hear the high-pitched *"ZIZzz"* of bullets passing by close over head or pinging into the gravel around us.

The sergeant dropped to the gravel writhing in pain and shouting, "I've been hit!" I knelt down beside him as he grasped his ankle with both hands and rolled on the ground. Then he pulled his hands away and I expected blood and jagged bone but it looked fine. We concluded it must have been a ricocheting rock and I took off again with sergeant limping along behind. We ran across an open field sloping up to the hillside. Several jeeps had gathered there and we ducked behind for shelter. Bullets continued to rain down on us. One of the jeeps had a 50-caliber machine gun mounted on it and someone, in frustration grabbed the gun and started firing up at the hills. Another guy dragged a 75mm recoilless rifle out of another jeep, loaded it and aimed up at the ridge line. Everyone behind the 75 scattered as he fired, blowing dirt, rocks and leaves for 100 feet behind. The shell landed among the trees up on the hill but we may as well have thrown rocks at the ocean for all the good it did.

Some sergeant hollered that he was "going to get the hell out of here," and "who's going with me?" I jumped up and we raced to a nearby jeep and climbed in. We tore off, throwing rocks with our spinning wheels, and headed straight down the slope toward the Chinese. After a couple of hundred yards, the ravine which had been blocking our way on the left, flattened out and my driver made an abrupt left turn down through the gully and up the other side. We roared up a trail across an open field on the other side, but the Chinese were not going to let us get away that easily. We were even closer now to the long ridge line above the blocked road on our right and it seemed every Chinese up there was now shooting at us, the lone duck in a shooting gallery. The bullets whined and zipped past our ears at an ever increasing rate, others whammed into the side of the jeep. I could see holes appearing in the hood and sides and clearly felt the jarring impact of one bullet which went through the door right under my seat.

I still could not bear to look up at the hillside and directly into the hail of copper jacketed lead. I felt that if I did, a bullet might smash directly into my face. Finally, I could stand it no longer and raised my rifle, aimed up at the ridge line and began pumping shots in their direction. Some of the intense fear gave way to anger and I felt better, at least I was doing something instead of cringing in my seat waiting for a slug to slam into me.

Ahead of us, a 6x6 loaded with artillery shells sat in the middle of the dirt road. It was burning fiercely. A body lay sprawled face down in the road 50 feet before the truck. The driver slowed momentarily, and then we both saw the yellowish tinge of the skin on his outstretched arms and head. He was already dead.   The sergeant gunned the engine, bounced over the body, then swerved around the burning truck. I kept my fingers crossed, hoping it wouldn't blow up until we were past. We could now see other vehicles up ahead on our left. They had gathered at the foot of a small ravine leading up the hill to the east. We could also see why they had stopped; a deep ravine blocked the way south a few hundred yards ahead.

We pulled up, abandoned the jeep and started running for the ravine. The bullets were still following us as persistently as ever. I passed a jeep and noticed, on the seat, the largest pair of field glasses I had ever seen - like those used on ships. I started to grab them then changed my mind. I don't know why I even thought of picking them up. A few soldiers had gathered at the foot of the ravine. One standing alone behind a jeep caught my attention. He had no shirt on and his face was ashen white and impassive; his eyes looked straight ahead in a wide-eyed glassy stare. His right arm, almost totally severed, was still hanging by his side dangling from one glistening white tendon. The flesh from the upper half of the right rib cage had been stripped away, exposing the lighter colored ribs contrasting with the darker flesh underneath. The ribs heaved slowly in and out with each breath. I noticed little blood. I couldn't comprehend how a human being could sustain such an injury and not only remain conscious but remain standing, unless my very brief glance overstated the extent of his injuries.

In normal circumstances, one would be almost overwhelmed with sympathy for someone in his condition, but now I only had time for a momentary twinge of empathy before running on past. I knew he was going to die, but there was little time for sympathy when at any moment you yourself expected to be killed.

Some men were climbing up the side of the ravine to the top of a low hill, maybe 200 feet high. Four soldiers had started up the path carrying a stretcher with a wounded man on it. Another stretcher lay on the ground with a soldier who had been shot in the foot. They needed more guys to carry the stretchers so I volunteered. By now I had become almost numb from the fear and adrenaline. I moved along, as in a trance, yet sharply aware of the others around me, aware of each bullet that sizzled past but no longer bothering to duck or take evasive action. Reality had a somewhat dreamlike quality. I knew that there were many Chinese in the hills to the west but I had inexplicably forgotten about the thousands of Chinese I had seen swarming toward us from the north and east. It made no sense at all for me to attach myself to a stretcher crew when we could not possibly outrun the hordes almost upon us. My mind apparently was overwhelmed by the situation and it no longer functioned in a rational manner. It tunneled in on bearing the stretcher as a job that needed doing; as a sane act in a world which, for the moment had gone insane.

We had six guys on each stretcher, four carrying while the other two carried the guns of the four carrying the stretcher. We struggled up the path for about 50 feet, and then I changed places with another guy. About half way up I saw the lieutenant from my old platoon in Easy Company. He passed us on the trail moving pretty fast. When he reached the top about 100 feet above us he turned around and made a sweeping motion with his arm as he yelled down: *"Come on men!"* then disappeared. That was the last American officer I saw that day.

PART TWO

THE MARCH

CHAPTER FOURTEEN

Captured

The four of us struggled with the stretcher on up to the top of the small hill and were glad to see that the path ahead followed a gentle, almost level slope through Sumac bushes which were about 5 feet high. We set the stretcher down and the guy spelling me handed me my M1 back along with two other M1s. I walked ahead, my M1 on my right shoulder and the other two rifles slung on my left shoulder. Suddenly we heard strange voices ahead on our left. It sounded like Chinese. The guys carrying the stretcher dropped it and dove into the bushes without even taking the time to get their guns from me. I ran straight ahead, hoping to pass the Chinese before they could cut off my escape route.

I hadn't gone a hundred feet when I rounded a slight curve in the path and stopped dead, staring into the muzzle of a Burp gun about 20 feet away. At the same instant, the young Chinese soldier holding it barked some order at me. A warm wave of panic washed over my face and down my body. I felt faint, almost dizzy. He couldn't miss at this range. I instantly remembered that one word of Chinese that they had taught us six days earlier in reserve. I shouted "*TOWSHUNG!*" as I jerked my thumbs out from under the rifle slings and raised my hands. He answered with a burst of machine gun fire aimed it seemed, right at my face. I clamped my eyes shut and tensed my body expecting the impacts. I was going to die! I did not relive my past, instead my mind just ceased to function. For one second, there was only oblivion.

Figure 16: Chinese Burp Gun

I felt nothing. How could he miss? He barked another order and I opened my eyes. He had moved closer and was now pointing the barrel and looking slightly off to my left. I snapped my head around to my left rear just as he fired another burst, clipping and cutting through the tips of the Sumac bushes behind me. I heard a shout and one of my stretcher buddies came out of the bushes with his hands held high. The Chinese motioned him over by me with a wave of his gun barrel. I guessed he wanted our weapons so I unslung my three rifles and laid them on the ground. I assumed my buddy had also, but my gaze was riveted on the Burp gun barrel. It was not enough. He pointed at my waist. I took my cartridge belt off but it also carried my canteen, bayonet, ammo and first aid pack. My poncho was slung over the back of the belt so that it also dropped to the ground. I gave absolutely no thought to losing my canteen and poncho, something I would later regret. I was still too petrified with fear to think of doing anything but following orders.

The soldier was now standing about 4 feet in front of me. I detected the unmistakable, pungent odor of garlic on his breath. Next he wanted to see what I had in my pockets. I removed the contents one at a time. I handed him my wallet, wrapped in plastic. He waved his left hand back and forth like a semaphore while with the other hand he kept the Burp gun leveled at my gut. I figured he didn't want my wallet. I took off my watch and again he waved it off. I had a jack knife in one pocket. That he took! He poked at my breast pocket. I had brought some of my own tools with me to Korea. I had put a small diagonal wire cutter, needle-nose pliers and two small screw drivers in the fingers of a leather glove and this I carried in my breast pocket. I hated to lose them, but I wasn't about to argue about it.

The soldier now motioned up the path with the gun barrel as he grunted, "*duuh! duuh!*" We guessed that he meant to get going so we started walking up the path. We began to see other Chinese soldiers and soon it was crawling with them. Sporadic gunfire crackled ahead and off to our right. We crouched down. Nearby, a badly wounded Chinese soldier lay on a stretcher. He had no shirt on and blood soaked bandages covered his stomach, arms, and legs. He was moaning continuously in a low voice as he looked at us. I tried to guess the meaning of that look. Would he kill us now if he had the chance? I thought he probably would.

In the present war in Iraq, whenever commentators are discussing our soldiers who have been taken prisoner, they almost always call them "heroes". In that moment in time when someone gives you a few hundred milliseconds to decide if you want to live or die, most choose to raise their hands. There is absolutely nothing heroic about this in my opinion.

We moved on since the gunfire didn't seem to be coming in our direction. Another soldier brought four more POWs to add to our little group. Now there were six of us. I began to think maybe they're not going to shoot us after all. The sun was getting low on the horizon and from it I could tell that we were being taken eastward. We came to a treeless grassy hillside. The path cut across the south side just below the crest of the hill. Chinese soldiers were scattered all over the hillside and three of them had a heavy machine gun set up no more than 20 feet from us. They were firing random short bursts at another hill just south of us. Suddenly one of our 30 caliber machine guns on the other hill opened up, firing long bursts. Whoever he was, he was good because the bullets began to whack and thud into the dirt all over our hillside. We dropped to the ground but there was no protection since we were lying on the south slope facing the machine gun. We could only grit our teeth and hope none of the bullets found us.

A Chinese officer was standing on a small rise nearby and waving his arms while screaming orders. The soldiers around him returned the fire then some soldiers came running up with another machine gun and quickly set it up. They joined the others in firing at the American position. The Chinese officer was just like our officers; he was standing up in a fully exposed position shouting orders and totally ignoring the bullets flying around. I guess officers, American or Chinese, are all alike.

The firing stopped and our guards motioned us onward until we were halted by another soldier who ran up brandishing a Burp gun. He looked to be about 50 with a wrinkled, weather beaten face and he also looked mean and angry. He shouted at our guards and made threatening gestures toward us with his gun. Our guards seemed to be afraid of him. He motioned for us to get down on our knees with our hands on top of our head. He pulled back the slide on his machine gun and then I heard it snap forward, as he braced it at his side while pointing it down at us. They were going to kill us after all, just like some of the stories we had heard about the North Koreans. Should I run? Maybe he wanted us to run so he could shoot us. Fear made the decision for me. I felt weak all over - paralyzed into inaction. I couldn't open my eyes.

We heard another angry voice. I opened my clenched eyes and saw a younger Chinese soldier who now seemed to be berating the older one who I had thought was about to shoot us. They argued for a few seconds, and then the older man stalked off. The younger Chinese, who I guessed to be an officer of some type, now impatiently ordered our guards to get us moving. I'll never know what that was all about. He may have intended to shoot us or he may have only wanted to give us a good scare.

The sun was rapidly approaching the horizon as we were brought up to a bunker on the hillside. We were ushered in, one at a time. When my turn came, I stooped low to clear the logs over the entrance and stepped cautiously inside. It was a low-ceilinged room about 6 feet on a side, lighted by a kerosene lantern. A Chinese officer sat on a stool at a tiny writing board under the lamp. A guard stood by the door with his rifle at the ready.

The officer asked my name, rank and serial number in excellent English. As I gave the information, he transferred it to his papers on the writing board. Next he asked for my unit. I told him Headquarters Company of 2nd Battalion, 23rd Regiment of the 2nd Division. I didn't even think of trying to hide any information from him. (John Wayne would not have approved, I'm sure) He then asked for the names of my regimental, battalion and company commanders. I said that I didn't know their names since I was new in the unit. I was telling the truth but I was afraid that any moment he would start threatening or beating me. He then proceeded to tell me the names of all my commanding officers. As he mentioned each name, it jogged my memory and I knew he was probably correct. Obviously he had already gotten the information from others and was only trying to verify it or else he was testing me to see if I was lying. Next, I was asked how many men were in a company. I honestly didn't know, because I didn't want to know. I was fed up with the Army and ignored anything about the army that didn't interest me. The officer made no effort to force an answer from me. Again, he just informed me of the number of men in an infantry company. After a few minutes, I was returned to my original guards.

The Chinese were rounding up more and more of our guys. We were gathered into a large group of about 100 as the sun set. It was rapidly getting dark as they herded us close together under the trees. It started to rain. I made an attempt at gallows humor mostly to buck myself up, but some of my fellow POWs snapped back that they "didn't see anything funny" about our situation. After that, I kept such thoughts to myself.

Our guards began to form us up into a column. They were tying each man's left hand to the right hand of the guy in front, and then repeating the process with the guy behind. I immediately thought of the incidents I had read about where they tied your hands before they shot you. They were using strips of cloth from torn-up captured marker panels. These are the panels we used to mark our position on the front lines to prevent our own airplanes from strafing us.

When we were all tied together, we were marched along a narrow path. It was now very dark, and it would have been easy to escape if we weren't tied together. Though if we had escaped, we probably would have soon run into some more Chinese soldiers. As we stumbled along, you could hear the voices of other Chinese in the darkness beside the path and occasionally see the glow of a cigarette. The hills seemed to be literally crawling with Chinese. We finally arrived at what seemed like the top of a small tree-covered hill. Our hands were untied and we were crowded together with other POWs already on the hill.

It got very dark and the rain fell steadily. There was no wind and the night was quiet except for the patter of raindrops on wet ponchos or helmets and an occasional soft whisper. We all huddled together under the trees and some shared their poncho with a buddy. No one near me had a poncho so I could only huddle on the ground against a tree trunk using my helmet to keep some of the rain off. It didn't much matter - I was already soaked to the skin and shivered uncontrollably.

One of the POWs in our group must have been badly wounded because he kept moaning continuously. I never did see who he was or how he had been wounded. Sometime after dark when the rain started, he began to softly call, "mama, mama." Hour after hour this went on. I didn't blame him for keeping me awake, I wouldn't have been able to sleep anyway and besides, I probably couldn't have endured it any better than he.

It must have been after midnight when suddenly I sensed a stirring among the figures nearby; the soft rustle as one wet poncho brushed past another. I made out a figure moving almost silently among the other figures huddled on the ground. This new figure would pause over the form of one of the POWs on the ground, stoop down, then after a brief moment, he would straighten up and move onto the next.

He approached me. I could tell from the odor of garlic that it was probably one of the Chinese guards. The hump on his back told me that he was carrying his rifle slung over his shoulder upside down under his poncho. I tried to anticipate what he was going to do. Just then, his hand found my arm, and then slid down to my wrist. He felt my watch. It clicked in my mind. I remembered that first Chinese soldier who had refused to take my watch and noted now how quiet this one was trying to be. He was stealing watches and I guessed he could be in big trouble for stealing from POWs. He grasped the watch and as it slipped off my wrist I clenched my fist firmly around the band. He pulled gently. I pulled right back. For a second I considered hollering, then - no, I had a better idea. I grabbed his poncho with my right hand and started to pull it off of him. He resisted. I became more insistent. The cold and wet had bolstered my courage and also I sensed that I had him at a disadvantage. I grabbed the poncho by his neck and started to pull it over his head, my hand brushed against the butt of his rifle. This time he did not resist as I pulled the poncho free. I then released my grasp on the watch band and he stole quietly away.

We had made a deal and not a word was spoken. I was very satisfied and I suspect that also he wasn't too disappointed, because he could easily get another poncho. On a night like this, a dry poncho was worth much more to me than a twelve-dollar Bulova. In the weeks ahead, I'm sure that poncho saved my life several times.

I slipped the poncho over my head and put my helmet back on, and then crouched down again. I was still wet but at least now I might dry out in a few hours. As morning approached, our wounded buddy weakened noticeably. His cries of "mama" became weaker and less frequent. Just before dawn there was only silence. I wondered what his mother would have done if she could have heard him.

The CCF attacked the 23rd again that night, May 18 around midnight in the rain. The 2nd division stopped the Chinese Advance only a couple of miles south of where I was captured. (**Munroe**, p.134) That night the two battalions of the 23rd reported 886 men missing, this was just half of all the men in those units. However, in the next few days many stragglers wandered in. The final toll for May 17 and 18 was 417 missing and presumed captured, 159 wounded and incredibly only 21 listed as killed. I found that hard to believe since I myself saw about 10 killed. The 38th was said to have lost more than 1000, and many of their men were mixed in with ours, so maybe some of those I saw were from the 38th. The 23rd alone also lost 117 vehicles and 76 trailers. The most incredible however is the statement of one historian that "the 23rd infantry remained intact as it fought its way out of the encirclement and thus they escaped disaster." The two regiments lost more than 1500 men and all their vehicles. If this is "escaping disaster," I would hate to go through one. (**Blair**, The Forgotten War, p. 882)

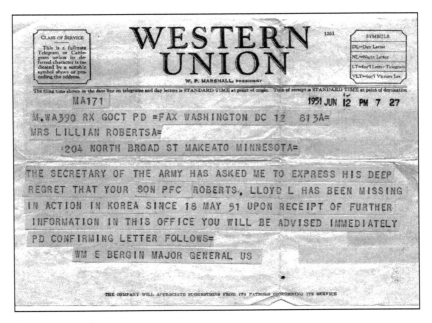

Figure 17: Missing

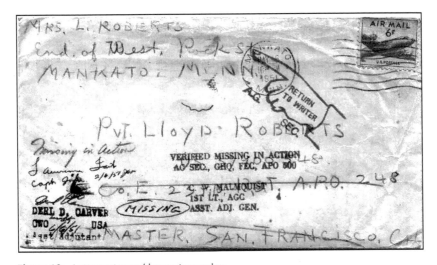

Figure 18: Letter returned home to sender

CHAPTER FIFTEEN

The March North Begins

A s it became light, on May 19th our guards moved us off the hill and down a winding path through the trees. As we walked past, Chinese soldiers handed each of us captured weapons to carry. Some were given BAR's but most were given two M1's tied together with telephone wire. There was some grumbling, because it just didn't seem right that we should be helping the Chinese carry their captured booty. I did not count noses, but I guessed that there were somewhere between 200 and 400 men in our group. We seemed to be heading more or less northwest. Finally I recognized something familiar, the wreckage of our trucks on the Hongchon-Inje road. They were taking us back the way we had come. (See **Figure 19**)

We climbed up a path and onto the road headed northeast. All we could see in both directions were the burned out hulks of 6x6's, jeeps and trailers. As we walked single file along the road, we had to pick our way through the scattered wreckage strewn over the road and in the ditches. Every vehicle had been burned; the entire road and surrounding hillside were also blackened. Obviously the equipment had been napalmed by our own planes to prevent the Chinese from getting it. It must have happened the day before on May 18th, probably not long after we had abandoned the vehicles, because the debris was now cold.

Here and there a few bodies lay amid the wreckage, all burned beyond recognition, as was usual with napalm. Some may have already been dead, killed by the hail of Chinese bullets raining down from above the hillside; others were probably wounded and left with the trucks by their buddies. From the remains of their burned boots we could guess that they were most likely Americans. As we passed the remains of another burned-out hulk of a 6x6, I noticed a charred body underneath. He was still frozen on his knees and elbows with hands covering his face. I could visualize that he probably hid under the truck, afraid to brave the hail of bullets from the Chinese, and then realized too late that he was being napalmed by his own airplanes. That could very easily have been me.

Figure 19: View of May 18 ambush when recaptured on May 23rd

The decision to napalm was probably made by some general in the rear echelons: it was better to end the suffering of a few wounded men and perhaps kill a few others too timid to leave the safety of their hiding places, than to allow those weapons and equipment to fall into the wrong hands. I'm sure it was the right decision, given the circumstances, but the circumstances should never have happened.

The Marines routinely fought their way out of many roadblocks in Korea. If our troops had been better trained, motivated and led they probably could have also fought their way out without losing so much equipment.

Some of the guys managed to snatch a few scorched cans from the trucks as we walked past. I didn't see anything worth grabbing. As we headed north past the tail end of the column, I saw the last burned-out truck which I guessed was our old Headquarters Company truck. Nothing on it remained unburned.

We filed up the road and turned northwest. We were crossing the small valley which lay just below the hill occupied by the 23rd on the night of May 16 when the Chinese attack first started. I remembered that this was the place where we had slaughtered hundreds of South Korean soldiers who had tried to retreat through our lines.

We now saw the results. The guards were walking us right through the middle of the killing field. Every ten or fifteen feet, no matter which way you looked, there lay the crumpled remains of a body dressed in US issue uniform. They appeared to be South Koreans, although in this war they could just as well have been North Korean infiltrators dressed in stolen uniforms. Hundreds littered the valley floor. We could have taken other routes. I got the impression that our guards were deliberately taking us through these areas so that we could see the destruction. Maybe they were trying to humiliate or demoralize us.

About midday we stopped for a half hour rest in a quiet wooded glen. It was overcast and cool and the lush vegetation was still dripping from the previous night's rain. The woods were silent and there was no hint of war. The guys who had scrounged some cans from the wrecked truck convoy now took the time to see what they had. They opened them with the small C ration can openers we all carried. Great! They had two one-gallon cans of yellow mustard and one gallon of ketchup. We hadn't eaten in 24 hours. They started tasting the mustard or ketchup; some just dipped their fingers in the cans then licked them off. In a few minutes the cans were empty. I could only watch, because they only shared their booty with their closest buddies.

As we walked, one of the POWs began singing what sounded like a hymn. He knew only two or three verses and most of the verses were, "*Lord let it be, please Lord let it be*" or something similar. He kept it up all day until I just wanted to tell him to shut up. As it later turned out, he kept singing throughout the whole march. Soon I wasn't the only one sick of hearing him.

We marched all day, stopping only for short five minute breaks. I became so thirsty I couldn't stand it much longer. Even the guys who had canteens had emptied them long ago. I hadn't seen a river or stream close enough to allow getting a drink. Finally the trail crossed the edge of a rice paddy. A small rivulet was flowing through the paddy. I knew I shouldn't, but I quickly stooped down and scooped up a hand full of the cool, clear looking water. It tasted good, so I drank my fill. The guard prodded me on with his usual "*duuh! Duuh!*" I regretted now that I hadn't kept my canteen and I would regret it much more in the future.

Our route wound through wooded ravines, along back country trails, and footpaths and sometimes narrow roads fit only for a team of oxen. We moved single file at a steady, brisk walk. Often we could look up along the hillsides and see hundreds of Chinese soldiers sitting under the trees and bushes, waiting for nightfall - their safest time for traveling. We seemed to be traveling west or northwest. Some of the other guys agreed with me. They also had the impression that we were being exhibited to the Chinese troops, perhaps to build their moral. We walked along, with our eyes cast downward most of the time, talking very little, and then only in low voices or whispers.

Our path coursed along a steep wooded hillside, just a few feet above a rushing mountain stream which tumbled over rocks and large boulders on its way down a very narrow canyon. The hillside and boulders by the stream were literally crawling with Chinese soldiers. There must have been thousands. Every bush or tree had at least one and sometimes three or four soldiers resting or sleeping underneath. Others were cleaning weapons or eating from small porcelain glazed metal bowls with chopsticks or spoons. We had not eaten in 24 hours.

It was very quiet. The Chinese soldiers watched us intently as we filed past. Some laughed softly and pointed at us and made, what I assumed, were derogatory remarks about us to their comrades. Our guards let us stop and go down to the stream to get a drink. I leaned the captured weapons I had been carrying against a rock and clambered down to the stream. The water was cool and clear. Suddenly we heard a distant shout, "*Fiji Laala!*" Then we heard the sound of an airplane engine. All the Chinese froze wherever they were and they motioned for us to freeze also. I jumped from a rock in midstream to the bank and the soldiers shouted and pointed their weapons at me so I sat down on a boulder and remained motionless.

An AT-6 single engine observation plane came into view flying low along the canyon. It circled our position at about 500 feet, and I could clearly make out the helmets of the pilot and his back seat observer as he banked in our direction. The plane disappeared from view behind trees then returned again. My face was looking directly up at the pilot as he banked again. I didn't see how he could have avoided seeing us or some of the Chinese. The plane circled a couple more times then flew off. We knew he was a spotter plane and we knew that if he had seen us, the next thing we could expect would be artillery or napalm. I grabbed the two M1s wrapped with telephone wire and our guards hurried us off along the trail.

Figure 20: AT-6 Observation Plane

It began getting dark. The guards halted and started tying us together again. This time, they tied us together by our waists using rope and telephone wire in single file groups of five or 10 men, then we picked up our weapons and continued on. It was a cloudy night and began to drizzle. We stumbled along in the dark. The man ahead of me whispered that he was going to "drop" his weapons, and I heard it thud softly into the bushes beside the trail. I thought about doing the same but was too fearful of the consequences. For all I knew, the guard would shoot those who were no longer carrying captured weapons in the morning.

We kept marching all night, stumbling along the path, brushing against bushes and struggling to keep up with the guys in front and behind. Occasionally we could hear the murmuring sound of a nearby stream or the low voices of Chinese soldiers along the path or see the glow of their cigarettes as they took a long drag on them. The night was obviously filled with Chinese. I couldn't imagine breaking my rope and trying to escape. I was sure that I wouldn't get more than 100 yards before blundering into some soldiers and getting recaptured or maybe even shot. I was beginning to get weary. I hadn't' slept in two nights and now hadn't eaten in 30 hours.

As the sky got light, we could begin to take stock of our situation. The terrain was still low wooded hills and we were traveling over narrow paths or trails. I finally noticed that one POW, who had been in our group ahead of me, was missing and several of the guys were no longer carrying weapons. The guards halted and began counting noses. As soon as they discovered the missing guns and especially the missing POWs, they became very angry. I didn't know what to expect, but nobody was shot or even hit with a rifle butt. Of course, our guards looked very young and naive and it might have been a different story if they had been older battle hardened soldiers.

With daylight, (May 20) everyone was untied and we continued marching. Later we were relieved of our captured weapons and then resumed the march in a west/ northwest direction. Just as the day before, the hills were full of Chinese soldiers waiting for the night. Instead of heading north, we were again being paraded westerly along the front so they could show-off their captives to the troops.

The rain pelted down heavily throughout the day. I was beginning to think our guards were trying to walk us to death. I now hadn't eaten or slept for 48 hours. At least we no longer had to carry any weapons. Until then I had kept going on fear and adrenaline, but I didn't think I could keep going much longer. At first we had marched along at a very brisk walk but now everyone just slogged along through the mud at a slow walk. We pressed the guards for frequent rest but only got 10 minute breaks every hour or so.   Night had come again, and again we were tied together but this time they seemed to be a little more careful. The rain had abated as we continued our shuffling journey northward. Life was reduced to almost one step at a time and the future consisted of just hoping that the next rest break would come sooner rather than later.

In between, my thoughts were obsessed with food. I remembered everything I had ever enjoyed eating and even some things I hadn't. Visions of roast beef, mashed potatoes and gravy with all the trimmings, followed by heaps of vanilla ice cream smothered in syrupy mashed strawberries filled my mind. When I closed my eyes, I could almost taste them. I was not alone; others around me began wishing out loud for a large juicy hamburger smothered in onions or a quart of fresh, icy cold milk or whatever their mind had fastened on at the moment. From that day on, food became the number one topic of conversation and occupant of our thoughts. Home ran a close second. Food was our immediate concern; home could wait a while.

At dawn on May 21, we straggled into a small valley with a few Korean huts clustered under some trees near the southern end. We were crowded into the small rooms of the mud walled houses, 10 to 15 men per room. I was so exhausted, I just collapsed on the floor among the other bodies; they could have been dead for all I cared. The floor was plain hard-packed clay but it didn't matter, I was asleep in moments. From time to time during the day I was dimly aware of occasional jostling and shoving as those around me sought to find a more comfortable position or got up to go to the bathroom. One couldn't move or turn over without awakening at least the two on either side and going to the bathroom would wake up half the room. Again, it didn't matter; a half-opened eye, a little grumbling, and you would be back asleep immediately.

In the afternoon we began to awaken and stir ourselves. Someone said we were going to get fed. That got my attention. Soon one man from each room was sent to the kitchen hut to get our ration. Our man walked in carrying a 3-gallon bucket of boiled potatoes. We had no bowl or mess kits, so each, in turn, would reach in the bucket and grab a couple of small potatoes about the size of eggs. I managed to get about four or five before the bucket was emptied and devoured them, skins and all. They tasted terrible and one or two guys were too finicky to eat any. This was my first food in seventy-two hours and I wasn't going to risk passing anything up. Little did we know that this would be some of the best food we would have for months.

As dusk approached, we were gathered outside our huts. For the first night we were not tied to one another as we were marched in a scraggly column north. I was getting sick. I guessed it was probably due to the many times in the past days when I had drunk water from rice paddies and roadside ditches. It was beginning to catch up with me. When diarrhea hit, I only had time to quickly drop my pants by the side of the road. There wasn't even time to wipe as the guard prodded me on. But many of us were in the same boat and it began to slow the progress of our march.

We could hear trucks on a main road ahead and as we got closer, we also made out the rhythmic beat of hundreds of human feet. As we climbed up on the shoulder, we could tell we were on one of the main supply routes (MSR) somewhere in Central-Korea. In the blackness, we could feel the gravel under our boots and make out a strip of road about 10 to 12 feet wide which was only slightly lighter than the deeper black of the ditches which bordered it. The guards kept us on the right shoulder marching north at a normal walk.

Hundreds of Chinese troops were moving four abreast in the opposite direction to our travel. They came toward us in great black bunches in the night, marching at a quickstep or dog trot - about two beats per second. The deep, rhythmic, hypnotic thud of hundreds of feet hitting the ground in unison was blended with the slightly less rhythmic, rattle and jangle of pots, pans, weapons and whatever other metal objects they were carrying. As they passed, the ground shook beneath our feet. Each group was marching in step with one another and led by an officer a few paces ahead. They were totally silent except for the occasional order barked by some leader. Each group was like some giant black machine. The heavy silence implied either dedication or fear, or maybe both. I couldn't imagine any unit of American troops marching like that, like automatons.

As each group passed, we could hear another approaching no more than 100 yards behind the first. Behind each group we could dimly see the outline of other men, one behind the other, trotting along at the same pace, cast iron cooking pots slung from a pole between them. Other pairs of men appeared to be carrying heavy weapons, boxes and sacks and all moved at the same inexorable pace. If we got too close, we were jostled or bumped out of the way sometimes with a low curse and sometimes we would be knocked down. Other single Chinese soldiers would now and then come running either north or south through our ranks pushing, shoving and cursing us as they made their way, probably carrying orders between different units. Often the road was as crowded and chaotic as a busy Christmas shopping mall and all in almost total darkness. Escape would have been no problem at all at almost any moment you wanted to choose, as long as one of the guards wasn't walking directly behind you.

Every 10 or 15 minutes one could hear the growl of a truck approaching in medium gear without lights. Then we would spot the looming black hulk bearing down on us at five to 10 miles per hour. They did not slow or stop for anything. The Chinese soldiers trotting down the center of the road would just crowd over to their right shoulder, barely slowing their jog as the truck passed. This went on hour after hour. At least a division of troops, 10,000 men, must have been passing us every hour.

Sometime before midnight we heard the, by now, familiar shout of "*Fiji Laala!*" along with scattered rifle shots to warn of an approaching plane. Almost immediately I heard the drone of twin engines, it was a B26 bomber. As he passed overhead at about 1000 or 2000 feet, I heard a low pop and instantaneously the valley around us was bathed in white light. Several more pops followed, as a string of flares was dropped northward from our position. The pitch of the motors increased as the B-26 made a 180 and headed back in our general direction. The entire valley was flooded in white light as bright as daylight. The MSR ran south through a small valley with low hills on both sides. Hundreds of Chinese troops were jogging south in groups of about company size, about 200 to 300 men. Their columns stretched as far as I could see to the north and south in the light of the flares. They didn't stop, scatter or slow down as the B-26 approached from the north, flying well to the east of the road.

There was suddenly a series of three or four bright flashes, then the thud of tremendous explosions on the hilltop about 600 yards to the east. All the POWs immediately scattered across to the west side of the road and dived into the ditch. Some of us went even further, running a hundred feet or so into the adjoining field. Our guards were frantic as they followed us waving their guns and shouting. We paid almost no attention to them. I dropped flat on my belly in the field about 100 feet west of the road as I heard the B-26 returning, this time directly overhead. I would have run further out into the field, but I was sure the guard would have shot me in the back.

First I heard a low whistle, rapidly increasing in pitch, and then I remembered to clap my hands over my ears and open my mouth. Somewhere I had read that this could sometimes keep you from having your eardrums broken. The first concussion seemed to raise my body straight up from the surface of the ground at least an inch; the next ones were almost as bad. Small clods of earth showered down over me. I glanced quickly up. The first bomb, probably a 500 pounder, had impacted on the other side of the road from me; the others had hit a hundred or more yards to the north, on the road or on either side. As the last flares winked out I could see that some of the closer Chinese troops had apparently scattered to the ditches but most of them just kept on trotting south at their usual pace as if nothing had happened.

Figure 21: B26 Medium Bomber

The B-26 engines droned off to the south so I guessed we were safe for the time being. Our guards ran up and down in the darkness screaming and shouting to try to round everybody up again. I stood up and groped my way back toward the road until my night vision had returned. I didn't even think of trying to escape; what would be the use with the thousands of Chinese around? We collected on the right-hand side of the road as the guards ran   and down, apparently trying to count heads. They must have been satisfied that they had most of us, because we soon continued the trek north. I was sure some of our guys and many Chinese must have been killed by the bombs but in the darkness we had no way of knowing. By daylight we would be long gone and if a few were missing, most of us would never know the difference. The next day, some Chinese would come along and bury the pieces and they would then join the list of all those who just disappeared.

Most of the night we struggled north against the tide of bodies tramping south but as dawn (May 22) approached we were almost alone on the road. The Chinese didn't dare try to move that many men on the MSR in daylight. We slept exhausted most of the day in some Korean houses, and then moved out again on the MSR at dusk. We had not been fed since the boiled potatoes we had been given about 24 hours previously. Our guards didn't starve; however, they seemed to make sure they got their two meals a day. They carried a long cylindrical sack, made of canvas, about 3 inches in diameter and maybe 5 feet long - looking not unlike a long sausage. It was filled with some sort of ground up dried powder which they would mix with hot water to make a thick gruel. I later found out that each sack held about 10 days' supply of food. But we POWs never got any of that.

After dark, the night became almost a repeat of the previous night. Again, we had to fight our way north against hordes of Chinese marching down the MSR toward the front. Every few minutes another truck would come plowing its way through the black sea of humanity which only parted long enough for its passage, then closed in behind.

In five days, I had only eaten about five small potatoes and had slept very little. Now my dysentery was getting worse. We only moved at a normal walk but after an hour most of us would be exhausted. At each ten minute break, we would collapse on the shoulder of the road or on the side of the embankment. Many would fall asleep immediately.

Sometime in the night, the guards called another halt. The embankment was steep so I just dropped to the road with my feet stretched out down the slope into the ditch, my head on the gravel shoulder and my helmet beside me. I didn't care about anything; the thudding feet of the Chinese soldiers, the trucks, nothing bothered me. I just wanted to sleep. I didn't notice the truck until its tire brushed the top of my head and ran over my hair. The guy beside me said his buddy had been hit. He didn't move. He was dead; his head had been run over and crushed by the big dual wheels.

The break was over and the guards rousted us up again. We just left our buddy, whoever he was, laying by the road. As we started north, we heard the shouted warnings of airplanes again. One of our nearby guys still had his wrist watch and said it was about 10:00 P.M. and time for another B-26. We soon learned that the B-26's were very regular, 10:00 P.M. and 2:00 A.M. every night. We started calling them "Bed-check Charlie." But this night, they didn't bother us.

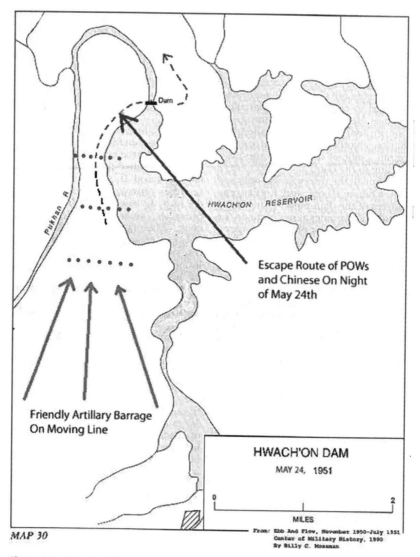

MAP 30

Figure 22: Hwachon Dam

CHAPTER SIXTEEN

Hwachon

After the debacle of May 17 and 18, the 2nd division and other units consolidated their positions on a more or less east-west line at Hangje. The weather was clear and sunny on the 19th, then rainy for the 20th through 23rd. The Chinese kept up heavy pressure on the 2nd division on the 19th and 20th and took very heavy losses, especially from artillery. On the 21st, the 23rd launched a limited counteroffensive, inflicting heavy casualties. The Chinese attacked the 23rd at 0200 on May 22, and this was their last attempt during the Spring offensive. On May 23rd a big offensive was launched on the central front with the 2nd division, a major participant. On the 24th, a tank spearhead reached the Soyang River on the Hangje-Inje road followed by the 23rd regiment on the 25th. Also, on the 25th, Hwachon was recaptured by the 17 Infantry Division with the 7th division blocking the escape of the Chinese to the west of Hwachon Reservoir. Six thousand CCF were captured. I did not know it at the time, but I also came close to being liberated. Some of our guys who escaped at this time were probably killed by their own artillery.

In summary, from the middle of May to the first week of June, the 2nd division sustained heavy losses but then counterattacked and regained all the lost territory. In this period, the Chinese had thrown 12 divisions against the 2nd division alone and had suffered 65,000 killed in 20 days of fighting. (**Munroe**, p. 138)

After resting during daylight, we moved out at dusk, again without being fed. For five days and nights I had nothing but five small potatoes. The few, who were too fussy, hadn't even had that. We were all hurting now. It was difficult to tell how far we walked each night but a good guess would be ten miles. This night was different; we had left the MSR and were following trails through the hills again. It was still early, maybe 10 P.M., when we were led up to what appeared to be a very large bunker.

I could feel the log revetments leading up to either side of a low log entrance. I could make out a large mound of earth silhouetted against the night sky as I ducked down into the bunker. Immediately inside the doorway there was only total blackness. We were being pushed and shoved one at a time into the bunker by our guards. Everyplace I tried to put my foot, I felt a body and one could progress only by squeezing your foot down in between two sleeping persons. Every step awakened at least one sleeping soldier and I was rewarded with strings of curses in Chinese. The floor was literally carpeted with Chinese soldiers. I stumbled my way about 15 feet back into the bunker and finally found a small area where I could just manage to squeeze down between two Chinese and their rifles.

We must have awakened half the sleeping soldiers before we settled down. The rest of our guys must have been put into other bunkers, because this particular one was already stuffed with humanity. I lay for a minute on my side, wedged in among my enemies, cramped and uncomfortable and listened to the snoring, coughing and heavy breathing. The stink of sweating, unwashed bodies and garlic breath permeated the dank atmosphere. I wondered 'how the hell' did I ever get in such a situation, and then fell asleep.

Some unknown time later I was awakened by a terrific commotion. This time I was the one being stepped on. It was still just as black as ever, with only the entrance visible as a slightly lighter shade of black. The Chinese soldiers all seemed to be bailing out as fast as they could. It was total bedlam. Then I heard the pounding thud of incoming artillery. I scrambled out the door and somehow found one of our guards or else he found me. They were assembling us into a large group in front of my bunker. The Chinese soldiers were all running off into the darkness down what looked like a road.

The sounds of exploding shells were getting louder every minute. We could hear the distant rumble of hundreds of guns all firing just as fast as they could reload thus forming a constant background sound like continuous thunder storms many miles away. Then much closer, we heard the whistle and crump of incoming shells exploding somewhere to our left, right and front as we faced south. It was what was called a walking artillery barrage. Hundreds of guns were all fired simultaneously and aimed to land every 50 or 100 feet along a line. Each time they fired, the line was moved forward 50 to 100 feet. The effect was of a line of explosions walking forward through the enemy positions. Someone in the open didn't have much chance of surviving such a barrage, even in a trench you could get hit by shrapnel if the shells were set to explode 50 feet above ground.

As we hurriedly gathered in the darkness, one of our buddies, Francis Burke, whispered in my ear that he and three others were going to escape and head toward the sound of artillery which he knew to be our lines. He asked if I wanted to go with. I told him I was too sick and exhausted to keep up and wished him luck. Burke was a big friendly, happy-go-lucky guy from Chicago and everybody liked him. I figured if anybody could make it, he could.

The artillery was getting close and the guards shouted at us to "*RUN! RUN!*" I ran, trying to keep up with the others in the darkness. I sensed Burke slip away to my left but I kept running straight ahead along a gravel road. I ran as fast as I could and I was aware of others running behind and ahead of me, but the artillery was rapidly gaining on us. There seemed to be a low hill on my left and on the right the road followed a black expanse that appeared like a lake or large river. I guessed it was probably Hwachon Reservoir.

As I ran, suddenly the shells seemed to be exploding on all sides at once. A large white geyser erupted with a roar on my immediate right and drenched me with the spray. A fish, about a foot long, appeared on the road in front of me, flopping furiously. I kept running. The barrage moved on ahead of me as fast as it had approached. I slowed down to a walk and began to locate some of the others. After a few minutes the artillery stopped abruptly.

Our guards ran up and down the road gathering up all the stray POWs and also probably trying to determine how many they had left. I had no idea if anyone had been killed. Dozens could have been hit and probably were. Most of us only knew the names of one or two or at most a few other men. Each of us had all we could do to try to save our own skins; fellow POWs came in a distant second. In short, it was very easy to die on the march and not be remembered or missed by anyone.

On May 25th, the 24th, and the 7th Divisions plus the 17th infantry recaptured the area around Hwachon Reservoir. Six thousand Chinese were captured while trying to escape to the west around the reservoir. (**Blair**, *The Forgotten War*, p.898) Our guards evidently succeeded in sneaking us around the west side of Hwachon before it was retaken by the 17th infantry. The artillery barrage was part of, and preceded that offensive. If I had known how close our troops were, I probably would have also tried to escape. After the war, I learned from Francis Burke's parents that he did not make it out that night. Some bones and his dog tags were found in a shallow surface grave near Togumi, Korea. Togumi is not on any of my maps. A surface grave means that someone just threw a little dirt over his body, probably someone who didn't give a damn - like some Korean or Chinese soldier.

I later determined that the distance from Hangje to Hawachon is about 40 to 50 miles. This means that we had covered this distance in five days, or about 10 miles per night.

CHAPTER SEVENTEEN

F80's

At dawn we trudged into a valley with low hills around it and settled into a group of Korean houses. Korean houses were all remarkably similar. They would start on a level plot of ground by laying out a long rectangle of large rocks about one foot in diameter and all the same size. The rectangle was usually about 10 feet wide and 40 feet long. This level bed of rocks formed the floor and foundation for the house. The top of the bed of large rocks was then filled in with smaller rocks to fill up the tops of all the cracks and spaces, and then the whole thing was covered with a smooth layer of clay to form the floor.

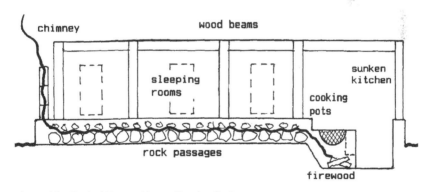

Figure 23: Typical Korean House Heating System

Next a sunken kitchen about 3 feet deep was dug on one end of the rectangle. It was not intended so, but the sunken kitchen formed a natural foxhole in each house. Steel cooking pots were now built low into this sunken kitchen with small fireplace openings right on the floor. The smoke and hot gases from the fires curled up around the bottom of the pots and then percolated out through all the small spaces and crevasses in the large rocks under the floor, and finally out the other end of the house through a chimney which extended from the ground up on the other end of the house. The whole purpose was to heat the floor in the winter time. Finally, a three-room house was then built on top of the heated floor. The walls were made of hand hewn pine timbers held together by mortise and tenon, wood peg construction. Willow branches were woven between the upright timbers and plastered with clay to form three or 4 inch thick mud walls. The sloping timbers of the roof were covered with clay tiles or thatch. There were no windows, and only one or two doors in each room. The doors consisted of thin slats of wood covered with thin paper and opened by sliding horizontally. Inside, the walls were generally papered with newspapers. The ceiling was a thin grid of slats also covered with newspapers to keep the warm air in during the winter. It sounds primitive, and it was, but it was also a very efficient way to heat a house. The Koreans call this type of heating 'ondol'.

Breakfast was a cup of boiled soy beans in a salty, dark broth. I choked it down even though it tasted terrible. I knew I needed every bit of nourishment I could get. I could feel myself getting weaker every night as we marched. One small meal a day, the 10 mile hike every night and the ever-present dysentery were taking a toll. I squeezed into a spot on the floor, covered with a bamboo mat, and tried to get some rest. The guy next to me on my left was the sergeant who had been my squad leader in Easy Company. He was just a kid, no older than I, named 'Emil Erdman' who had been born and raised on an Iowa farm. He was a really nice guy and well-liked by everyone when we were both in Easy company. He was also very religious and not a bit embarrassed to admit it. When he spoke of his parents, he said he was grateful to them for the type of upbringing they had given him.

Figure 24: F80 Jet

The guards would always pack us into the rooms so that there was never quite enough space to lie down and stretch out on, but by then we were usually so tired we could care less. This house was a little different from the usual, the sunken kitchen was located on the side rather than the end of the house, and it had doors opening into two of the rooms.

I slept fitfully until about midday when shots rang out nearby and I heard "*Fiji laala*" again. In a moment I could hear the distant roar of jet engines along with the intermittent rattle of their 50 caliber machine guns. It sounded like two or more F80's coming south down the valley from an excursion further north.

Our guard stepped quickly into the doorway and waved his rifle with its ever-present bayonet in a way that made it clear that we were to stay down. I had started to get up and move into the kitchen for more protection but stopped when he pointed the gun at me. I lay down again and noticed that Emil beside me was lying flat on his back, his hands clasped over his chest and his eyes closed as he mumbled a prayer.

The jets were now approaching very rapidly and the intermittent bursts of machine gun fire continued. One could tell just from the sound of the guns when they were pointed toward you. The F80 was probably traveling at half the speed of sound or more, so that the pitch of the gunfire when approaching was doubled and when flying directly away, the frequency of the sound was almost half what it would have been from a stationary gun. This change in frequency or pitch of the sound due to the Doppler Effect was very noticeable, and we quickly learned when we should duck.

The next thing I knew, parts of the wall on my right exploded with a series of sharp whacks as each 50-caliber slug slammed into the mud wall beside my head. The supersonic crack of the bullets was followed immediately by the high-pitched rattle of the machine guns. Emil, his head only inches from mine, emitted a loud "*UUFF!*" as a slug struck his chest.

The guard's bayonet was forgotten as I leaped into the adjoining kitchen and hit the dirt floor on my belly. The air was filled with a cacophony of snapping, crackling bullets and the dust from their impacts as I huddled on the floor, then two F80s roared overhead very low. A few seconds after passing, they fired another burst and this time the sound of the guns had changed dramatically to a very low pitched growl. I knew the danger had passed for the moment and began picking myself up and brushing off some of the dirt.

I crawled back into the room and as the dust settled, it was quiet except for the distant rumble of the departing F80's. I knew Emil had been hit, so I checked to see how he was. He was dead, killed instantly. He was a nice guy. So much for the power of prayer; I'll take a sunken kitchen any day.

Two other guys were also killed which was really amazing considering the literal hail of bullets sprayed at 200 or 300 POWs in several houses. You could conclude that aircraft with machine guns are not very effective against personnel, especially if the men are able to take cover in trenches or foxholes. They did scare the hell out of us, though.

We buried all three of our guys in a garden behind one of the houses at dusk. The Chinese let one of our people say a few words after we had tamped the earth down over their graves, then we gathered our stuff together and headed north again.

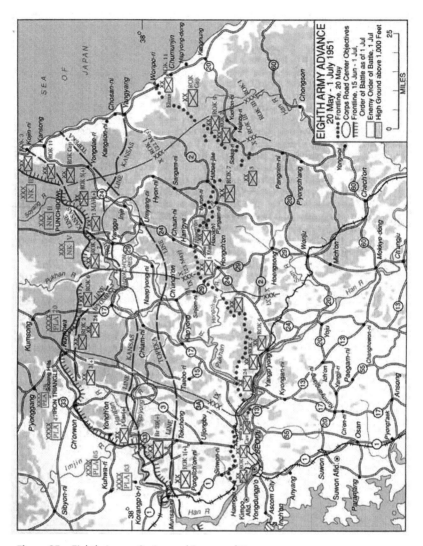

Figure 25: Eighth Army - Spring and Summer '51

CHAPTER EIGHTEEN

Spots

Many of us were getting sick, mostly from dysentery, and were having trouble keeping up with those who were better off. Although, with the near starvation rations, lack of sleep and walking all night, no one was unaffected. We had been marching all night through a more hilly area and had stopped at a small group of Korean houses for the day. We were in a narrow valley with steep hills climbing above us on either side. A small shallow river with wide gravel banks flowed past our huts.

At midmorning, pails of boiled soy beans were brought around but as I sat up, I found that I was too sick to eat any. I was already nauseous and I knew if I ate anything, I would just throw it up. I lay back down, but couldn't sleep. As I stared up at the papered ceiling, the room seemed to swim and rock slowly as if I had too much to drink.

I thought I might be dying and began to panic as I wondered what would happen in a few hours at sunset when I would have to get up and start the night's march. I knew I couldn't make it. I wondered what they would do with me. So far, everyone had been at least able to keep up with the rear of our marching column. I thought of the stories I had read of the Bataan Death March and how the Japanese had shot or bayonetted POWs who couldn't keep up.

I dragged myself to my feet and staggered outside. It was a beautiful, bright, sunny day. As I looked around, the whole world swam before my eyes and I noticed, for the first time, large objects or spots drifting around in my vision. They seemed to be yellowish-brown and filled maybe 20% of my field of view. I couldn't get rid of them; blinking had no effect. Whatever they were, they seemed to be inside my eyeballs.

I didn't know what to do. In my panic, I felt I must do something besides lie on the floor of our hut and die. I lurched slowly down to the river, about a hundred feet away and sat down. The water felt cool and looked clear. I scooped up several handfuls and drank it. The nausea subsided for a few moments.

I heard a guard shouting and looked back, he was gesturing for me to come back. I thought, what an idiot, did he really think that I might be able to escape in my condition. I shuffled back to my room and lay down again. By nightfall I was in even worse shape and was almost resigned to whatever was going to happen.

Fortunately we didn't have to march that night; some of our guys had been told that we were going to stay a few days. More food was brought around that evening, but I couldn't eat and went back to sleep. Morning was another sunny day and I wasn't quite as sick to my stomach but the spots in my eyes were still there. I forced myself to eat some boiled sorghum when it was brought around later.

The sorghum plant looked just like corn except there were no ears. The seeds, all contained in a large bunch or tassel at the top, are reddish-grey, and are about the size of BB's. When boiled it looks bad, smells awful and tastes worse. I believe that back in the 'States. We sometimes fed it to the chickens.

For the first six months of captivity almost the only food we got was boiled sorghum and boiled soybeans, and not very much of that. We stayed in our little valley for another night and day then we walked to a nearby road and continued our march. I was feeling a little better and at least the spots were gone.

CHAPTER NINETEEN

Pneumonia

Our road wound through low hills down into small valleys and then back into the hills. It was gravel and narrow, with only room for a single vehicle, obviously not the MSR. We met no trucks or columns of Chinese soldiers, most of the time we were alone with our five or six guards. It would have been easy to escape but we wouldn't have lasted long.

It began to rain, generally a light drizzle, sometimes a steady rain. It was now early June but the nights in the rain seemed unusually cold. I was very glad now that I had a poncho. I had long ago thrown away my steel helmet but I kept the lightweight plastic liner, which was still shaped just like a steel helmet. As the rain fell, it would run off the helmet liner down onto your poncho and then off onto the ground. The only things that got wet were your face and your lower pant legs and boots. Still, as the evening wore on, I developed the chills and my chest became very congested. I thought I might be getting pneumonia. My lungs began to feel heavy and I couldn't take a deep breath. I had to breathe in short, rapid panting breaths. If I tried to breathe deeply, I was stopped almost soon as I had started. My lungs were obviously already full of something else besides air.

The sickest POWs all gravitated to the end of the marching column and some of us got better acquainted as we struggled to keep up. There was always one guard bringing up the rear and he would keep urging us on with his "*Duuh! Duuh!*" Sometimes he would get exasperated and poke us in the back with his rifle butt and once or twice he even poked me lightly in the rear end with his bayonet. It hurt, but I never noticed any blood later so I guessed he hadn't broken the skin. I got the message though, and would always speed it up; for a little while anyway.

I remember one little runt, Carleton Durden, from somewhere in Georgia. We began talking about food. Food probably accounted for 80 or 90% of all the conversations among the POWs. He would describe in great detail, through chattering teeth, all the favorite food his mama used to fix for him when he was a kid and then I would describe roast beef, mashed potatoes, gravy, etc., etc. He was no more than five feet, six inches and probably not over 120 pounds. I knew I was in bad shape, but in spite of that, I felt sorry for him. He had no poncho and was soaking wet, with chills even worse than mine and shook uncontrollably as he walked along. It was dark but I could tell by the way his teeth chattered and his voice trembled.

Less than half the guys had ponchos so when it would start to rain, we would try to share it with someone who didn't have one. They could walk along beside you and duck under the edge of the poncho and maybe keep some of the rain off. I knew that there, but for my twelve dollar Bulova, went I and I would have wanted to be treated the same. As it got light the rain changed to drizzle and we stopped for the day at a couple of small houses. The first guys to arrive, who were also generally the ones who were in the best shape, filled the houses and those of us at the end of the column had to sleep outside. Trenches and foxholes covered the hillside and backyards of the houses so we decided to try to sleep there. By now I had the shakes almost as bad as Durden, so we decided to try to share our body warmth under one poncho. We found a trench which didn't have any standing water in the bottom and both curled up under the poncho, front to back. I remember thinking, at the time, that I wouldn't have been caught dead in such a position with another guy under normal circumstances, but these were different times.

We tried to sleep but only dozed. I was beginning to get anxious about my pneumonia. I felt that each breath required a conscious effort on my part and if I fell asleep I might not wake up. Every half - hour or so, we would turn over, in an attempt to get warm and to dry out the other side of our bodies. We didn't have to worry about F80's since the drizzle kept up all day. By evening, I was almost glad for a change as we began walking again. That night was the same as the previous except that now I was more out of breath than ever. With each step I was conscious of the weight within my chest and just the act of breathing began to occupy most of my thoughts.

We slogged on through the night and I somehow managed to stay up with the very end of the line. At daylight it was still raining and no houses, that weren't destroyed, were in sight. The guards did not stop and we just kept going. I was beginning to feel a little dizzy. The world began to seem a little unreal, I just wanted to sleep but at the same time I was afraid to.

Late in the day we arrived at a group of Korean houses beside the road with several barns or sheds for animals adjoining them. They said we would stay the night. We were herded into the houses and we collapsed wherever we could find room on the floor. I tried to lie down but found that it was more difficult to breathe then when standing so I tried to sleep sitting up.

Buckets of soybeans were brought around and I managed to force myself to eat about a cup. The hot salty broth almost tasted good. It was getting dark and the rain had started down a little heavier. The room was packed with snoring bodies but I couldn't lie down. I felt like my chest was filling up and slowly suffocating me. The room was cold and I had the chills and shakes and wished I could get warm.

I remembered the barn I had passed as we were led into the houses. I had seen several mules tied up inside and eating from a large pile of hay in the corner. I took my poncho and sneaked quietly out, stepping carefully over prostrate forms as I went. I slipped along the side of the house then into an open door into the barn about 20 feet away. I groped in the dark until I felt the warm rump of one of the mules. He stamped his feet a little and moved over. I burrowed deep into the hay pile with my poncho wrapped around me, quickly gave up the struggle to breathe and fell asleep.

When I awoke in the morning, I at first didn't know where I was, and then I remembered the hay and thrust it off only to find myself staring a mule in the face. The hay had been warm and soft and it was the first good night's sleep I had in more than two weeks. I felt much better as I returned to my room in the house. The guards, if they had seen me, gave no indication.

I now noticed an older Korean "Mamasan," working in the kitchen adjoining our room. Apparently civilians were still living in some of the rooms of our houses. Curious, I went into the kitchen to see what she was doing. She had a small tank heating over a fire. She was sitting off to one side next to a small tube. A tiny stream of clear liquid came out of the tube and emptied into a small bowl. After a few moments, she smiled, held a large tablespoon under the stream and then handed me the spoon full of liquid. I took it, placed it to my lips and sipped it down in one gulp; it was steaming hot Soju, a very powerful Korean drink made from distilled fermented rice. It burned on the way down but also seemed to warm me all over. I smiled back and thanked her with a little bow of the head and returned to my room. I hoped it would help my pneumonia and it was reassuring to see that there are nice people no matter where you are.

CHAPTER TWENTY

More F80's

W̲e had stopped for the day and some of us were put up in a group of three houses nestled up against the hills but right next to the road with the usual river paralleling the road on the east. I was in the middle house of the three houses, with one about 100 feet to the north and the other about 50 feet southeast. It was another bright and sunny day and we knew from past experience that about midmorning we could expect F80s somewhere in the area.

We had finished breakfast (if you could call it that) and I was just lying down to try to get some rest when the half expected "*Fiji laala!*" was heard. I looked out the open door to my right as I lay on my stomach on the hard dirt floor and caught the glint of sunlight off the bright aluminum of a single F80 as it made a descending left turn to the south. It rolled level at 1000 feet altitude and headed right for us about a mile away. I was on the wrong end of the house and this time could not dive into the kitchen. There was no place to hide.

I watched spellbound as the silhouette rapidly enlarged; he was diving precisely at our location. First, came the winking flashes of his four 50 caliber machine guns in the nose; and then milliseconds later the staccato cracking and popping sound as the bullets slammed into our roof and the houses around. This time I didn't close my eyes and duck but instead watched fascinated as he bored in on us.

A small swirling black cloud erupted underneath the jet and the first thought was that he had been hit, and then I saw that it was a rocket approaching even faster than the F80. At the same moment, a dark, oblong tank separated from one wing and began tumbling end over end toward us. I just had time to cover my face with my hands when the lights went out. There was no sound, no light, no feeling; just nothing.

I don't know how long I had been unconscious, but it was probably not more than ten seconds. At first I became aware of total darkness with the sounds of people around me, then the darkness slowly faded into a uniform grey and finally light. I could see timbers and other wreckage around me through the thick choking pall of dust. I tried to get up but couldn't move my lower torso. Instantly, I feared I was paralyzed but as the dust cleared, I saw that one of the large roof beams had fallen across my thighs. I tried to move it, but it wouldn't budge. I called to some of my buddies who were picking themselves up from the debris nearby. It took four of them to lift the beam off me. I got up and we all scrambled out of the wreckage, making sure that everyone got out.

The building had been totally destroyed, only a few of the upright and roof timbers were still standing. The rocket must have made a direct hit on the roof about 10 feet above our heads. The building 100 feet to the north was burning fiercely; a mule was standing in the front yard, head hung low, half his body burned black with black shards of skin and flesh hanging down. He was still alive. The napalm tank must have landed short of our house and hit the first one. I didn't see anyone come out of it.

The other house just south east of us was also burning, as well as the trees and hillside beyond. After I had closed my eyes, the F80 must have released a second napalm tank during his pass. It had to have just barely skimmed over our roof in order to hit the house to the south of us. If I had to get hit by something, I would choose almost anything but napalm.

We milled around in the front yard of what was once a large Korean house for a few seconds. Two of our guys had been dragged out of the debris by their buddies and were lying on the ground. Both had been hit in the legs and one lay half sitting up, screaming at us to "kill me! Kill me!" Both his feet, with boots still attached, appeared to have been nearly severed, and lay at strange angles with respect to his lower legs. Dark, red blood oozed out over the ground and seeped up through the thick layer of dust on his fatigues. His buddy lay quietly dazed and silent.

Figure 26: Chinese 40mm AA Gun

I had only a second or two to take in the scene, when our guards began hollering "*FIJI!*" and shooing us out onto the road. We left our buddies to their fate and stampeded out on the road and north. As we ran, I could see two F80's coming around again for another pass at us. About 200 yards north of our compound, I ran past a 40mm antiaircraft gun crew who were firing furiously at the two jets. I tried to put as much distance as possible between myself and the gun.

On their second pass I wondered if the pilots could see all those small figures in dark clothing running along the light gravel road in the bright sunlight. If they did, they chose instead to concentrate on the *Ack-Ack!* gun, which was okay with me. We were finally rounded up by the guards and began an unplanned march north in broad daylight which was something we hadn't often dared to do. We now began to take stock of our own situation. A few of the guys had been hit by shrapnel. One had two dollar-sized holes in his back and another had a large nasty wound on his back near the right shoulder. I noticed a little blood oozing out on my right forearm and they said I had a couple of small holes in the middle of my back. It didn't hurt at all, so I was not worried. My ears were ringing, however, and I couldn't hear well for months.

I had no idea how many of our guys, if any, may have died in the napalmed houses. We couldn't stick around and the Chinese never discussed it. Survival was mostly just a matter of dumb luck but occasionally you had the brief opportunity to make an intelligent 'zig' instead of a 'zag'. But there were always a few who got religion and credited a benevolent God for saving their necks. I remember one regular army soldier, we'll call him 'Calvin', who used to brag how he would steal cases of cigarettes in Japan and sell them on the Black Market to finance his visits to the whore houses. Anyway, after this particularly close encounter, Cal got religion, and swore that God had answered his prayers and so, if he ever made it back to the 'States, he would faithfully attend Church every Sunday, and even sit in the front pew. Cal gave no thought to the burning houses we had left behind and how many of his buddies may have been cremated there or the other buddy who writhed on the ground in such pain that he begged us to kill him. No, Cal only thought of his own scrawny, ignorant neck. I always thought it was unfortunate that it was only survivors like Cal who are allowed to heap praises on God for saving their lives, but we never get to hear from all those guys who didn't make it.

CHAPTER TWENTY-ONE

P51's

The weather was getting warmer and we very seldom saw any rain. Somewhere I had lost my poncho - probably back at the house where the F80 rocket hit us. It didn't matter now. It had served its purpose. I don't think I would have survived my bout with pneumonia without it. I still had my helmet liner though and it would become more useful in the next few weeks to keep the hot sun off my head.

The march now became more unpredictable. Where before, we had always slept in the daytime and walked at night, now we sometimes reversed that and instead, slept at night. We had walked about 10 miles that day and had seen very little air activity. As dusk approached, we descended into a small valley. Up ahead we could see numerous fires which seemed to be right on our route.

We entered a small city well after dusk, and could see that it had been heavily hit by our planes sometime that afternoon. As we walked along the main street through town, a river was on our left and many one and two story buildings were on our right. Some of the buildings were still burning, and others were only smoldering. Big two wheeled carts loaded with supplies and equipment were scattered and overturned everywhere, and numerous dead mules, which had been pulling the carts, were lying in the street.

Our guards decided to stop for the night. I guess they figured that if it had just been bombed, it should be fairly safe for the time being. Supper that night was the usual boiled soybeans, but some of the guys in another house said they had been given boiled mule meat. Some said it was almost as good as beef. I got none of it. The next morning we moved on early.

As we got further north, we no longer saw the F80 jets; apparently they were restricted to about 25 to 50 miles north of the front lines because they couldn't carry any more fuel. We now began to see P51's during the day, replacing the F80's, but the P51's only did low level strafing with their six 50 caliber machine guns. They flew lower and slower, so we had a much healthier respect for them. The B26's still came over twice a night in good weather but they didn't bother us as long as we weren't near any trucks, troops or trains.

Figure 27: P51 Mustang

We were stopping for the day in some houses on the west side of a long, broad north-south valley. Four P51's were raising hell about 2 miles east of us on the MSR. I couldn't see what they were shooting at, but they must have found something interesting. The guards were making sure we didn't stray outside because we still had dark-green fatigue uniforms on and presumably a pilot, even at low altitude, couldn't tell the difference between us and North Korean or Chinese troops. Korean civilians typically wore pure white shirts and pantaloons and you could easily spot them a mile away. We noticed that the Korean civilians would usually just keep on working in their field whenever a plane came over; they apparently knew the pilots could see their white clothes and wouldn't bother them.

I didn't see it, but one of the guys said he saw a P51 get hit and go down in flames. The other 51's circled the area for a while without firing and then headed south. That night after supper, as we were getting ready to march for the night, four Chinese came in carrying the pilot of the P51 on a stretcher. He had a broken leg in a splint and was surprisingly chipper since I'm sure he hadn't been given any morphine for his leg.

We soon discovered that we were expected to carry the pilot with us on our march and it caused some grumbling. Few of us were in any shape for this and the four POWs carrying the stretcher would usually set it down after five or 10 minutes and turn it over to another four who, in turn, were lucky to last another 10 minutes. This went on all night and slowed our progress considerably. The guys carrying the stretcher were used to heading up our column, but now they found themselves bringing up the rear with me and all the other sick and lame POWs. The grumbling got louder, but the guards didn't relent.

At daylight we stopped at another group of houses which seemed to be on the west side of the same north-south valley only further north. I ended up in the same room as the injured pilot. I'll call him 'Hans'. While waiting for chow we swapped war stories. He was still very upbeat. He said he was part of a group of South African pilots flying P51's on low level interdiction missions, in other words, shooting up truck and troop convoys.

Hans explained how he was shot down on the day before. They had been flying up the valley looking for targets of opportunity when ground fire must have gotten lucky and hit his engine. It caught fire and quickly got too hot to remain in the cockpit, so he popped the canopy, released his seat belt, stood up and jumped out. But he said he had committed one of the cardinal sins of all pilots, he had failed to zip up one of his leg pockets. He showed us his flight suit which had zipper pockets all over; on the calf, thigh, arms and several on his chest. They were used to hold maps, pencils, and whatever else they wanted handy during flight. As he attempted to jump free of the falling aircraft, the zipper caught on a canopy latch. He found himself plastered against the side of the aircraft, unable to reach back and free himself. The ground was coming up rapidly, so he just jerked the rip cord of his parachute to let it tear him free. As the chute blossomed, it ripped the pocket free and smashed his leg against the horizontal stabilizer, breaking his leg in three places. He still had his flight suit on and showed us the torn zipper which was the cause of it all.

Breakfast was Hans' first taste of POW food, boiled soybeans, which he ate. He seemed a little disturbed by the shape many of us were in and wondered how he would fare. About midmorning our rest was disturbed again by the guttural sound of airplane engines. Hans said it was undoubtedly his buddies in their P51's since this area of north-central Korea was their assigned sector. The 51's cruised north up the middle of our valley then in a few minutes we could hear them returning, this time they seemed to be on our side of the valley. Hans began to curse them as they approached, low and slow. He said he knew what they were looking for, vehicles or anyone that looked like a North Korean or Chinese soldier. I asked him how it felt now to be on the other end of his six 50 caliber machine guns. He didn't answer but he also didn't look pleased.

The four P51's flew south past our open door, at very low altitude, they couldn't have been more than 600 yards away. Hans recognized the tail markings and named the pilots who were most likely in the planes. They disappeared to the south but later we could hear them working the area further to the east.

Later that afternoon some of us sat around and quizzed Hans a little further. We were especially interested in just what he could see from his cockpit. He said it was easy to spot trucks and large groups of soldiers but people hiding or sitting still in brush or woods were impossible to tell from the bushes. He also advised us not to run out of the houses when the 51's were around because any movement of a person in dark clothing was sure to draw their fire.

It wasn't long, however, before we got onto our favorite subject - food. We wondered what types of food they ate back in South Africa. He said his ancestors were Dutch so the food was generally of a Dutch-German origin. Hans couldn't really appreciate our interest in food because he hadn't been starved sufficiently. He still missed his evening drink in the bar back at the base in South Korea. He said his favorite was a "German Alexander," and he gave me the recipe which I wrote down on a slip of paper and put in my wallet, fully intending to try it if I ever got home.

We lugged Hans again that night a few more miles north and stopped in some Korean houses which were set out in the middle of the fields. We had a few trees by the houses, but otherwise we were hundreds of yards from the nearest woods or hills. We had never been so exposed and I didn't like it.

Hans' friends appeared again that morning. It was a warm sunny June morning and all the doors were open. One P51 came over very low with his engine throttled back. When he came into view through the open door, he was in a shallow bank at an altitude of no more than 200 feet and about 300 yards away. I could clearly see his white helmet through the Plexiglas canopy and he appeared to be looking our way. Everyone was still as a mouse except for a few muttered curses hoping he would go somewhere else, anyplace. I thought if we could see him, then surely he must be able to see us through the open door. A Korean farmer, in white, working in the open field, stopped what he was doing and just watched. The P51 circled a couple of more times, and then flew off to join the others without firing a shot. He was so low and slow that I'm sure I could have hit his plane with my M1 if I had wanted to and had a rifle. I concluded that the Chinese just felt it wasn't worth all the trouble they would bring down on themselves, so they either didn't dare or didn't bother shooting at the planes.

CHAPTER TWENTY-TWO

Pizza

We were getting into summer in Korea. The night marches were warm and the air was pleasant, reminding me of summer nights back home. There was no moon, but the stars seemed especially bright and we had no trouble making out the general features of the country side as we walked. At one place we wound up a narrow road through the mountains with the smell of pine forests on all sides and the sounds of frogs and crickets from the bushes; there were even fireflies and an occasional hoot owl.

I would sometimes slip away from reality and imagine myself on a hike in the North Woods but it never lasted very long. I had only to look ahead, as the column of dark figures shuffled slowly around the hairpin turns in almost total silence, to remember where I really was. Or I could look subjectively at myself in the dark and feel the ache in my gut and the shear weariness of my entire body and I would know where I was. In quiet moments like this, I thought of all the things I wanted to do in life but I knew that death was close and that thought created an ache worse than all the others, an ache I couldn't place my hands on. When you're young, you don't die easily.

We stayed that day in some houses on a quiet hillside. As we waited for chow, most of us sat around and discussed food. I remember Johnny Tricomo, a little Italian kid from Detroit. Like a typical Italian, he talked a blue streak, as long as his hands were not tied, and he began describing all the Italian dishes his mother used to fix, most of them unfamiliar to the rest of us. He said he remembered his father would send him out on a Saturday night to get a pizza for supper. No one in our entire room knew what a pizza was, although some had heard of it. So he proceeded to describe how you made a pizza and we were all converted; we couldn't wait till we got home and found a pizza parlor. Maybe this had something to do with the rapid spread in popularity of Pizza after the Korean War.

I also got acquainted with Bill Pfleegor about this time on the march because we were both in bad shape and this meant we would both gravitate to the end of the column. Besides food, we discussed home and he told how he had joined the Army after two years of college. We both decided that we wanted to go back to school if we ever made it out.

After breakfast some tried to sleep and others just sat around and quietly talked. Joe, who had been wounded by shrapnel near his right shoulder, during the F80 rocket attack, mentioned that the wound did not hurt as much anymore and now it had started to itch. In fact, he said, it almost felt like something was crawling in it. I said itching was a good sign that it was healing so we decided to have a look at it. He had tied an old undershirt and some other rags around it as a bandage and Tricomo helped him peel the rags back carefully so as not to pull any scabs off. Johnny was like that, always trying to help somebody else, even though he was in worse shape than most. When he got the bandage about half off, we could see why it itched. It was full of fat little white maggots. Joe took one look at the writhing mass and let out a low wail. Then he began blubbering incoherently, something about "why me."

It took us a while to calm him down but after one or two guys laughed at him he began to listen. I said, that I had read that in the Civil War they used to deliberately put maggots on wounds because the maggots cleaned the wound better than any doctor could. It seems they only eat the dead flesh and detritus and don't touch the living flesh. And that was exactly what we saw; the wound was clean and pink and seemed well on the way to healing. Johnny tied the bandages back up and Joe, looking a little sheepish, lay down and tried to sleep while ignoring his "visitors."

In the afternoon one of the guards came around looking for strong men to go and get some rice. He pointed at the healthier guys and motioned for them to come along. One of those who volunteered was a soldier captured from the French battalion which had been attached to the 23rd regiment. He said he had been hit three times in the leg by a Chinese burp gun when he was captured on the same day as I was. It didn't seem to slow him down at all, or at least he had no trouble keeping up with us. In fact, he was usually up near the head of the column, so I didn't see him very often. During the day, he would often pull his pants leg up and show us the three bullet holes through his calf muscle. It must have hurt like hell, especially at first, but I never heard him complain or ask for any help.

The guys were gone over an hour and it was close to dusk when they returned lugging two of the biggest sacks I had ever seen. The sacks were hand made by sewing rice straw mats together at the edges, leaving a small hole at the top. Rice was then poured inside and the hole sewn up. They were about 3 feet square and our guys who had to carry them guessed that they weighed more than a hundred pounds. We couldn't wait. This would be our first taste of rice. I remembered, again, the rice I had thrown in the garbage can just a few days before I had been captured.

.

CHAPTER TWENTY-THREE

First Bath

As we got further north, we seemed to be getting out of the range of the P51's, which only scoured the roads within 50 to 100 miles of the front. This meant that if our route took us over narrow little used roads or mountain trails, we could travel in daylight without much worry about being strafed. For the first two or three weeks of captivity, we had been harassed by airplanes day and night when the weather was clear.

About noon we came to a broad shallow river flowing down from the mountains. It was probably late June by now and the temperature felt like it was in the 80's. The guards indicated that we were going to stop awhile and clean up. Most of us waded into the cool water up to our knees and began trying to scrub some of the crud off our faces and hands. We had been prisoners now for over a month and this was our first chance to bathe.

I took my shirt and undershirt off to soak them in the water and for the first time I saw what a month of pneumonia, near starvation and continuous dysentery had done. I knew I had lost weight, but now I was stunned by the extent of it. My arms were thin and spindly, every rib stood out clearly and most scary of all, my gut had almost disappeared under my rib cage. I remembered the pictures I had seen of prisoners liberated from the Nazi camps such as Buchenwald and the Japanese survivors of Bataan. I looked just the same and guessed that my weight must be less than 100 pounds.

The first sight of my own body was profoundly discouraging. I seemed to be getting weaker every day and this had only confirmed my worst fears. I looked at my belly again and wondered where it had all gone. I distinctly remember, as I stood knee-deep in that river, that I took both hands and placed them on either side of my waist at the narrowest part and squeezed them together. I was able, without much effort, to touch my fingertips both front and back. This would have made my waistline about 18 to 20 inches.

We had come down from the mountains into a level plain and were approaching a large city or more precisely, what was left of a large city. It had been almost totally flattened with only a few chimneys and telephone poles sticking up here and there. We marched in a long scraggly column up a broad main street through the middle of the city. It was a warm, clear day and very few Korean civilians were anywhere in sight. I was the last man in the entire column; in fact, the next POW and the guard bringing up the rear were a couple of hundred yards ahead of me.

I had dysentery constantly since the first week of capture and my gut was always in turmoil. As we walked, about every hour, I would have an almost irresistible urge to go. As luck would have it, another urge came on me right in the middle of the city. I had stopped and dropped my pants by the side of the street and was straining to eliminate a paltry amount of liquid when several young Korean men ran up and began beating me with sticks and clubs. I don't know if it was because I was desecrating their city or because they just hated Americans. Any way I picked up my pants and tried to fend off the blows as I hobbled to catch up with my buddies.

Fortunately, the Chinese guard noticed and he ran back shouting something at the Koreans who then scattered. The guard then began rapping me on the back with his rifle butt and poking me in the rear with the tip of his bayonet. A few minutes before, I had thought I was incapable of moving any faster; but now I found some additional energy and was able to catch up with the other guys.

That night we had moved into what looked like a developed or urban area but it was too dark to tell for sure. Some of the guys guessed that we were near the North Korean capital of Pyongyang. We began seeing a lot of truck traffic after it got dark so we must have been on one of the MSRs. We finally halted at the edge of a very large river and waited as a group of trucks crept slowly out of the darkness in what seemed like a very shallow river.

It was our turn next as the guards drove us down into the water. The water was only about a foot deep and I could feel the boards of a wooden bridge under my feet as I sloshed along. Somebody had a flashlight which they only turned on a few times and then only for a few seconds. It now became obvious that we were crossing a fairly deep river on a wooden bridge built just beneath the surface to hide it from our bombers in daylight. It impressed us as a very clever idea. In the few brief moments of light from the flashlight, I could make out the roiling yellow-brown waters of a large river flowing over the timbers, but I could not see the bridge itself beneath the ripples.

There was a shout and the guard flicked his light downstream, one of our men had either slipped or jumped off the bridge and was rapidly floating down the river. There were no shots. They just let him go. Somebody would spot him when it got light. If he was trying to escape, he picked the wrong place and the wrong time.

On the other side of the river some of the stronger POWs were given wooden boxes to carry. They were about the size of a small suitcase and they carried them slung over their backs on rope shoulder straps. We all wondered what they contained; many thought we were carrying food for ourselves or for the Chinese, but it was dark and we could only speculate. When we stopped for a break, one of the men managed to break a board off his box and pull out what he said felt like small hard cakes. Thinking it was some sort of dried Chinese wheat cake, he ate one.

We continued our march and it wasn't long before the POW who had eaten the "wheat cake" got violently ill. We stopped for another break as he writhed on the ground and vomited. After a short while he died. We just left him there and moved on. Someone said the guards told them that the "wheat cakes" were explosives, probably TNT. They could have told us that earlier and prevented such a stupid death, but then they probably knew that POWs should not be carrying explosives and didn't want us to know.

CHAPTER TWENTY-FOUR

Old Camp

We were in a more mountainous region again and had stopped in a large village. We were placed in a large block of houses with a central courtyard. The walls of one row of rooms bordered a street in the village. There were no doors facing the street, but a few small holes had been knocked in the mud walls facing the street. We were to stay in this one location for a few days. It may have been a collection point for POWs.

The food was no better or more plentiful there than it had been on the march up, so some of our guys began trading whatever they had of value for food. The Korean civilians would come up and peek through the holes in the wall to dicker for watches, rings or whatever. One POW traded his watch for a large sack of turnips and shared them with his close friends. I wasn't one of them. Others traded for carrots, onions, potatoes, etc. I had my gold Mankato High School class ring, but I didn't even try to see what it was worth.

The first day, an American dressed in normal winter clothes consisting of wool Khaki pants and shirt and a field jacket appeared at the hole outside our room. He gave us his name and rank and said that he was the sole survivor of a group of about 400 POWs who had been kept there during January and February of the previous winter. They had all died of starvation, malnutrition and disease, every last one of them except for him.

He had survived only because the Chinese found out that he was a demolition expert and had kept him off in a separate part of town. He was kept busy in that region doing road construction and repair, blasting tunnels and whatever demolition work the Chinese needed. He said he was fed very well, plenty of rice and all the canned beef he wanted. He hadn't even lost any weight. He came back every day we were in the camp and helped us get fair trades of food for our watches, rings, etc., from the Korean civilians.

This POW's survival by doing demolition work for the Chinese seemed to be out-and-out collaboration - if not treason. Other men told me that they had been forced at gunpoint into the cabs of US 6x6 trucks towing 155mm howitzers and ordered to drive them away from the battle area. It was apparently fairly common for the Chinese to use POWs to help them retrieve captured booty, but if you were being forced at gunpoint, I would guess it couldn't be called collaboration.

The Chinese often told us that we got the same food as their troops did and that this was all that's required by the Geneva Convention. But they also knew that the POWs were dying by the hundreds on that diet and we felt that they had the ability to get better food for us if they had really wanted to.

I have since read that an important part of the brainwashing method is to take a person to the brink of death, then if he survives, his mind is often easier to manipulate because he will feel grateful for survival. What does it matter if a few hundred die in the process? In retrospect, I think there is much truth in the idea. Later, in lectures, the Chinese would tell us, with pride, that the end justifies any means; the individual didn't count; only the goal, the collective good was important. I think most of them actually believed it.

In the winter of '51, the Central Intelligence Agency (CIA) intercepted a report by a Chinese Communist inspection officer. He had traveled throughout North Korea and reported back that their troops were sick, starved and frozen and surviving in the sub-zero winter on a few unthawed scraps of potatoes. Thousands of their men were immobilized by pneumonia and intestinal disorders. (**Goulden**, p.463)

This shows that the Chinese didn't treat even their soldiers very well. But by the spring of '51, I still believe that they could have fed us much better than they did.

CHAPTER TWENTY-FIVE

Boxcars

We left our temporary camp after a few days and were again making our way through rugged, hilly, wooded terrain. It was very early and the sun had just risen somewhere beyond the hills, but the light hadn't penetrated to the narrow ravine our path was following.

0

Figure 28: C119 Flying Boxcar

Very suddenly I heard a rumble which seemed to be coming from all sides. Then a large airplane roared down the canyon just above the trees. We all looked up, too startled to move or duck. It was an American C119, also known as the "Flying Boxcar. The fuselage was shaped much like a large rectangular boxcar and twin booms on the wings held large radial engines. The booms extended straight back to hold the large horizontal tail and twin vertical stabilizers. The large clamshell doors on the back of the fuselage were wide open, indicating that he was just about to drop something or someone or that he already had. He was very low for such a big airplane, for that matter, for any airplane. I guessed that he was only 100 or 200 feet above the trees.

There was a flurry of excitement as a rumor spread like wildfire through the POWs; maybe they were going to drop paratroops to rescue us or maybe they were dropping food for us. The sound of the engines quickly faded and was gone; our elation faded with it.

The CIA had training bases for spies, and saboteurs on Yongdo Island in Pusan Harbor and in Japan. Korean operations were headed up by a man named Hans Tofte. When interviewed 30 years later, he admitted that the CIA had as many as 1200 agents in North Korea, most of these were dropped and supplied by parachute. This is probably what we had seen that morning. (**Goulden**, p.473)

Our path joined a narrow road which followed both a small stream and a railroad northward. Most of the time as we walked along the road, the railroad ran along the opposite bank of the stream. Every few hundred feet or so large bomb craters scarred the railroad bed, the stream bed and the road we were walking on. Debris littered the area. Every hundred yards we would see sections of rail twisted into odd pretzel shapes or wrecked railroad cars and even the rusted remains of a few locomotives lying on their sides half submerged in the stream.

We rounded a bend in the road and up ahead a group of 15 or 20 Korean civilians were just finishing repair of a 500 pound bomb crater which had all but obliterated the road. The bombs had probably been dropped the previous evening by a B26, our friend, Bed Check Charlie, which we heard almost every night. This didn't say much for the effectiveness of our bombing if they put a team of workers like that on every crater. They could have the crater filled-in almost before it had stopped smoking.

At dusk we arrived at a small village near the rail line, surrounded by rugged low hills. We were led along the tracks toward what once probably was a rail yard. Scattered everywhere were the remains of boxcars and locomotives. As I passed, I noted that most of the cars had heavy steel ends, about 3/8 inch thick with floors, sides and roofs made of wood. I could see numerous holes in the ends of the cars made by 50 caliber bullets from strafing planes. The bullets had sliced through the steel like it was soft butter. Even the heavy steel boilers in the locomotives did not stop the 50's.

As it got dark, an old coal fired locomotive backed up to a string of cars and coupled-up. Our guards began loading POWs into the big open doors of the cars. I was too weak to climb into the car so a couple of stronger POWs grabbed my legs and hoisted me up onto the filthy, straw-covered floor. I struggled to my feet and moved back toward the opposite side. I was trying to avoid being shoved back into the far ends because I wanted to be close to the door in case we had to get out in a hurry.

Over half of the guys needed help getting up into the car; we were all getting pretty weak. They packed us in until each of us had just enough room to sit with our legs pulled up under our chins. One Chinese guard sat in the open doorway with his legs dangling over the edge, hanging on to the door with one hand and his rifle with the other.

The Train started with a lurch and quickly got up to speed, which in this case I thought was only about 20 or 30 miles per hour, at the most. Even at this speed the car dipped and swayed over the rough tracks. I could imagine how many old bomb craters we must have been passing over. It was pitch black inside the car as we lurched and swayed through the night. Sitting on the floor soon became unbearable, because I no longer had any fat or muscle on my buttocks. I finally had to stand up and hang on to the door. We stopped often and sat with our engine quietly chuffing for many minutes for no apparent reason before eventually moving on

For latrines, the Chinese had provided a couple of buckets which were passed back and forth in the dark when someone needed them, which was often. I began to suspect that some of our guys were not bothering to ask for the bucket but instead they were going on the floor or in their pants. Well, it wouldn't be the first time for many of us.

Around 10 P.M., right on schedule, we heard shots and a warning of airplanes. The train quickly braked to a halt but the engine kept panting quietly. The guard told everybody to stay in the train and be quiet. If shooting had started, I was determined to ignore the guard and leap out the open door any way I could. I heard the motors of a B26 coming closer, then he passed directly overhead at maybe a thousand feet and faded away in the direction we had been going. A few minutes later we jerked to life and resumed our way.

About midnight it began to get light as a full moon rose and now we could see the countryside through the open door as we passed. I figured we hadn't seen the last of "Charlie" for the night and I assumed we would be much easier to see in the moonlight. Sure enough, after an hour or so, there were more shots and the train screeched to a sudden stop and I could already hear the B26 engines. This time he seemed even lower, maybe only 500 feet, as he passed directly overhead, flying slow with his engines at low power settings. I wondered what would be the best thing to do if I heard the whistle of bombs. Fortunately I didn't have to decide because he just kept on going. The train did not start again. We could hear him coming back. Again he flew south at low altitude directly over the tracks and then on, quickly fading into the distance. This was one time that several hundred GIs were definitely not rooting for their side. I'll never know how the B26 failed to see us. I thought they had radar or infrared scopes to spot the heat of a train engine in the night. Later one of the POWs on the first car said that when they stopped, the Chinese covered the hot box of the locomotive. Maybe this was enough to make the difference.

Later research confirmed that the B26s used for night patrols in Korea had SHORAN (Short Range Radar Navigation) on board. This allowed them to follow railroad tracks at night but apparently they couldn't always distinguish trains among all the clutter on their scopes.

CHAPTER TWENTY-SIX

Yalu

Before dawn, the train halted and we slowly dismounted from the cars. I dared not jump, but lay down on the floor and carefully lowered my legs to the ground. Getting out of the cars took us almost as long as it had taken to climb in. We struggled into some empty houses in a small town. We hadn't slept for 24 hours, so I found a spot on the floor and quickly went to sleep.

We were awakened about midday for chow, so I sat up and looked over our room. Through the open door I could see gravel paved street passing by our house and other houses across the street. After chow a maroon 1940 Buick drove up and parked in front and two men dressed in rather unkempt suits, striped shirts and nondescript ties got out. They were escorted into our room and remained standing as they introduced themselves in good English as Russians from the local consulate.

They began asking us questions, such as when we had been captured and what units we were from. They would look around the room for someone to volunteer an answer but if no one did, then they would address their questions to some POW they had singled out. They asked me, "Why are you fighting in Korea?" I answered truthfully, "Because I was drafted." They asked several others the same question and got answers which ranged from; "I don't know," to "fighting for my country." After 15 minutes, they climbed back into their American-made Buick and left.

Later study of maps of Korea show a railroad running from Pyongyang, northeast through the mountains along the Chongchon river to Kanggye and then Manpo on the Yalu river. I would guess that this was probably the route of our train after we had picked it up somewhere north of Pyongyang.

The next morning we were roused early for chow and then assembled in the street in front of the houses. As we marched off down the street, I could see a very large river winding through the low hills past the town. We all thought it had to be the Yalu. At the river we were loaded into large flatboats, about 10 feet wide and maybe 30 feet long. They were handmade of wood with heavy plank sides and plain boards for seats. Each boat held about 50 POWs plus a couple of guards and one Chinese oarsman who steered and propelled the boat with a single, large, sculling oar which protruded out the back of the boat.

I had found a seat on the right side of the boat just ahead of our oarsman (who I'll call 'Ling') where I could hang my hands over the side and feel the cool water. Ling was one of the most happy-go-lucky Chinese I ever saw. He was often laughing and kidding around. We didn't know what he was saying but sometimes we could guess. We moved out into the center of the channel and began drifting down with the river current, other boats were either ahead or behind us.

It was now probably early July and as the sun rose higher it got very hot and my only shelter was my helmet liner. It felt like it was in the 90's and I began to overheat. I was getting dizzy and sick and then began to have intermittent chills and sweats. Every half hour I would dip my liner in the river and pour a quart or so of cool water over my head. If I hadn't been able to do this, I probably would not have survived the day

Whenever someone had to relieve himself, he would just hang his butt over the side of the boat and let fly. This seemed to greatly amuse Ling, and I soon realized why; he thought it funny that Americans had this problem, while he, a poor Chinaman, was apparently immune. He would scoff at us and then take his cup and dip it right into the Yalu river water and take a big drink. He didn't even seem a bit concerned that at the same time, several POWs might have their rear ends hung over the side of the boat a few feet ahead of him. I guess he had been born and raised on the Yalu and drank the water all his life. It either kills you, or you survive.

Later that day, our "driver" sculled over to the north side of the river and beached us on the bank, near a small town. The guard took a few POWs into town to get more rice or sorghum. I took the opportunity to get out of the boat and go on shore. That side of the Yalu was in Manchuria, which is a province of China, so I dropped my pants and left a token of my esteem on Chinese soil.

After a while, the guys came back carrying sacks of something and we re-boarded the boat. Our guys were excited, while going through town they had passed a small bakery and had seen bread and some type of cookies in the window. We all began to speculate that maybe now the food would improve.

Sometime after dark, we docked and were led off the boats for the night. It was a POW camp right on the river (probably Pyoktong) because some of our people said they had seen and talked to other Americans. I was exhausted and hoped that this was the end of the line but early next morning we were marched out on a wide gravel road lined with tall Poplar trees. From the sun, we seemed to be heading south or west.

The road wound through increasingly rugged hills, the trees lining the road on either side provided much needed shade. All the roads in Korea were lined with Poplars, planted by the Japanese before World War II. At least the Japanese did something useful during their occupation of Korea. In the early afternoon, the head of our column had rounded a curve below a small round hill and headed into a narrow valley filled with houses on both sides of the road. Beyond, the valley spread out into what was left of a larger city.

A rumor flew back to the rear of the column. There were Americans in the village ahead. I hoped this was it. I couldn't continue much farther. When I reached the small village, I could see hundreds of American POWs sitting listlessly in doorways, along the sides of the houses or under trees. A few were standing beside the road asking us what units we were from, but most wanted to know how the war was going and if we knew when it would end. Most of them looked terrible; dirty, emaciated and pitiful. They even looked worse than us. My heart sank, I had hung on up to this point in the hope that once we got to a permanent camp the food and conditions would improve. But from the looks of these men, it was going to get worse.

Later study of maps has allowed me to estimate the various distances involved. I estimate that we walked from the point where we were captured below the 38th parallel, to somewhere north of Pyongyang, the North Korean Capitol, where we were put on a train. This is about 225 miles airline, but we followed winding roads and even more twisted foot paths snaking through narrow canyons and along mountain streams; thus the actual distance was probably more than 250 miles. The train was a one night journey of about 130 miles and the subsequent trip down the Yalu by boat was about 75 miles. The three segments of our journey, on foot, by train, and by boat, are marked on the map located in the front of this book (see **Figure 1**)

PART THREE

POW CAMP
The First Year

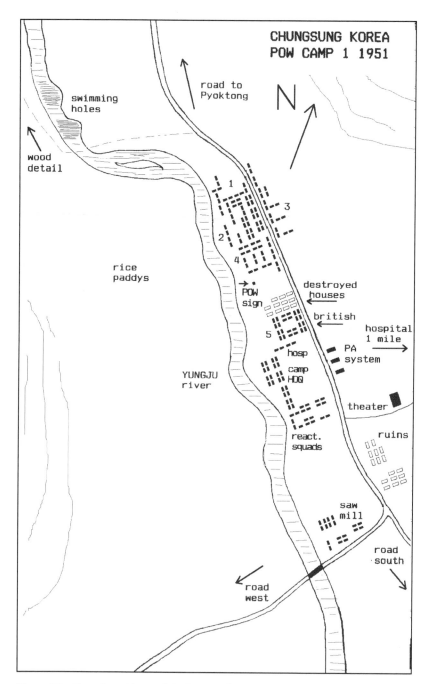

Figure 29: Camp 1 and Immediate Surroundings

CHAPTER TWENTY-SEVEN

Camp

W e entered camp in a long bedraggled string of weary men. It was the end of June or the first week of July. The camp consisted of clusters of mud-walled, tile roofed, typical Korean houses situated on both sides of the main road which ran south east. Most of the houses were located on the west side of the road and bordered a shallow river to the west. The river ran in a north/northwest direction and I assumed that it eventually emptied into the Yalu about 10 or 15 miles to the north. The loose collection of houses we called camp #3 was maybe 100 yards wide at the most and about a half mile long in the north-south direction. The valley widened about a half mile south of camp into a more spread-out city which bore the scars of heavy bombing sometime earlier in the war. What was left of that section of town was used by the Chinese and Korean civilians and military.

The adjoining map depicts the camp and its surroundings. The various companies are numbered 1 through 5. The main part of town just south of the camp (much of which was destroyed) has not been shown. A more detailed map of the central part of camp is shown in Chapter 40. The definitive source for information about POWs in Korea is U.S. Prisoners of War in the Korean War, by A. Rowley. In addition to very detailed information about all aspects of prison life, it has US Air Force aerial photographs of all the camps. (**Rowley**)

As usual, I was bringing up the rear as we were collected at the south end of the camp. The guards assigned us rooms in a group of vacant houses on the southwest corner of camp and about 100 feet from the river. Ten men were put in each room which measured about 10 feet by 10 feet. The floor was smooth hard dirt covered with a woven bamboo mat.

We were all sick but some of us were in much worse shape than others. I stumbled slowly through the single small east facing door into the dim interior and collapsed on the floor among the other bodies. I reflected on the hundreds of gaunt, hollow-eyed skeletons lining the road as we had trudged into camp. As we approached the end of our journey, we had all hoped for better food and living conditions, but now all those hopes were dashed. Chow was brought around, the same old stuff; boiled sorghum.

After chow I slowly made my way down to the river to scrub-out the tin can I used for a 'bowl'. No soap, just sand and polluted river water. As I headed back to my room, I checked-out the nearest latrine - an eight by 3-foot pit with small 3 inch diameter logs placed across with about one foot spacing between them. I knew I would have to pay several 'visits' there during the night; provided I could make it all the way. The procedure then would be to drop your pants as you were backing carefully onto two of the round and shaky logs in the dark. This required all the skill and finesse of a high-wire artist and perhaps more courage, because we didn't have a safety net to catch us should we slip. The whole exercise was difficult enough on dry logs but then some of my less proficient fellow sufferers from rampant diarrhea cheated a little and backed up only to the edge of the pit. They then proceeded to blast the ends of the logs with the watery remains of whatever they had eaten the day before. This was, of course, precisely where a more conscientious person such as myself, expected to stand. On a bad night, I had to negotiate this treacherous obstacle course as many as ten times; on a 'good night' maybe only 4 or 5 times.

As it got dark, we all settled in for the night. Five of us were lying with our heads to the north wall and the other five were stretched-out with their heads against the south wall. Ten pairs of feet overlapped by about two feet in the middle and there was not enough room in the east-west direction for everyone to lie flat on their backs; some of us were forced to lie on our sides. The floor was hard as rock and the lack of fat, or even meat, on our bones made lying down sheer torture after more than 15 minutes. When you fell asleep, you were soon awakened by the excruciating pain in your bones and had to roll over to the other side or onto your back, if there was room.

This went on all night, every night, and between being jostled by the guys on either side of you or stepped on by someone either going to the latrine or coming back, you got damn little sleep. We soon learned to place the guys with the worst diarrhea closest to the door. I was awarded a place next to the door by acclamation. The 'honor' now allowed me to make a relatively quick exit when needed, but it also meant that now everyone else stepped on me on the way out and when returning. It seemed our days were now dominated by thoughts of food in between meals and by the ritual of eating when chow was brought around. Our evenings, on the other hand, were occupied with the other end of the food chain as the days meal made its all too rapid trip through the gut.

After four months or more of continuous diarrhea, many of us began to experience bleeding of the rectum and worse. I began to notice that each time I squatted on the latrine part of my rectum would pop out and hang below. When finished, I would then have to stuff it back up inside. One of the men in our company had it so bad that each time he went, about four or five inches of rectum could be seen dangling below his anus. I believe the medical term for this condition is a complete prolapse of the rectum. It was disturbing and painful, but later, as the diarrhea subsided, our bowels returned to normal as well.

When we arrived, we had been issued five blankets for each room. These blankets, when held up to the light actually resembled cheese cloth more than blankets. We were expected to share the blanket with the next guy. The Chinese, whoever he was, who decreed that five blankets should suffice for 10 men, sleeping five on a side, obviously couldn't divide. The two guys sleeping on the end either had no blanket or else they could only cover their feet. But of course, it was also possible that this nameless Chinese was really just a cynic, and knew that shortly there would be more than enough blankets to go around. But, it was summer and we really didn't need blankets on most nights. We also received a small porcelain metal bowl and an aluminum spoon. I could now set my tin can aside for other uses. One never threw away anything as valuable as a tin can in prison camp.

In the first days, we were issued POW uniforms. These were dark blue cotton pants and shirt plus a small soft blue cotton cap. Our shoes were canvas top, rubber sole tennis shoes; the same type as worn by the Chinese soldiers at the front. They also collected our GI uniforms except for the underwear. Our combat boots were also confiscated, however, a few of the guys managed to hide theirs.

I soon discovered another disadvantage to sleeping next to the door. This position placed my head in the corner next to the wall and when facing the wall, my nose was very close to a small hole which looked suspiciously like a rat hole. Later that night a large, dark rat skittered out of the hole and brushed past my face, then disappeared. From then on, I tried to sleep with my back to the wall. Sometime during the night while I was awake, I heard our rat moving around on top of the papered ceiling. The Koreans would place light wooden slats across the ceiling and then glue newspapers to the slats to seal the room and prevent loss of heat in winter. Anyway, this particular rat got careless and stepped on a weak area, then fell through right into the middle of our room. Somebody let out a yelp and then it became total bedlam as everyone thrashed around trying to clobber the little devil; but he got away. Before getting back to sleep we began to seriously consider catching him and having roasted rat. In fact, some of the men caught a few sparrows and ate them, and one man in our company somehow managed to catch a crow which he cooked and ate. Soon afterward, he got violently ill but did not die. I guessed that he probably hadn't cooked it long enough.

The ten men in our room, or squad, were; myself, Bill Pfleegor from Williamsport, PA., Johnny Tricomo from Detroit and seven others whose names I don't remember. We were all sick and weak when we had arrived and now there was a tremendous letdown as we all realized that the food was not going to improve. Most of us lay around all day, only stirring ourselves to go to the latrine or eat chow and wash your bowl.

About this time, we began to notice things crawling around inside our clothing at night. Inspection in the light of morning revealed small, white, little buggers about the size of a grain of rice - lice!

If you were able to get around, this then became one more daily chore, along with getting chow and washing your bowl. What we would do, is remove our shirt in the morning and turn it inside-out. The little devils would all scurry to the nearest seam to hide and we would then come along with our two thumb nails and squeeze them till they snapped. When done with your shirt, you had to repeat the whole process on your pants. You had to do this at least every other day, or else they became numerous enough to keep you awake at night.

As you can imagine, the poor guys who were too sick to take care of themselves soon became absolutely infested with lice. Some of the very sick men were so full, that all you could see was a seething white mass when you pulled their shirt back. In fact, we often suspected that the lice may have sometimes sucked enough blood out of their victim to be the immediate cause of death.

A couple of the men just gave up and would eat only a few bites of their food. Tricomo would hover over them like a mother hen, trying to get them to finish their chow. After chow he would take their bowls down to the river so they didn't even have to get up for that chore. Soon they even stopped getting up to go to the bathroom. They would just foul their pants and then lie in it.

Johnny was a saint, as much so as any person can be. We all had our 'accidents' from time to time, but when we did, we would go down to the river and wash out our own pants. Johnny, however, cheerfully gathered up their soiled clothes, wiped up the mess and then took everything down to the river, washed it and hung it up to dry.

After a couple of days of this, some healthier POWs came by with stretchers and carried our two buddies up to the 'hospital'. The hospital was nothing more than an old Korean temple about a half mile southeast of camp, and about the only medicines were charcoal for diarrhea and Mercurochrome for sores. A few days later somebody said both men had died. They were buried on the hillside behind the temple.

Johnny now concerned himself with another of our roommates who was rapidly going downhill. He also became incontinent and refused to eat. The next day, he too went to the hospital and then died the following day. Bill Pfleegor, Johnny Tricomo and I were now probably the sickest of the remaining seven men in our room. Johnny was getting more depressed. Despite his best efforts, three of his friends had died in less than two weeks. Our squad was no exception; men were dying all over camp. Someone who came back from the hospital, after carrying a patient up there, reported that about 10 or 15 men were dying every day.

Bill was now going downhill. He picked at his food and sometimes wouldn't eat anything. We had gotten acquainted on the march because we both often ended up near the end of the column. He said he had enlisted in the army after two years of college. He showed me a picture of his girlfriend which he carried in his wallet. He was anxious to get back home, finish school and get married.

There was excitement in the camp. We were going to get our first meat ration. They brought in live pigs which our cooks butchered and cut up into small chunks. These were boiled in a large pot and each squad was given their portion in, what we called our "side-dish" pan. This was just a pan such as we used to use on the farm as a wash basin. It was about 14 inches in diameter and 3 inches deep. Each squad would assign one man the duty, each day, of picking up the chow. We would get our rice or sorghum in a bucket and boiled soybeans, vegetables, etc. in the side-dish pan.

We would all wait anxiously, sitting in a large circle in our room, with our spoons and bowls at the ready. Our roommate came down the street gingerly carrying the pan loaded with its precious cargo. He stepped carefully through the doorway and set it down in the middle of the floor. Woe onto the man who tripped and spilled his cargo. His very life would have been in danger. Each man placed his bowl next to the pan forming a ring of bowls surrounding the steaming hot soup. Whoever brought the food, also had to dish it out. A GI spoon was usually the 'official' tool used to ladle out food.

Each bowl might get filled with five spoonfuls on the first round and so on, until the dish was empty. All eyes in the room would be riveted on the server, noting carefully whether each spoon was level or heaping, and whether he seemed to give himself or his buddy a little more heaping spoonful then the next guy. Many fights broke out over such things as the number of soybeans in a spoonful being put into your bowl, compared to the number of beans he was giving himself. And finally, at the end, there was a final reckoning to compare each bowl and make sure that the level of beans and broth was the same in each.

This day the air of expectancy was especially great. We watched as the hot broth was parceled out to each bowl until its level was low enough to expose the chunks of pork on the bottom. The meat had been cut into small cubes, about one inch on a side and we could see that there weren't very many. At the final tally, each had received two small pieces of mostly fat and skin. The two pieces in my bowl were solid fat with a thick section of the pig's hide on one side. Short black hairs still protruded from the pieces of skin.

It was tough to chew, but I ate every bit, not wanting to waste any of the precious protein. Bill was having difficulty with his ration which was just like mine; fat and skin. He chewed on if for several minutes but just could not bring himself to swallow it. He complained that his mouth was sore and his gums were bleeding and that it was just too tough. He then spit it out into his hand and I told him not to waste it, so he gave it to me. I promptly ate what remained of his chewed-up ration and then finished my sorghum. I was determined to eat everything I could lay my hands on, especially anything with protein in it.

.

CHAPTER TWENTY-EIGHT

Dumplings

Another rumor came through the camp. We had been issued flour. Almost every day we had a new rumor - the war would end in 30 days, prisoner exchanges had started, or the Red Cross was bringing in food parcels. But this rumor was true. The cooks were going to use the flour to make "dumplings." It sounded great.

The cooks mixed water with the flour to a thick doughy consistency and then formed it into little balls about one inch in diameter. These were then dropped into boiling water for about 10 or 15 minutes. At chow, our side-dish came heaped-up with 'dumplings'. Each man got at least eight or 10 in his bowl. As I bit into the first one, I soon realized that they weren't going to be that great. Cooking hadn't done much to change anything; they still tasted like balls of almost uncooked dough.

Someone in one of the other squads had traded some of his valuables for a couple of extra rations of 'dumplings'. He stuffed them all down at one sitting and not long after, began to get sick. In the afternoon I saw him lying on the ground near the latrine moaning and writhing in pain. His stomach was all bloated-up and I was reminded of one our cows being in the same condition when I was a kid living on the farm. At that time Aaron, the owner of the farm we lived on, punctured the cow's stomach with a sharp object. As the hole was opened, a stream of foul-smelling gas hissed out, much like a tire that has been punctured. But here, no one seemed to be trying to help our buddy and he died later that night.

I spent much of my day in my room and only went out to go to the latrine and wash my bowl. On the way down to the river one day, I met Johnny Ford. The weather was very warm, so many of us did not wear our shirts. Almost everyone was a walking skeleton. Johnny was a little guy and looked as thin as anyone but he had a chipper attitude and was often smiling. I must have looked down in-the-dumps, because he told me to cheer up. He said you got to have a positive attitude and keep fighting. It sounded like good advice and we soon became friends. If some days I didn't feel up to making the trip down to the river to wash my bowl, he would stop by and insist that I stir my butt and get out of my room.

He had been captured much earlier in the war and had survived the previous winter as a POW. He told of being kept in a large schoolhouse with a hundred or more other POWs. One day while he was outside sitting on the latrine, jets had come screaming in and hit the brick schoolhouse with rockets. Johnny was knocked into the latrine by the concussion. He said he had crawled out, covered with excrement and then went back into the ruins of the schoolhouse. Everyone was dead.

Pfleegor was worse. He wouldn't eat and he wouldn't get up at all. We all tried to get him to eat the food anyway. I told him he had to force it down no matter what it tasted like or how he felt. He wouldn't listen. We all pleaded with him, trying different tactics, but to no avail. Finally in desperation, I thought I would try insulting him. If he got mad enough, maybe he would get up and eat his chow.

I accused him of acting like a baby and feeling sorry for himself. Then I said, "Maybe what you need is your mama's tit." At this he got boiling mad, struggled to his feet and staggered out the door trying to hit me with his fists; but I managed to stay just outside his reach. He then took his bowl and sat down on the stoop outside and began to eat his sorghum. When he was done, I took his bowl down to the river with mine and washed it out.

The next day, Bill was back to his old tricks, he wouldn't eat and wouldn't get out of bed. Tricomo and I couldn't budge him. I considered Bill my best buddy in camp and I hated to see him just give up like that. It hurt to insult him by saying things about his mother, that I really didn't mean, but the tactic had worked in some of the other squads.

That night I had just come back from the latrine and lain down by the doorway. Bill was lying next to me. I began to notice him mumbling and talking to himself. I finally realized what he was saying. He was talking to his mother, and sitting down to a large meal. He talked of roast beef, mashed potatoes and gravy, pie and ice cream. He began making slurping sounds as though he was actually eating the food he was talking about. I poked some of the other guys and told them to listen. Tricomo heard it also and we wondered if he was asleep or awake and hallucinating. The words seemed almost too distinct for someone who was asleep.

The next day they carried him off to the hospital. He seemed only half conscious as he was being put on the stretcher. I told him I would keep his wallet, bowl and his prized GI spoon until he got back. I didn't know if he even understood me. We all knew that Bill would never come back. I now had all of Bill's possessions and I began to feel guilty. Taking them without his clear consent was perilously close to theft. But it was the same for everyone, whenever one of our buddies died, his most precious possessions simply devolved to the closest survivors. Whether we wanted to or not, we all benefitted when someone died. We now had more sleeping room, more blankets, and maybe a good pair of combat boots or a knife. Such inheritances didn't ease the death of a friend; they only added guilt to sorrow. A few days later Tricomo was very depressed, he said he had been told that Bill had died.

After the war I picked up my new '54 Chevy in Detroit and visited my Aunt Florence. Then I continued on to Williamsport, Pennsylvania to see Bill's folks and give them his wallet which I had brought back. His father was Chief of Police for Williamsport and they were very nice. They insisted that I stay overnight. At dinner that night I met his entire family. We sat around a very large dining room table which must have seated 15 or 20 people. He had carried a picture of his girl in his wallet and I also met her that night. I remembered looking at her picture while in prison camp, and noting that she had signed the photo with; "May God bring you home safely to me"

They all asked many questions about POW camp and about Bill's health and why he died. I answered all their questions to the best of my ability without getting into any of the sordid details. His mother, his girl, and some of his brothers and sisters started crying and then it was all I could do to keep from crying.

I left the next morning after breakfast. His brother came out to the car to see me off and we got into a further more detailed discussion about Bill's death. I told him that we had tried everything to get Bill to eat but it was no use. I even told him what I had said about his mother in an attempt to get him mad and that even that only succeeded in postponing the inevitable for one more day. We were both crying when I left.

Now Tricomo just seemed to suddenly give up. He no longer bustled around trying to help someone else. He began to stay in the room more and would pick at his food. He rapidly went downhill from there. Just like all the others, he lay in bed all day, wouldn't eat and began to soil his own pants. After all the help he had given others, now no one went out of their way to help him. He lay in his own excrement until he too, was carted off to the 'hospital', never to return.

Now there were only five of us left. We each had our own blanket all to ourselves. Maybe that Chinese who had issued the blankets was a cynic after all.

It had only been a month since we had arrived in camp and now half of our squad was dead. I would be the next one to die. I was quite sure of that. I didn't want it to happen but I could see it coming, since I was now the sickest one in the squad. I would still try to take care of my own chores but just walking was now very difficult. Some days I probably would have just lain there all day if Johnny Ford or one of the other guys hadn't come by and insisted I get off my duff. We would then head down to the river at a slow creep. The river was only about 100 feet away, but it would still take us about an hour to wash our bowls and make it back to the room.

I was now so weak that I began to notice the two small steps up into the door of our room. As I placed one foot on the 6 inch flat stone used for the first step, I had to then shift my weight to that foot and then straighten that leg to lift my body up to the level of the step. This is an action that one is normally oblivious to, but now it required so much of my available strength that I began to quiver with the effort. I had to pause on that step and then repeat the operation for the next step.

I had no explanation for my loss of weight other than my continuous diarrhea. My appetite was fairly good and the food was beginning to improve a little. We now got some vegetables each week, such as boiled celery cabbage, in addition to the usual boiled soybeans and sorghum. The sorghum tasted awful, so some of the men who were not as sick as I, would sometimes not finish all of their rations. Sometimes in this way, I was thus able to get a little extra in my bowl. I never threw anything away and ate all the food I could get, but I still seemed to be losing the battle.

It was hot now, maybe early to mid-August, but I didn't sweat - my body was too dehydrated. One day ran into the next and the only difference, if anything, was that each day seemed hotter than the previous. At midday the dust and heat hung like a pall over the compound. The air was permeated with the stench of excrement and urine as the sun heated the nearby latrine. Many of us tried to sleep in the suffocating atmosphere of our rooms while others sat in the shade of the eaves and stared listlessly through sunken eye sockets at nothing in particular while quietly brushing away the clouds of incessant flies. The flies were everywhere; they gave you not a moment's peace. They even sought you out as you tried to sleep in the dim interiors of your room. And in addition, as you entered your room to lie down, the subdued light seemed to be a signal to the hundreds of lice hiding in the seams of your clothing to emerge and get an early start on the evenings feast.

I've often heard it said that starving to death is painful, that one suffers. I've also read that you couldn't consider cutting-off nourishment to a terminally ill patient, because that would be cruel. Those who make such statements don't know what they're talking about. Starvation is not physically painful; it is really very easy, in fact, too easy. If one is old and ill, I suspect one would go easily and willingly.

Some days, I too became despondent and just lay in my room, but even then I still retained that little spark of 'dignity' or whatever you want to call it, that prevented me from deliberately soiling my pants. I somehow always managed to struggle down to the latrine and back. Those who became incontinent never seemed to survive more than a few days. But I was young, and most days I wanted very much to live.

One morning I got up to go to the latrine and as I headed back to my room I stopped to rest by our 'front porch'. It was just getting light, low clouds and mist shrouded the surrounding hills. Our valley was eerily calm and no one else was stirring. I was reminded once again why they call Korea the "Land of the Morning Calm." It was a peaceful and beautiful scene until I returned to reality and reminded myself that I would probably be dead within the week. I became profoundly depressed by the thought. There were so many things I had wanted to do in life, and this was a helluva way to end it. Somewhere up on the mountain to the west, a cuckoo bird began to call. It almost seemed as if he were mocking my plight. It was a slow, mournful call, somewhat like a mourning dove, and only exacerbated my melancholy mood.

Then I became angry. I didn't know who or what I was angry at, I was just angry. I wouldn't let it happen. I resolved that day to not go back and lie in my room, instead, I would move around our area, go down to the river, check out the kitchen, or whatever; anything to keep active.

I think that day was the beginning of a turnaround in my health. I had been very close to death. If I had developed bleeding gums, if I had caught pneumonia again or some other disease, or if the food hadn't started to improve a little, I would have died just as Bill had. I soon found out that, for some reason, it was important to stay active. Moving about, though tiring, seemed to make me feel better and seemed to reduce the constant turmoil in my gut. Lying flat on your back in bed and feeling sorry for yourself only got you an early grave.

Somewhere between six and nine years of age, I had discovered that Santa Claus was just 'make believe', but I allowed my mother and others to continue the charade for a few more years because I didn't want to hurt their feelings. About the same time, I also decided that God was just a mythical character too. In all the intervening years, I saw nothing to change that conviction, and during these worst of times, prayer never once entered my mind.

Since returning home I have read statements by some of the other POWs where they gave God or their religion credit for bringing them through. Hogwash! I met many who professed to be religious, who didn't survive. And I remember at least one other fellow atheist who also didn't make it.

As I saw it, the ones who survived the best were the tough kids; the ones from the wrong side of the tracks. American Indians also seemed to do well. One in our company didn't even lose any weight. He never got diarrhea and he seemed to thrive on the slop that killed many others. Tough kids like that were exposed to the diarrhea bug many times while growing up and like Ling, our Yalu boatman, it either killed you, or you survived.

For all the rest of us, it required will power and a little luck; will power to eat food that in normal times would make you retch and luck to avoid some of the bugs going around that would kill you no matter how much will power you had. Where some survived and gave religion credit, I think it was really their subconscious will power which pulled them through - God only got the undue credit.

The death rate among American POWs in Korea was higher than any war in American history, including the Civil War. Raymond Lech (**Lech,** *Broken Soldiers*) has made a study of POWs in recent history and determined that the following percentages of POWs had died during captivity in the noted wars.

- 4% of American POWS held by Germans and Italians in WWII.
- 14% of Americans held by the North Vietnamese.
- 34% of Americans held by the Japanese in WWII.
- 43% of Americans held by N. Koreans and Chinese in Korean War.
- 45% of Germans held by the Russians in WWII.
- 60% of the Russians held by the Germans in WWII.

CHAPTER TWENTY-NINE

Beginning

I now began to stir myself. I would creep slowly about the compound talking to others and stopping often to rest under a tree or on some rock. I went down to the river and bathed for perhaps the first time in two months. The weather was very hot and the water was quite warm in the shallower parts. I sat in the sun by the river bank for over an hour while my pants dried.

I met a guy from another squad on the other side of our company area. We hit it off right away. He was very bright and we would sit in the shade and discuss many subjects, from science to philosophy and religion. He was also an atheist, and made no bones about it. That was one subject we couldn't argue about, because we both seemed to be in complete agreement with one another.

A couple of weeks after we had first met, I spotted him one morning tottering in the direction of the latrine. As he walked, he was quivering and shaking like a 90 year old man, but he also had a very determined look about him. He said it had come on him suddenly. The next day, he did not leave his room and the following day he was dead. Somebody thought maybe it was meningitis. He was a really sharp kid and if he had lived, he could have amounted to something, and I don't even remember his name.

In camp we were organized into squads and platoons, and the platoons were then collected into companies of about 200 or 300 men, just like the army. In the whole camp there were maybe five companies, including the remnants of the British Gloucester regiment.

Each company resided in a cluster of houses often adjoining two or three other companies. At first the Chinese would post a guard on the company boundary. If you tried to cross over to visit a buddy in another company, he would *shoo* you back, but many guys just snuck across when he wasn't looking.

By now I was wandering all over our company area, but I wasn't fast enough to sneak over into an adjoining company without being spotted by the guard. One day they had gotten some more rice in at Headquarters and were measuring out our company's ration for the week. I had shuffled up to Headquarters to see what was going on.

They were weighing our rice using large balance scales. These were long heavy poles made of some dark hardwood like ebony. The object to be weighed was suspended from one end of the pole and counterbalanced on the other end by known test weights. When ready to weigh something, two strong men would slip another heavy pole through a ring in the balance pole and lift the entire contraption up. A third man would then add or subtract balance weights until the ebony pole was balanced horizontally. The number of test weights times their distance from the end then was used to calculate the weight of the rice suspended from the other end.

When they had finished weighing, I asked Shen our camp interpreter, who happened to be standing there, if I could weigh myself. He said, "Sure, just hang onto the end of the pole while they lift you up." It required all my effort to hang motionless while they adjusted the weights, but it was all over in a few seconds. He gave me the weight in some Chinese unit of measurement and then said that it was about 96 pounds in American units." He should know, because I later found out that he had been a Professor of Physics at Shanghai University. By now I had started to regain some of my strength, so a few weeks earlier I may have been down to about 90 pounds, without clothing.

It had been a warm, hot night and it was pitch-black as I got up to go to the latrine. I managed to find it, half by instinct and partly by the vague outline of a dark area on the ground. As I hurriedly backed onto the logs spanning the pit, I slipped and fell feet first into knee-deep soupy excrement. I let out a low moan and climbed back out as quickly as I could. I was now so mad that tears were streaming down my face.

I slogged down to the nearby river, still crying with rage, and began washing myself off in the cool water. Before I could complete the job, I was blinded by the sudden glare of a flashlight and made out the form of the guard standing on the bank. He was hollering "*DUUH, DUUH!*" which means "*GO, GO!*" I guessed. I was still so angry that I tried to ignore him as I continued to wash my legs off. Finally he started in my direction, so I decided I had better comply. I went back to my room and used the dipper in our barrel of drinking water outside the house to finish cleaning myself. Fortunately it was a warm night, so it wasn't too cold as I crawled back into bed soaking wet from the waist down. The next day, my buddies thought it was all very funny.

A short time after this incident, we heard shots one night. The next day we found out what had happened. A POW in one of the other companies had apparently gone berserk and started walking down to the river. He was walking across the shallow knee-deep water when challenged by the guard. He ignored the shouts of the guard and even a warning shot. After this, the guard just shot him dead. He had told someone in his squad that he was going home.

I had developed a large boil on my neck which had been festering ever since the march. I suspected that maybe a small piece of shrapnel had entered when we were strafed by the F80's. I heard that they had set-up a clinic to handle minor health complaints, so I decided to check it out. It was being run by a British medic from the Gloucester's.

He cut it open and cleaned out all the pus, all without any anesthetic, and then he daubed some Mercurochrome on it. It hurt like hell, but I wanted to get it over with. They also gave me something for my diarrhea - powdered charcoal. It sounded like quack medicine, but I took it anyway. A week later my diarrhea hadn't improved one bit.

The day was bright and sunny. We were told to fall out and assemble in a large square on the east side of our company. This was unusual and anything unusual was all that was required to start a flurry of rumors. Everything from; we're going home, to; we're probably going to hear a lecture. The latter was the closest.

The interpreter explained that we had to write our autobiographies, from our early childhood up to the present. They wanted to know what type of family we had grown up in, what our fathers and relatives did for a living and what we had done before joining the Army. They gave us paper and pencils and said there was more paper if we needed more.

I sat down and briefly described my childhood on the farm, then our move into the city. I told of studying electronics in High School and also at Dunwoody Institute and my work in TV repair before being drafted into the Army. I don't think I needed more than two sheets of paper.

When we had finished, we were allowed to return to our squads. As we sat around our squad area, some of the guys were joking about the wild and fantastic stories they had made up. One said that his father was a millionaire and that he had been a rich playboy. It never occurred to me to do anything but tell the truth.

Later we fell out one more time and this time we were told to bring all of our belongings. This really started the rumors flying. All I had, beside two wallets, were my blanket, bowl, spoon and an old tin can. We were moving to another company. I hadn't realized it yet, but when the Chinese made a big change like this, they usually had a 'political' reason for doing it. The entire camp was reshuffled, squads were broken up and guys were separated from their buddies. I never did see a good reason for it.

At any rate, I had been in 4th Company, (I guess), in the southwest corner of the camp and was being moved to First Company in the most northern end of the camp. First company was a triangular shaped group of houses forming the northern tip of Camp #3, Chungsung, North Korea. It was about mid-August, 1951.

We had been in camp now for about a month and a half. All this time the Chinese kept us totally ignorant of what was going on in the outside world, especially the Korean situation. When viewed in hindsight from a distance of 40 years, it becomes obvious that events in Panmunjom often motivated the Chinese to change the way they treated us POWs. At the time, however, we were unaware of any ulterior motives although we often had our suspicions.

On June 30, 1951, General Ridgway broadcast a message on Radio Tokyo, proposing the start of Peace Talks. Peking responded, and the first meeting occurred on July 10th. The talks were on again-off again until they resumed on July 25th to discuss the establishment of a truce line and POW exchanges, among other things. The food began to improve throughout the summer and my health right along with it. I believe this was more than just a coincidence.

Still, the US kept the pressure on. On July 30, the Air Force conducted a massive raid on Pyongyang employing 370 warplanes. Despite this, the Chinese came back to the talks on August 10th and continued until August 23rd, when they were suspended for two months. (**Blair**, *The Forgotten War,* pp 933 – 946)

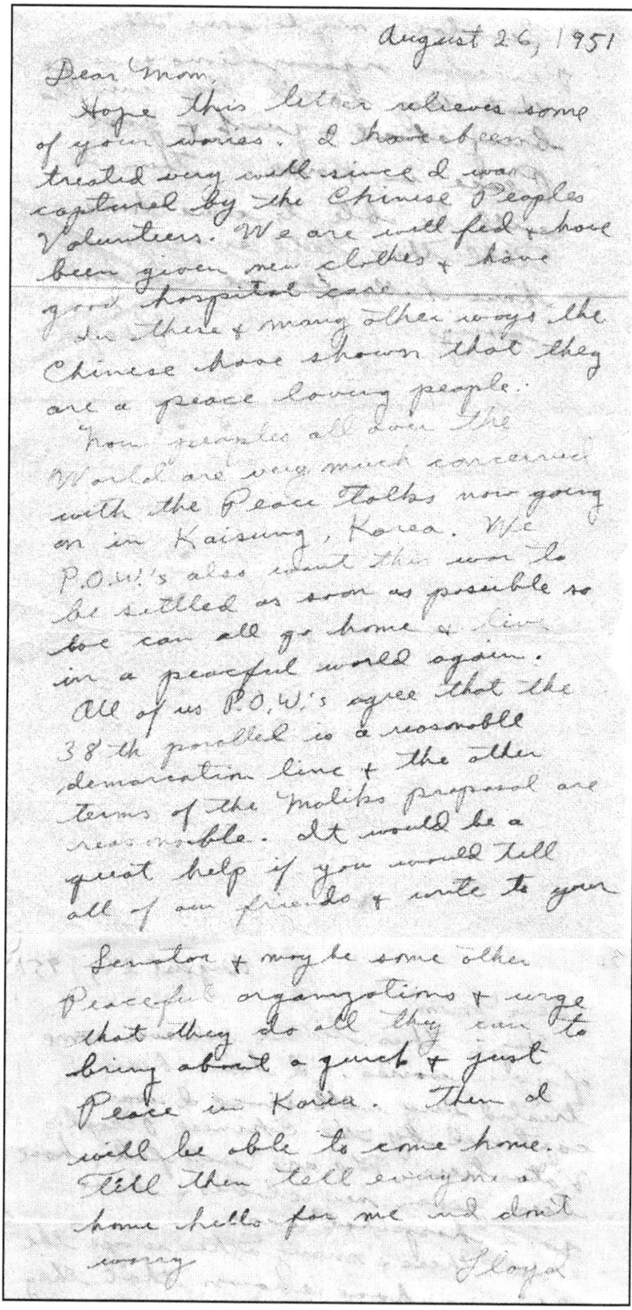

August 26, 1951

Dear Mom,

Hope this letter relieves some of your worries. I have been treated very well since I was captured by the Chinese Peoples Volunteers. We are well fed, have been given new clothes, & have good hospital care.

In these & many other ways the Chinese have shown that they are a peace loving people.

Now peoples all over the World are very much concerned with the Peace Talks now going on in Kaisung, Korea. We P.O.W.'s also want this war to be settled as soon as possible so we can all go home & live in a peaceful world again.

All of us P.O.W.'s agree that the 38th parallel is a reasonable demarcation line & the other terms of the Maliks proposal are reasonable. It would be a great help if you would tell all of our friends & write to your

Senator & maybe some other Peaceful organizations & urge that they do all they can to bring about a quick & just Peace in Korea. Then I will be able to come home. Tell them tell everyone at home hello for me and don't worry

Lloyd

Figure 30: First letter home

CHAPTER THIRTY

Letters

I had begun to make myself 'at home' in my new Company - First Company. We were located at the far northern tip of Camp #3. I was now in a room, or squad, with ten men again. Our room was one of three in a small house very close to the river and right next to the company cook house. It was now nearing the end of August, 1951.

After we had settled in, the Chinese felled us out in the small courtyard of First Company. They announced that we would be able to write letters home. A murmur of excitement swept through our gathering, and then the interpreter began to qualify his statement. He came right out and stated that we should tell our folks that the Chinese were a "peace loving people who had a lenient policy" when dealing with the POWs. He said we should describe the good food, hospital care and clothing we had received. He said that Peace Talks were going on in Kaesong, Korea and that the Russian ambassador to the UN had proposed that the 38th parallel was a fair and equitable demarcation line.

The following is a copy of the first letter to my mother: (on the **next page** and also see **Figure 30**)

August 26, 1951

Dear Mom,

Hope this letter relieves some of your worries. I have been treated very well since I was captured by the Chinese Peoples Volunteers. We are well fed and have good hospital care. In these and many other ways the Chinese have shown that they are a peace loving people.

Now peoples [sic] all over the world are very much concerned with the Peace Talks now going on in Kaisung, Korea. We POWs also want this war to be settled as soon as possible so we can all go home and live in a peaceful world again.

All of us POWs agree that the 38th parallel is a reasonable demarcation line and the other terms of the Maliks proposal are reasonable. It would be a great help if you would tell all of our friends and write to your senator and maybe some other Peaceful organizations and urge that they do all they can to bring about a quick and just Peace in Korea. Then I will be able to come home. Till then tell everyone at home hello for me and don't worry.

Lloyd

I also wrote a letter to my sister Ethel which contained almost the identical words. The first and last sentences were my own; all the rest was merely a parroting of the list of propaganda statements our interpreter suggested we include in our letters. They were just 'suggestions', but I and many others, had the distinct impression that we had better include them if we wanted to assure that our letters were delivered. In addition, I knew that the words and phrases I was using would appear stilted and phony, so that people would know that I was not saying what I really thought.

When captured, I was well below the 38th parallel. None of us had any idea that the UN Forces had subsequently pushed the Chinese up to 25 miles north of the 38th over much of the front and close to 50 miles on the east coast. It was blatantly dishonest of them to keep these facts from us, while at the same time, using us to promote their position. This is just one example of how devious and sneaky the Chinese could be.

The North Koreans were often cruel and crude; conversely, the Chinese were more civilized. Where the North Koreans sometimes shot prisoners whose hands were tied behind their backs, the Chinese would just let men die of benign neglect and then try to convince the survivors that they had a most generous "lenient policy" toward POWs.

Lies like these had some temporary success with us because they closely controlled our access to news, but I'm sure that similar lies were very effective with their own people who never got to hear a dissenting point of view.

A few of the guys grumbled that they "weren't going to put that crap in their letters." Some even said they weren't going to write any letters. However, I didn't have a problem with including their propaganda in my letters. At that point I was 'missing in action' and had nearly died and in fact, I was still a very shaky 98 pounds or so. I just wanted to make sure that my letters got out.

When I had arrived in Korea, I was not enthused about fighting and I also wasn't really sure what the war was all about. After I was captured, I was relieved to be alive and grateful to that Chinese soldier, whoever he was, and who didn't shoot when he easily could have.

After that, we were bombed, napalmed, rocketed and strafed by our own side and starved by the Chinese. I was a relatively passive person at that time and I thought that this was just the way war was. I didn't blame our pilots for shooting at us and I didn't blame the Chinese for not giving us enough to eat. This was just war, and I was thankful each day to be alive.

Now by late August, I had been a prisoner for three months and had seen five of my buddies die. I had almost joined them. Men were still dying every day but I now began to have a glimmer of hope that I might make it. But I still hadn't laid much blame on the Chinese for my precarious condition or for my friends' deaths. Again, this was war and this is what one had to expect as a POW. At least they weren't beating us as the Japanese had done in WWII.

In addition, the fact that the Chinese lived right among us, was an important factor in influencing our opinion of them. Each company was relatively independent of the other companies. We had our company commander, who spoke no English and he, in turn, had his interpreter who usually spoke quite good English. Each company was further broken down into what they called 'platoons', and each platoon also had its interpreter, who usually was not very good at English. The commander, along with his interpreters and their cooks and helpers always occupied a couple of houses within the company area proper. There were no armed guards within the company, although the company commander usually did wear a pistol.

Our company commander generally remained aloof, but the interpreters, cooks and helpers were usually very friendly. Our interpreters, especially, would stroll around the area and engage us in conversation about everything from life in America to automobiles. Any attempts at interjecting a little propaganda were generally rather low-key.

Later on, as our health improved, basketball or volley ball equipment was installed and the interpreters as well as the Chinese cooks and their helpers would often join some of the POW's in a game of pickup basketball. Even people who fiercely hated the Chinese on the front lines, found it difficult to hate these people when you lived with them every day. It is likely that this was just a calculated part of their indoctrination or 'brainwashing' scheme.

I began to get acquainted with the guys in my new squad, most of whom I had not known before. I still had severe diarrhea and was forced to get up half a dozen times each night, not to mention the numerous trips during the day. One night I awoke and hurried out the door on the way to the latrine, but it was so dark that I became disoriented and couldn't find the latrine. But diarrhea waited for no one and I got no further than the path outside our door.

Well, needless to say, I was not the only one who had to make a trip to the latrine that night, and the next morning the recriminations flew left and right. Several guys had stepped in my mess during the night and to say that they were mad, would be an understatement. I, of course, was one of the prime suspects, but I was too embarrassed to confess. Some, who hadn't stepped in anything, even saw some humor in the episode.

Some nights later, another of our roommates had a similarly violent attack of diarrhea, only he was sleeping in the far corner of our room, at least 10 feet from the door where it was always difficult to negotiate your way over all the supine bodies and tangled legs without waking half the room. Well anyway, our buddy must have been lying there for some time debating whether to hold it or incur the wrath of his roommates by stepping all over their feet.

Eventually, the inevitable could be delayed no longer. He jumped up, dropped his pants part way in preparation, and then leaped over the sleeping forms as he bounded for the door. Well, as you can guess, he had waited far too long, and his leap over his buddies may have been partly jet propelled as he deposited a stream of repugnant fluid behind him. By the time he had reached the door, the need had largely dissipated but he continued anyway.

By now the entire room was awake and the air was filled with howls and curses. It took at least half an hour to clean up all the mess in the darkness. Mostly, everything was just thrown outside to sort out in the daylight. Our friend was reluctantly allowed to return, but he was not allowed to ever live down his mistake. Eventually most of us saw the humor even in this event, which proves, I guess, that a situation has to be pretty grim before people fail to find at least something funny in it.

Almost everyone had diarrhea, except for one or two tough young Mexican kids and a couple of American Indians. Apparently they had developed some sort of immunity due to their exposure at an early age. The Chinese did not provide any type of toilet paper until the winter of 1951, so that summer we had to make-do with whatever we could scrounge. As a result, all the leaves had been stripped-off the lower branches of the trees in camp and all the broad-leafed weeds had also disappeared.

One day, I even saw one discouraged POW use two ten dollar bills as toilet paper, and after he had finished, a more optimistic POW reached down into the pit and retrieved the bills and took them down to the river to wash-off. Another guy in our squad solved the problem by always keeping an old rag hanging out of his back pocket. About once a week or oftener, depending on how much his squad members bugged him, he would take the rag down to the river and wash it out, then hang it up to dry while he used his spare rag. Another man in the adjoining squad was a former prize fighter. He still seemed to be in very good shape and seemed to have lost little weight. He was tough and even managed to do a few pushups every day to try to keep in shape.

He began to complain about a sore mouth and bleeding gums. I had read enough about vitamin deficiencies to know that it was probably scurvy or beriberi or some such disease and that the solution called for fresh fruit and vegetables. Fruit was out of the question, but we were beginning to get some vegetables, although they were always boiled. I remembered that cooking can destroy some of the vitamins.

We were getting some Chinese cabbage, eggplant and squash; all boiled, of course. But this didn't seem to be enough for our boxer friend who rapidly got worse. His mouth became so sore and ulcerated that he could not eat, just like Pfleegor a month earlier. About two weeks after the onset of his symptoms, he was dead.

This had a profound effect on me; I knew that I was not out of the woods yet. If a healthy, strong, tough guy like him could go so quickly, what chance did I have if I got scurvy. I began to redouble my efforts to scrounge food wherever I could.

CHAPTER THIRTY-ONE

Monsoon

The date was probably early September and the rains had started. This was the monsoon season and it rained for almost a month with little letup. The little river that ran past our camp that was normally only about a foot deep- was now a raging torrent from four to eight feet deep. The roiling brown water now lapped at the base of a box elder tree about twenty feet from our back door.

On one of my foraging excursions around the company area, I had noticed some onions and other vegetables growing behind the company headquarters. I was still desperate to get some fresh vegetables to preclude getting scurvy, as some were showing signs of. One night I was awakened early by the sounds of a violent thunderstorm. I had an idea, and quickly got up and sneaked out, ostensibly to go to the latrine.

The rain was coming down in buckets as I slipped quickly past the cook house and headed across the courtyard. Every few minutes, the area was brilliantly lit by tremendous lightning bolts. The guard usually stood on the road entering camp from the north and I knew he probably wasn't more than 100 feet away, but probably taking shelter under the eve of one of the buildings.

As I approached the road, I dropped to the ground and began crawling on my belly in the pouring rain and mud. When I reached the road, I waited until just after a large lighting flash, and then I scooted across the road and dropped to my belly again on the other side. I then crawled between the two headquarter buildings and emerged in their backyard.

I located the garden in the next flash, and then crawled quickly through the mud to the onion patch. I pulled up about a dozen nice large green onions and rapidly retraced my path. When I got back to our hut I stood under the eve where the rain water was pouring off the roof and washed the mud off my person and off the onions. I waited outside the doorway a while to let most of the water run off my clothes, and then I slipped as quietly as I could back into my room. The ceiling had been papered with many layers of old newspapers and I had remembered one of several holes just above where I had been sleeping. The ceiling was low enough that I could reach up and stuff the onions through the hole and back out of sight on top of the papered ceiling. I then lay back down and went to sleep.

The next morning I was dry enough so that no one noticed. At chow that morning, the sun was trying to break through so everyone sat outside to eat the sorghum and side dish. I stepped quietly inside and reached up into the ceiling and pulled out a couple of onions and quickly broke them up into small pieces and mixed them into my bowl. I then went outside to finish my meal.

Apparently no one ever noticed all those dark green things in my sorghum or the smell of onions on my breath. I repeated this scenario every meal for the next couple of days until I noticed that the onions were being chewed by rats and they also were developing a thin coating of slime. At that, I took the remaining ones down and shared them with my buddies in the room. They never asked where I had gotten them.

After the onions were gone, I began to cast about for other 'fresh' vegetables. Our cooks had been given some cucumbers to cook. As usual, they cut them up into small slices and tossed them in a large iron pot, where they were boiled until they became soft and mushy. I figured that all that cooking probably destroyed most of the vitamins which we really needed. While snooping around the cook house, I noticed that the cooks had dumped all the small ends of the cucumbers into a drainage ditch behind the kitchen. I picked up a bunch of the larger pieces and washed them off in the river. At chow time, I mixed them into my bowl with the sorghum.

About a week later I became very sick. I felt dizzy and nauseous but I still forced my food down. The next day, the guys commented that my skin seemed to have a yellow tinge. Then I noticed that my arms were definitely yellowish, and also my urine had become orange colored. I moped about the room for about a week before I started feeling better. It was probably hepatitis which I had gotten from the uncooked cucumbers. After that I stuck with nothing but cooked food.

Recent blood tests in our clinic show that I test positive for "non A, non B and non C" hepatitis antibodies. As of now, five strains of viral hepatitis have been identified; A, B, C, D and E. All cause jaundice, but only B, C and D can develop into a chronic form of the disease. My jaundice could have been due to many other causes other than the hepatitis virus, but if it were a virus, the "E" type is the most common in the Far East.

The food was now definitely beginning to improve. Every meal, we were now getting some type of vegetable such as; eggplant, cucumbers, squash and even watermelon. Our cooks apparently knew only one way to fix anything - boil it. They even boiled the watermelon.

We also got more rice now and along with the rice, a little bonus - beetles and beetle larvae. The beetle larvae weren't too bad, they were white and about the size of a grain of rice, so it was easy to ignore them but the beetles were black and again about grain of rice size. They were a little harder to ignore, but we rationalized that we were getting a little vital protein.

The side dish also began to include more meat. One day we had little popcorn shrimp, and another day we had egg soup which actually had a few wisps of egg visible in it. Other days we got fish. I always seemed to get the head, which I nevertheless ate, brains, eyeballs and all. Another day we had chicken. Naturally I got a complete head. The eye balls popped like small grapes, and then I sucked the brains out through the eye sockets. After that, I proceeded to finish it off by gnawing off the combs and tearing out the tongue. I was still being true to my earlier solemn resolution to eat everything I could lay my hands on, but my resolve was being tested.

The next time that we had chicken, I fished in my bowl and pulled out one foot. About the only thing edible there, were the small pads on the bottom of the feet. I now began to wonder where all the rest of the chicken was going - who was getting all the good parts? We suspected the cooks but we didn't have enough evidence to lynch them.

Another Chinese delicacy which sorely tested my palate was dried fish. We would see these long, dark brown dried fish hanging up under the eaves of the cook house. They were about three feet long and looked like eels. They seemed to have been dried in the sun and then heavily salted to help preserve them. All of this didn't deter certain small white maggots which had taken up residence in the dried carcasses despite the salt.

If anything could be screwed up, our cooks would find the way. Instead of soaking the fish in water first to dissolve the salt and then draining off the water, our illustrious chefs just dumped the whole thing into a vat of boiling water; salt, maggots and all. The result was a thick, dark-brown soup swimming with a few shards of flesh, a jumble of bones collecting on the bottom and a few white maggots floating on top.

Nevertheless, I dug in, determined to pick every bone bare, until I had one taste of the broth. It was so salty, that even I couldn't stomach it. We continued to get this fare about once a week and the 'cooks' never did learn how to do it properly.

We also began getting Chinese steamed bread maybe once per week and this was a welcome change. At first, it was made from sorghum flour and sorghum always had a certain weird flavor about it which I never did come to like. Later, they used wheat flour and that was so good that fights broke-out over it until we got used to it.

And last, but not least, there were the garlic and hot peppers. We began to get more of these also in the fall of 1951, and they often helped to make dull and tasteless food more palatable. I knew that both garlic and pepper probably had some of the vitamins I felt I needed, so I ate all I could get a hold of. I remember sometimes eating as many as three whole bulbs of garlic at one meal and other times, I ate so many hot peppers that I could feel the burning the next day when sitting on the latrine.

Another reason for consuming so many peppers and garlic was the feeling that they might help to eliminate the diarrhea bugs in my gut. I reasoned that anything that strong just might kill some of the amoeba in my intestines. It could be just coincidental, but my diarrhea did subside that fall and eventually by November I was able to sleep through most of the night without having to get up.

CHAPTER THIRTY-TWO

Wood Detail

After arriving in 1st Company, we were called out for another formation, and addressed by the Company commander through his interpreter. Such formations were usually at least a weekly occurrence. In fact, we could have guessed as much when we were issued a small board and a single nail and told to make ourselves a small stool by nailing the board to a short piece of log. Anyway, this particular speech was concerned with the coming of winter and the need for lots of firewood to see us through the winter months. We were told that we were going to start having wood details, and everyone, except the cooks and those too sick to go, would be expected to take part.

Well, I liked to stay active and wander around the company but I certainly didn't think I was up to carrying wood in from the mountains about 2 or 3 miles away. By now I was probably a little over 100 pounds but still very weak and every morning when the detail left, I always begged off. I'm sure there were some who feigned more illness then they had, but I didn't feel that I was one of them.

As the weeks went by, those who regularly went on detail began to put pressure on those they thought might be malingering. At the suggestion of the Chinese, the companies began competing with one another to see who could bring back the most wood, and within the companies, the squads also began to vie with one another. Any squad with a lot of sick or lazy members couldn't very well compete.

Members of my squad began to make a few snide remarks about my loafing around the room while they were breaking their backs hauling wood. Finally one morning I had enough and decide to at least go along and see if I could just make it that far and back. We headed north out of camp on the main road a quarter mile then turned west on a foot path and crossed the river at a shallow spot using flat rock stepping stones. The path followed the river for another half mile, then turned west and began to climb through a sloping meadow with a few apple and peach trees before entering a narrow, twisting canyon. A cool mountain stream crossed and re-crossed our path as it tumbled and splashed over boulders on its way down. At irregular intervals, the waters of the stream collected in deep, tree shaded pools of quiet, dark water.

As the path continued to ascend, the dark woods closed in around us and the stream became a small brook which quietly bubbled and trickled over the rocks beside the path. The path finally petered out as we entered a deep wood filled with towering old hardwood trees mixed with some softer woods such as poplar, birch and pine. Everywhere I looked, I saw enormous black walnut trees, some almost 2 feet in diameter and big old oaks, many of them more than 3 feet across.

I had stopped to rest often on the way up and now I was exhausted from the climb. Many of our guys had gone much further up into the forest and were already on their way out carrying logs and branches from old fallen trees. For perhaps a half hour, I sat on a large boulder and drank-in the feeling of quiet and peace provided by the surrounding woods. I couldn't help remind myself that only two months before I had been at the brink of death and at least 5 of my friends would never know the simple pleasures of these woods.

I was in no hurry to get back to camp, as long as I got back in time for chow, so I explored the area a bit more. I was struck with the fact that there must have been 800 to 1000 POWs wandering loose in the woods around me. Two or three Chinese guards had accompanied us as we had started up into the mountains, but now they were nowhere in sight. We were on our own, if only for a few brief hours, but nevertheless alone. It was a refreshing and exhilarating feeling to put the camp and its sights and memories behind me for a few moments.

By now many other POWs had passed me carrying wood on their way back to camp so I decided that it might be prudent to find some wood and head back also. I searched and found a small broken branch, not much bigger than a broomstick, balanced it on my shoulder, and headed back down the mountain.

As I slowly picked my way down the rocky path and across the slippery, boulder strewn stream, I had to endure endless sarcastic comments about the "log" I was bringing back. I shuffled back into camp as the sun dropped below the mountains to the west, one of the last to return from wood detail that day. My squad said I should get the prize for the smallest piece of wood brought in that week.

I felt a little embarrassed, but I also felt a little triumphant; I had made it there and back. As I finished my meal with unusual gusto, I realized that I hadn't felt so good in months. Much of the ache and turmoil in my gut was gone, diarrhea was almost forgotten and I felt 100% better. I had no explanation for the change, other than the exercise.

I now became a convert - an exercise zealot of sorts. I started bugging some of my friends who were still lying around the room. I told them they should at least try going up into the hills, even if they only made if part way and even if they brought no wood back, but most of them just didn't believe me. After that, I never missed a wood detail, unless I had other duties, and that was the start of the real turnaround in my health.

On the next foray into the hills for wood, I made a small detour on the way up through a small meadow to check out what had looked like peach or apple trees. One tree had a few small green peaches on it so I picked one and bit into it. It was very bitter, but I ate it anyway as I continued on up the path. Then I noticed numerous low vines on the right of the path along the creek.

On closer examination, I found that they were loaded with small pale green bunches of fruit which looked very much like grapes. I popped one into my mouth and was pleasantly surprised. They were deliciously sweet, although more pulpy and mushy then grapes. Soon I was joined by several others and we quickly stripped the vines of everything we were able to reach.

By now I was stuffed and had removed my 'T' shirt to form a small sack which I had filled with another couple pounds of fruit before continuing on up into the hills for firewood. After returning to camp that evening, I finished off the remainder of my booty in addition to my chow. This was one day, at least, when I knew I had probably received my minimum daily requirement of Vitamin C and warded-off scurvy a little longer.

The fruit we had found on wood detail now became the talk of the camp. Some of the guys said they were a type of fig and not a species of grape. No matter, they were delicious and now some of the men, who had been too lazy to gather wood before, began accompanying us up into the mountains. However, I would have been the last one to criticize anyone else's motives. From then on, 'Figs' became my primary goal each day as we headed up into the mountains; bringing back wood was only a means to justify the trip. All in all, the hunt for figs, the excursions into the mountains and the moderate exercise became the only pleasures in my life as I struggled to regain my strength and optimism.

Each day I was glad to be alive, especially when I found myself alone in the woods. In the woods I seemed to be able to think; to get my priorities straight. I didn't hate anyone, I just wanted to survive - to go home and put Korea behind me. Every day as I could feel my strength slowly return, I felt grateful - grateful to no one in particular; certainly not grateful to the Chinese. At least it wasn't a conscious gratitude - a subconscious gratitude was always a possibility.

Sociologists have stated that there are four steps in brainwashing:

1. The victim has to suffer a profound psychic shock.
2. The victim must be removed from everything that makes them feel safe.
3. The victim is told what you want them to believe over and over again.
4. The victim is promised a reward.

Conditions (1) and (2) certainly applied to all of us in the summer of 1951. I can't imagine a more profound psychic shock then being brought to the brink of death and then surviving as a helpless POW.

In the fall of 1951, they then began to tell as what they wanted us to believe; to fulfill condition (3) and lastly, in regard to condition (4), I was given the greatest reward of all - my life. It's possible that we were being set-up for brainwashing and I didn't even realize it.

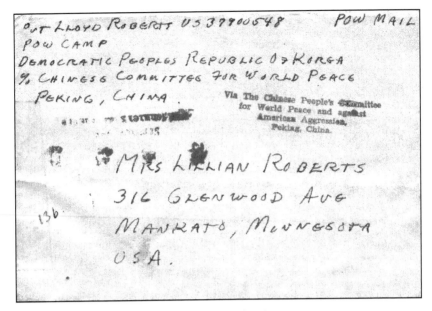

Figure 31: Typical letter home with propaganda address

CHAPTER THIRTY-THREE

Brainwashing

Sometime after moving to First Company, the Chinese began our indoctrination. Their methods were generally crude, unsophisticated and not the least bit subtle. They began by announcing that we were still soldiers and like soldiers we would maintain discipline, keep our rooms and area neat and clean and follow a schedule

We started by being aroused with whistles at 6 A.M., then we tidied up our area and fell in for calisthenics. I was just beginning to appreciate the benefits of a little exercise, but calisthenics for men in our shape, I thought was ridiculous. Nevertheless, we had to fall out every morning and at least go through the motions. I couldn't do one single push up and in fact, it was an effort to just get back on my feet after making an attempt at a push up.

As part of our calisthenics period, we also were ordered to learn and sing two songs: the Communist International in English and the Chinese National Anthem, "The East Is Red" - in Chinese yet! Everybody sang, or at least their lips were moving - there wasn't a single John Wayne among us. As testament to the effectiveness of rote learning, after 40 years I can still recite a couple of verses in Chinese.

After our exercise, we returned to our rooms for breakfast, then after washing our bowls, we had to return to our rooms for "study sessions." The study material would consist of short pamphlets in English describing the 'evils of capitalism,' how the workers are exploited, and the inevitability of the 'class struggle', to list a few examples. Our platoon interpreter would hand out the morning's material, and then get us started by reading some of it and asking us questions. He would then leave and go to the next squad after telling us to continue discussing the subject among ourselves.

As soon as he left, we would post a look out by the door and then begin either; ridiculing the pamphlets or discussing our favorite subject - food. The interpreter would return, periodically, to check on us and see how far we had gotten. We usually managed to skim through the material so that we had a general idea what the subject was and were then able to successfully fake a slight interest.

The study sessions and singing calisthenics didn't last more than a couple of months. The Chinese may have realized that they weren't getting anywhere or they may have just been trying to see if they could make us 'sit up and bark' on command.

Our platoon interpreter came by our squad one morning after breakfast and told me to come with him; I was wanted at Camp Headquarters. I racked my brain to remember if I had done anything wrong recently; then I remembered the onions I had stolen from Company Headquarters a few weeks earlier and I really began to worry. As I hurried along a couple of feet in trail behind the interpreter, I was very nervous and wondered if someone had ratted on me.

I was marched along the road all the way through the entire camp and even past the British POW's on the south side. As I passed through the various companies, I was subjected to curious stares from my fellow POWs who also probably were wondering what I had done.

Camp Headquarters consisted of a small cluster of houses adjoining the south side of British compound, and outwardly appeared no different than the ones we were living in. I waited outside one house while my guide went inside, then I was beckoned inside. I paused a moment at the open door and stared inside. The floor was light tan and almost as smooth and shiny as glass. It appeared to be lacquered or polished to a high sheen. I was told to remove my shoes before entering. I complied and stepped inside, noting that all the walls and ceiling seemed to be freshly papered and painted and everything was spotless.

An older, heavyset Chinese officer was introduced to me as the Camp Commandant and he motioned me to sit on the floor by the door next to a small radio. Through the interpreter, I was told that the radio had a problem and could I fix it? I plugged it in to a nearby socket and flipped the volume control switch in the normal clockwise direction to turn it on. After a short warm-up, I began turning the dial and found what sounded like a Korean broadcast. It was too loud so I reached over and turned the volume counter clockwise to lower the sound level, instead, it got louder. It was immediately obvious that, for one thing, the volume control was wired up backwards.

I then reduced the level and tuned across the band to see if it had any other problems. Everything sounded fine, so I told them what was wrong. They immediately brought out a small soldering iron, solder, a diagonal pliers, needle nose pliers and a screwdriver and asked me to fix the radio. The light inside was too dim for me to see well without glasses, so I asked to take the radio outside a moment.

I quickly found the two outside wires on the volume control and swapped them around and by then the soldering iron was hot so I soldered them back properly. I then checked out the radio one more time and they seemed happy with it.

I now knew that I had just passed a practical exam in electronics. It had really been ridiculously simple, but then maybe there was more to come. But as it turned out, that was all they wanted to see and I was marched back to my company.

On the way back I thought about the Commandant's house and how splendid it appeared compared to our rooms. In their lectures and in the study session material, the Chinese often stressed that under Communism, everybody was equal; class distinction had been abolished. But to me, it certainly appeared that the Commandant felt that he was a member of a somewhat higher class.

CHAPTER THIRTY-FOUR

Movie Stars

We had been gathered in the company area again to hear another speech by our Company Commander. We all sat there on our little stools and waited to hear the announcement whatever it was - usually another scolding for not keeping the area clean enough or some similar message. For me and many others, the commander's words just went in one ear and out the other. Many of us had collected bags of walnuts while up on wood detail and we used this opportunity to perform the tedious task of extracting the meat. They were wild walnuts and hard as rocks so we would bring two small stones with us which we used to break them open. We usually tried to hide the sound of the 'crack' by coughing at the same time that we banged the two stones together. There was very little meat inside, but it helped to make the lectures go faster.

However, this time the commander's words caught our attention. We were going to take part in a movie. A Chinese film crew was in camp and wanted to shoot some scenes with American Soldiers charging up a hill against a valiant, heroic Chinese machine gunner. We could guess who was going to win. They were asking for volunteers, and so, to make everything right, and also to make sure that they got some takers, the Chinese were going to give every man who took part two tailor-made cigarettes and an ounce of Soju. Now, Soju was a very potent liquid. I had actually tasted it only once before - on the march up to camp when a Korean 'Mamasan' had given me a spoonful from her little still.

I didn't care about the cigarettes, but the Soju, which was about 50% alcohol, represented nourishment; and I still needed every bit I could get ahold of. I quickly found two guys who felt that they wanted a good smoke more than a shot of booze, so we struck a deal. If everything worked out, I hoped to have three shots of alcohol all to myself. I wondered what the shock might do to my frail 110 pound frame, but I was also determined to find out.

The next day we fell out after chow and were all marched off to the low hills about a quarter mile east of camp. It was a warm sunny day and everybody was there, with the exception of the cooks and a few men who were too sick to even get out of bed. Even some of the cooks were envious, but their duties held them back. It served them right; I hoped we were getting even just a little bit for all the many times they must have picked the choicest morsels out of the pot before ladling it out to the squads.

I estimated that there were over 1800 men in camp at that time, and it looked like at least 95% had showed up for the movie. As we swarmed into the large open cornfield, we had to pass rows of trucks loaded with captured American rifles, helmets and stacks of musty uniforms.

There weren't enough to outfit everyone with complete uniforms so the healthier guys were given the most complete sets and told to lead off the charge up the hill when given the order. Some of the lead men looked very authentic with their wool khakis, field jackets, helmets and rifles with fixed bayonets. Wags in the group kept asking for ammunition, but the Chinese only smiled and ignored them.

All I got was a well-worn old field jacket and a steel helmet. I was surprised at how heavy the helmet felt in my weakened condition and how my bony frame rattled around inside the oversize jacket. To top it off, they gave me a well-used, but clean M1 rifle and a bayonet on a cartridge belt. I slid the bayonet out of its holder and snapped it in place on the business end of the M1. Probably more than a thousand other guys had done the same. I checked the cartridge belt; it did not have any clips of ammo.

Only a handful of armed Chinese guards were anywhere in sight on the hillside. They were vastly outnumbered and if a few hundred guys had wanted to be heroes, we could have taken over the camp maybe for an hour or so. A few guys kidded around, but I'm sure no one was serious.

We stewed around at the base of the hill for maybe half an hour while things were readied for the great battle. The Chinese had scattered bundles of corn stalks around the base and slope of the small hill and we could see the machine gun and camera crew getting set up on the top of the low 100 foot hill in front of us.

When all was ready, the corn stalks were set on fire and as the streamers of white smoke drifted across the hillside, we were told to charge up the hill, but not all the way. We were only supposed to go part way up and then fall under the withering fire of the heroic lone Chinese machine gunner. It was going to be a story to rally the millions back home, a story of how this stalwart young soldier had single handedly mowed down about 1800 armed American soldiers.

When the order to charge was given, I managed a feeble trot for maybe 100 yards and that was it - I was pooped. So I sat down on a nearby rock at the base of the hill, leaned my rifle against my knee and watched the proceedings with amused interest. Most of the men fell on the lower portion of the slope, and a few got within a hundred yards of the gun before dutifully collapsing. One joker, however, was in pretty good shape and decided to go all the way. As he charged the machine gun, I could see and hear the camera crew frantically hollering and waving at him to lie down, but still he kept going, head down and bayonet fixed.

At the very last minute he clutched dramatically at his chest, and then crumpled in a heap a few yards in front of the greatly relieved camera crew. That finished the shooting and our GI hero was congratulated for his great performance. Many of us wondered what they would have done if he had not stopped but had instead tried to capture the machine gun. But, at that stage, no one was ready to push the Chinese that far.

Our short movie career now over, we all ambled back to the trucks and returned our uniforms and rifles, then lined up for our pay. As we shuffled past several tables manned by Chinese, each man was handed two cigarettes then his ration of Soju was poured in the bowl he had brought along. I walked slowly back to my room carefully cradling my precious cargo.

In the room my two buddies showed up with their Soju and collected the two cigarettes after pouring the liquor rations into my bowl. I then transferred the entire amount to my spare tin can to free-up my bowl for chow; I didn't want to drink it on an empty stomach.

After supper, I began slowly sipping my Soju, about a teaspoon at a time. Each swallow burned all the way down, worse than the hottest peppers, and it must have taken me an hour to finish the three shots. By then, I was already feeling the effect and felt a little unsteady as I walked around the company area.

I wasn't the only one who had traded for extra rations and soon laughing and singing began to break out in various rooms. One of our guys had somehow traded for 6 Soju rations and now I noticed him staggering from room to room, barely able to stand up. But three was enough for me as I tottered back to my room and conked out. The next morning I awoke with few ill affects except for a slight headache.

One day another incident happened which provided an important insight into our captors minds. We had a POW named Dukovich in First Company who appeared to be a little deranged. He would wander around from place to place and almost never talked to anyone. Even in the hottest weather, he wore his long cotton padded overcoat. When not wandering around, he could often be seen roosting up in some tree like a large glum looking troll.

On this particular day, he was in his wandering mood and had decided to head north out of camp on the main road. Naturally, the guard, a young, baby-faced kid with an old Japanese rifle and fixed - bayonet, was not going to allow that. Several sharp, barked commands had no effect at all on old Dukovich - he just kept heading up the road past the guard.

With that, the guard charged at Dukovich, his rifle at the ready, and began jabbering excitedly in Chinese. Dukovich turned, grabbed the guard's rifle, wrenched it free of his grasp and proceeded to chase the guard back toward our company area. The poor guard ran like a frightened rabbit, probably expecting to get shot in the back, but instead, Dukovich chased him a few yards then threw his rifle down in the dirt.

In the following days, the Chinese never said or did anything to Dukovich as a result of the incident. This story quickly made the rounds of the camp and became just one more bit of evidence that maybe the Chinese guards had orders not to shoot unless absolutely necessary. From then on, the POWs would often probe and test the Chinese to find out how far they could be pushed and what we could get away with. In his own way, Dukovich had answered two questions we had been asking ourselves: (1) he really was nuts and (2) apparently the Chinese would no longer shoot someone trying to escape.

Near the end of my stay in First Company, the Chinese organized another big production. This time, they announced that we would be asked to "volunteer" to help the North Korean Farmers harvest their crops. The statement was greeted with near silence as they pointed out that our help was needed because many men had been killed and most of the remaining were fighting at the front.

Then they mentioned the 'magic word' - food! If we would "volunteer," they would provide extra food while we worked in the field. Again, nearly everybody who could walk turned out for the short march to a small valley just north of the camp. The entire valley, as well as the more gentle slopes of the hill sides, was covered with corn. About a thousand POWs quickly spread out through the estimated 40 acres of corn and began cutting and tying the corn into bundles which we then hauled back to the farmer's yard where a group of maybe a dozen Korean women and girls shucked the ears.

Around noon we took a short break and had chow which consisted of steamed bread and a meat and vegetable side dish. The food was good and there was more of it then we usually got back in camp. After lunch, we returned to the fields to finish the job.

About mid-afternoon it looked like we were going to finish early, so I thought I would check out a heavy grove of trees I had been eyeing up on the hill side. By now I had developed a 'nose' for figs and I was sure I had spotted some vines up in the trees. It was only a couple of hundred feet up to the trees and sure enough, they were loaded with figs.

The corn, the Chinese; all were now forgotten as I attacked the tree and struggled up through its branches until I had reached the coveted vines. I was still very weak and it required all of my effort. As I reached the fruit, I began stuffing it into my mouth as fast as I could, oblivious to the world around me and to the hundreds of men still working in the fields below - not unlike a big honey bear ignoring the stings of angry bees.

After a few moments, I became aware of shouts from the valley below, and then I noticed several Chinese running toward me waving their arms. I exited the tree much quicker than I had climbed up, still chewing the last handfuls of figs and headed back to see how much trouble I was in.

All they did was chew me out and then later back in camp, they singled me out as a prime example of everything a "socialist worker" was not supposed to be. I just couldn't seem to get along any better in the Chinese army than I had in the US Army. Never mind, it was all endured with a little feigned humility, and I hoped, without a smirk betraying what I really felt.

CHAPTER THIRTY-FIVE

Sound and Lights

Sometime in early October of 1951, I was again summoned to Camp Headquarters. They wanted to know if I would help install a public address system for the camp. I saw no reason not to, so I said yes. I was then introduced to a young girl named Foongee, who would be handling the PA and making the announcements. She showed me a small room behind the headquarters houses where an amplifier, microphone and record player were set up.

Foongee appeared to be about 18 to 20 years of age. She wore her hair in a long pigtail with bangs in front in the typical Chinese fashion. Like all the other Chinese, men or women, she wore the standard, army issue light tan pants and blouse, small slouch cap and rubber soled tennis shoes. She was shy, a little on the plump side, but I thought rather cute. Maybe I was regaining my health, after all.

Her English was very rudimentary; a small vocabulary and only the most basic grammar, but we were able to communicate okay. She said Bill Smith, a British POW, and an American, Sargent Brock, would help me string the wires and hang the speakers in each company. I asked Davis, a POW from my company, to help also.

The first thing I did, was check out the equipment. The amplifier was a large, heavy 100 watt unit made in China. The back of the amplifier had various connectors for driving just about any combination of speakers you might want. They had provided five speakers, one for each company, including the British and about a quarter mile of wire.

Next, I visited all the companies and figured out the best place for each speaker, then we began digging holes and setting up the poles. Davis, Brock and Smith did most of the hard work while I strung out the wire. I tried climbing one of the poles, but I still wasn't quite up to it. Maybe if there had been some figs up there, I might have managed it.

After a week, it was done. I made the final connections in the PA room, then flipped the power on and cautiously turned up the volume. It worked! All the dials, switches and knobs on the amplifier were in English so I explained everything to Foongee and made sure she didn't turn the volume up too far, and then I went back to First Company to listen to our handiwork.

Six o'clock sharp the next morning, we were abruptly awakened by the raucous strains of a Chinese opera. Chinese opera sounded somewhat like Italian opera, except that the singer was usually female and she always sang in a high screeching voice about two octaves above anything I was used to. She was accompanied by an intermittent series of pings, pangs, plunks and bongs from instruments which sounded as if they came from the kitchen rather than the concert hall. The "music" was followed by a chorus of howls and cat calls from the POWs in my company. They knew they had to get up, but the music didn't make it any easier. There was some talk of lynching the guy who installed the PA, but I hoped they were just kidding.

The next day I went around the camp to check everything out, and then went back to tell Foongee that it sounded great except for the Chinese opera. She showed me a big box of old 78 rpm records, some were Chinese or Russian, but most were pre-WW II American labels, such as Guy Lombardo and other well-known dance bands. She also promised to try to find some different, more pleasant music to wake us up with.

Later, I was looking through some of the Russian records. They all seemed to be brand new, with maroon labels and gold lettering printed in both English and Russian. I picked out Tchaikovsky's First Piano Concerto and suggested that it might be more appropriate for an early morning wake-up since the second movement begins as the composer's impression of a sunrise. In fact, the Russians had titled that side "Sunrise" in English. The next morning we were gently awakened by soft and beautiful piano music, but no matter how beautiful, in the setting of a POW camp, it was still bizarre.

Figure 32: Davis, Mac, Pete and me and the amplifier

The PA amplifier had a built-in radio, but I noticed that Foongee had also brought in a small short wave radio. She said she wanted to tune in the English language broadcasts from Radio Peking and Radio Moscow and re-broadcast them over the PA. I turned on the radio and began tuning through the bands. I stopped on one English language transmission which sounded like the Voice of America. Foongee shook her head and said we were not supposed to listen to that. She then turned the dial to a certain frequency and I heard the familiar sound of Radio Moscow, which I had often heard on my Ham radio back home. I saw that I wasn't going to be able to sneak a listen for news from home with her in the room and she also wasn't about to leave me alone with the radio for even one minute.

As we headed back to our companies, Foongee handed the four of us, (Davis, Brock, Smith and myself) each a small bag of hard candy as payment for installing the PA system. I ate a few pieces on the way back to my room then decided that I would share the rest with the guys in my squad. That was the first candy that I had tasted in over five months and my gut told me to eat it all myself, but my head decided I had better share it. Some of the guys thought that helping the Chinese set up a PA system bordered on treason but most felt that it was okay because we were going to get some benefit out of it.

That night we heard the first news in English since any of us had been captured. Some of the men had not heard anything from the outside world in over a year. There was total silence as we all strained to catch every word from the Radio Moscow announcer. We were especially attentive when he began discussing the Peace Talks in Kaisung.

After it was over, heated discussions broke out over just what had been said or implied. We knew the broadcast had to have been laced with propaganda but we also knew that certain basic facts had to be true. Our problem was separating the wheat from the chaff. But, at least we now had some idea of what was going on at the Peace Talks and in the rest of the world.

Not long after we had finished installing the PA, our camp interpreter Shen came by one morning and told me to pack up my things and come with him - I was moving to Camp Headquarters. Since I had been running back and forth every day, they decided it would be more convenient if I would just move to Headquarters permanently. I was not at all sure that I liked the idea - no more wood details and even more important, no more "figs."

The Headquarters buildings adjoined the British company on the south end of our camp. A couple of houses between headquarters and the British were used as a hospital during the winter months and still contained some very sick guys despite the improving food situation. The headquarters buildings themselves were mostly just typical Korean type houses identical to the houses in the main camp area.

When I arrived at the Headquarters area, I discovered that I would be rooming with three other POWs from the British company, Ron Allum, Bill "Smudger" Smith, who had helped install the PA, and another Bill, our typist, whose last name I have forgotten.

I soon found out that Ron was head of the camp "peace Committee." The Peace Committee was an organization of 'representative' POWs from each company whose purpose, ostensibly, was to promote "Peace." In reality, they were just a group of compliant young men, some gullible, some opportunistic, who were picked by the Chinese to promote the cause of the hour. One week it would be the signing of the "Stockholm Peace Initiative," and another week they might be asked to circulate some petition related to the Peace Talks.

If he could be believed, Ron had a rather colorful past. After discharge from the service in WW II, he had gone to Singapore and spent the intervening years running guns to rebels in Southeast Asia, before being recalled to active service with the Gloucester Regiment. He was a smooth talker and reminded me of a typical con man. In my opinion, he was just an opportunist and was only in the "Peace Committee" for what he could get out of it.

Bill "Smudger" Smith was something else. He had some function with the Peace Committee, but I was never really sure what it was. He was very quiet and didn't have much to say, but he seemed to be a very intelligent 'bloke'.

Bill, our typist, was a little more talkative, but he seemed to be trying to distance himself from the Peace Committee and anyone associated with it. He had been given a brand-new Olivetti typewriter, and his sole job was to type up petitions, notices and pronouncements. Most of the time, the typewriter sat idle so whenever we were allowed to write letters home, we would have Bill type while we dictated. As a result, I was probably the only American POW (at least in Camp #3) who sent typed letters from prison camp. I occasionally wondered how this must appear to the folks back home and to the Army censors.

At Headquarters, the four of us were assigned two rooms in a row of houses facing the main road but separated from it by a large yard. Adjoining houses on our left and right were used for some administrative purposes by the Chinese.

To enter our rooms, one had to step up about a foot to a stone and mud ledge which formed the outer boarder of the heated floor of all Korean houses. Then there was another step up to a narrow wooden porch which ran along the front of the house but underneath the overhanging tile roof. This allowed one to walk from one room to the next in rainy weather without getting your feet wet or tracking in mud.

Since the nights were getting downright nippy, one of the first things we did after moving in, was to check out our under floor heating. Smudger gathered a few sticks of wood from a large wood pile in back and started a fire in the kitchen of our house. As the fire got going, smoke began to seep out of numerous cracks in the dirt floor and soon filled the rooms with a thin, acrid, eye stinging haze. We opened all the doors, but it was still unlivable inside. We concluded that the concussion from the bombing in the nearby center of town had cracked the foundation, and nothing short of rebuilding the floor would fix the problem.

In a couple of days, the Chinese brought in a small metal stove made out of an old, rusty 10 gallon drum, and set it up in our 'living room' with a metal stove pipe protruding out under the eaves like some little shack in the Ozarks. If it was for the Peace Committee, the Chinese seemed to have no trouble getting whatever was needed in short order. Propaganda obviously had a very high priority. Now on cold days, we could at least huddle around the stove to warm ourselves, but the little stove did absolutely nothing to take the 'meat locker' chill off the adjoining room where we slept on the floor, especially since we had to let the fire burn out before we went to bed.

Two or three nights a week, members of the Peace Committee from all the Companies would gather at Headquarters and meet in our room. Some nights we had 10 or 12 guys hunched in a big circle around our little stove under the light of a single bare 25 watt bulb. These sessions usually amounted to about 50% bullshit and the remainder Peace Committee 'business'. On second thought, I guess that would make it 100%.

Bill, the typist, and I were not members of this elite group and we would rather have been somewhere else, but since the only source of heat and light was located in the meeting room/living room, we had little choice. But as time went on, I was drawn more and more into the conversations, especially the 'BS' part of the discussions. I had always found it difficult to sit and listen to someone make a statement that I considered "hogwash," and not then jump into the conversation with my "two cents worth." Anyway, the discussions did get rather lively at times and it did help to pass the time. I also got acquainted with a few interesting people and kept up on the 'goings on' in the different companies. It should be noted, that the Chinese very seldom showed up at any of these meetings, but I wouldn't have been surprised if they had eavesdropped now and then, since we had caught our company interpreter listening outside our door back in the main camp area.

One night we were jarred awake by the thunderous roar of airplane engines very low overhead, then the sounds of a series of small explosions as the engines faded away to the south. It was 'Charlie' again and this time it sounded like he had dropped something right on us. Up until that time, we had been living under the mistaken impression that our pilots were aware of the camp location, and would avoid the area.

The next morning, the Chinese fell everybody out for another lecture, during which, they lambasted the US for bombing a POW Camp. They told us that one American officer, two Chinese and several Koreans had been killed. The B26 had flown over low, following the main road which went right through the middle of the camp, and had scattered a string of small anti-personnel bomblets from the south end of camp and on further south into the main part of town.

We were then lined up and marched, one company at a time, through the damaged houses to see for ourselves, what damage had been done. The building structures had not been harmed much, but we could see the hundreds of small holes and gouges where the metal bomb fragments had sliced through the walls and doors and caught those inside sleeping on the floors. Afterwards, many of us, including many members of the Peace Committee, asked our interpreters, "why wasn't the camp marked and especially why wasn't it lit at night?" Their lame answer was that it would serve as a navigation beacon to our pilots. Very few 'bought' that answer. Our pilots never seemed to have any trouble navigating and finding the roads and railroads on the blackest of nights. They seemed to know exactly where they were, the problem, as we saw it, was that they just were not aware that there was a POW Camp at Chungsung.

Well, as can be guessed, the Peace Committee now had a new 'cause'; the "Indiscriminate Bombing of POW Camps." Meetings were held, letters were typed, and finally a petition was drawn up to be sent off to Kaisung. In each company, the squads were lined up one after the other, and marched into a room at Company Headquarters to sign the petition. It said something to the effect that, American Pilots dropped their bombs anywhere and everywhere without regard to civilian casualties. I didn't think that one in a hundred agreed with the words, yet more than 80% signed it. Most of us just were not prepared to make waves and challenge the Chinese but we felt that at least, it would draw attention to the position of our camp and maybe prevent a repeat of the incident. A few of the men who had refused to sign the petition and had also urged others not to sign were denounced publicly as "Reactionaries" by the Chinese and taken out of their squads.

I later found out that on November 3rd, 1951 Radio Peking broadcast a "**Protest Against Indiscriminate Bombing of a POW Camp on October 13, 1951,**" which they said had been signed by most of the POWs.

We had hardly finished installing the PA system, when I was asked to wire the camp for electricity. This was one thing I think everyone was in favor of. Up until then, most of us couldn't sleep more than eight hours per night, so we had to sit around after dark in our rooms and talk until the guards blew their whistles at nine o'clock as a signal for us to "hit the sack." Having a light in each room would be a welcome change.

Sargent Brock, the same POW who had helped me put up the PA, also helped install the lights. The job wasn't as big as it sounded, because most of the houses had once had lights and many of them still had wire strung along on porcelain knobs under the eaves. Most of the houses also still had a single pull chain type light switch hanging from the middle of each room and some even had light bulbs still installed.

We were given large rolls of copper wire labeled, 'Made in England'. The wire was about #12 size with heavy red cloth covered rubber insulation and was undoubtedly the worst wire I had ever seen. In some rolls, the wire had broken every 10 to 50 feet and then had been twisted back together again to form a splice. They had then run the wire through the machine that forms the insulation. Now every place where a splice had been formed, one could see a small lump in the wire like a little snake that had swallowed a mouse. In any other country in the world, that wire would have been scrapped. The British either 'pulled a fast one' on the Chinese or else the Chinese got it at a bargain price.

They also provided us with a heavy duty linesman's pliers, screwdriver and electrical tape. We started on one end of the camp and worked our way slowly to the other end. Most of the time we were working on "hot" wires but it was only 110 volts and no problem because we both had rubber soled shoes. I carried a light bulb with me as a means of testing each house as it was finished.

After about a week, we were done. I had studied the American Electrical Code back in the 'States' and I knew that the job we had just completed would never have passed inspection, but it worked and that was good enough for me. As for the Chinese, I don't think they would have known the difference between a good and a bad job.

When we were all done, the platoon interpreters in each company distributed light bulbs to each squad and that night there was light for the first time. After that I spent a busy few days running all over camp fixing lights that didn't work. For once, everyone was glad to see me and I got no 'flack' like I sometimes did about the PA system.

From that day on, the camp took on a different, less gloomy air in the evenings, but at 9 P.M. sharp, it was lights out. Bed Check Charlie usually didn't come around until after 10 P.M. and nobody wanted to try to find out what he might do if he saw a light on in one of the rooms.

CHAPTER THIRTY-SIX

Radios

I hadn't been ensconced at Camp Headquarters more than a month when one day an old Korean gentleman came by. He had a typical long grey beard, baggy white blouse and pants and a tall black hat. I guessed he was about 60 years of age and I noticed that he was carrying something wrapped up in a large white silk cloth tied with a black ribbon.

Our interpreter said he had a radio to fix and wondered if I could take a look at it. Would I ever! I welcomed the opportunity to do something interesting for a change. By now I had regained enough of my health and strength so that my mind could begin to focus on something other than mere survival.

A couple of months earlier, I had remembered what starvation had done to my body and I had then begun to wonder if maybe my mind might also have been weakened or damaged. As a simple test, I had tried to remember how to do simple arithmetic problems on paper. I was very disturbed when I failed completely. I didn't have the first clue on how to do long division. After several weeks of intermittent attempts, I finally figured it out again, but success did not bring comfort. I realized that my mind was only functioning at about a third grade level and I became really concerned whether it would ever return to normal.

That first radio now gave me another chance to test my mind on a more practical problem. The old Korean carefully un-wrapped his package to reveal a small tabletop radio in an old wooden cabinet reminiscent of the 1930's vintage radios I remembered from back home. I plugged it into an outlet in the light socket which hung from the ceiling and clicked the volume control switch on. It was dead, not even a trace of hum emerged from the speaker.

So I told the old Korean that he should leave it with me and I would see what I could do. After he had left, I got the pliers and screwdriver from the PA room and brought them back to our sleeping room. It was a warm day, so I opened the door to let in enough sunlight to allow me to examine the innards of the radio with my 20/240 vision.

I unscrewed the back and removed the chassis. I was pleasantly surprised; it looked exactly like some of the old radios I had repaired at home. The arrangement of the tubes, coils and tuning capacitors seemed to be an exact copy of the type of superheterodyne radio common in the 'states' during the 1930-1940 era. The tubes were the old glass type with metal plate or grid caps protruding out the top and a wire running from there into an adjacent coil. Even the tubes looked familiar, and I immediately recognized from their numbers, the standard RF, IF and audio amplifiers as well as the power rectifier and power output tubes. They were all lit up and all were in their proper places.

The standard 'trick' every radio repairman used first off, before dragging out his meters and test equipment, was to touch his finger on the grid caps to see if this caused a noticeable hum in the speaker. The hum resulted from the 60 cycle voltage which one's body picked up from the wiring in the house. I heard nothing and this told me, right off, that the audio output was not working, which could be due to a dead rectifier and no B+ voltage.

I then carefully turned the radio over, held it to let the sunlight illuminate it and squinted at the wiring and components underneath. Again, it was as familiar as the palm of my hand. The wiring was laid out the same, with the colors coded red for high voltage, green for signal wires, etc. Even the resistors were color coded the same as

American-made radios before WWII. At that time, I had worked on enough radios of this type that I could sit down and draw the entire schematic, including the values of all the parts, from memory.

I next wanted to check for proper voltages on all the tubes, but since I had no meters, I had to use another trick often used by lazy technicians; momentarily shorting out each point where voltage was supposed to be. A quick short to ground at a high voltage wire will generate a small spark and the size and brightness of the spark along with the loudness of the snap will give one some idea of the amount of voltage and current available at that point.

Starting with the power supply, I got a loud crack and a big arc. I also got a hefty spark at the plate of the output tube, but nothing on its screen grid. This could only mean that either the screen bypass capacitor was shorted, or else the screen resistor was open. With a small knife I cut the lead to the capacitor and *bingo*! - the radio began to squeal which in turn proved two things; the capacitor had been shorted and secondly, the screen resistor was okay.

I was now able to tune in music and speech, but the squealing due to feedback made it impossible to listen to. The radio needed a new screen bypass capacitor, but of course, I also had no spare parts. Then I guessed that maybe one of the other bypass capacitors in the radio could serve a dual purpose and tied a short piece of wire from the screen to the plate bypass capacitor. That did it! The radio now worked perfectly and I got several Korean or Chinese stations clearly as I tuned over the broadcast band. The quick success made me feel good for several reasons, but most of all because it showed that maybe my mind could bounce back from the effects of malnutrition. My earlier concern with the inability to work simple long division problems was greatly allayed by finding the solution to a rather subtle problem in 15 minutes with no tools and no spare parts.

There were no Chinese anywhere around and I hoped that no one had heard the radio as I quietly tuned in several stations. At that, I unplugged the radio and set it aside after first removing a couple of

tubes to disable it. Later that afternoon Foongee came by and I told
her that I hadn't found the problem yet. She seemed to accept my lie,
and walked off.

Smudger and Bill had been working in the 'living room' next door
on some typing and had heard the radio. I told them I wanted to keep
it a secret for a few days so I could monitor AFRS in Tokyo during
the evening. They were all very excited, and even our opportunistic
friend Ron, agreed to help keep the secret.

I had some scrap wire left over from wiring the camp, so that
afternoon I decided we needed an indoor clothes line in our bedroom.
I strung about 15 feet of wire from the north wall to the south wall of
our room and left the end hanging down to the floor where we
normally slept with our heads toward the south wall. In the meantime,
Smudger had washed out a few items of underwear at the river and
they were ceremoniously hung up to dry on our new 'clothes line'.

That night, the four of us could hardly wait for the last of the Peace
Committee members to leave. Some of them liked to hang around and
shoot the breeze even after the official lights out at 9:00 P.M. I
couldn't wait that long, and went 'to bed' early at about 8:00 P.M. I
replaced the tubes, hooked up the antenna and plugged in the radio,
then crawled under my blanket and cotton padded overcoat with the
radio.

Carefully keeping the volume at the absolute minimum, I
cautiously tuned the band. As I slowly approached each station, I
reduced the volume to prevent those in the next room from hearing.
Finally, I heard some familiar Western music and then the cheerful
voice of the announcer identifying the song and then the station -
"Armed Forces Radio" Tokyo Japan.

Later they came on with several minutes of 'World News' and I
heard, for the first time in months, the straight news without any
heavy handed propaganda. The news from both Radio Peking and
Moscow was always so obviously slanted. Each news item, even each
sentence seemed to be molded and crafted with its propaganda affect

in mind. They never reported anything just for the 'hell of it'. They not only did not report stories such as; 'dog saves master from burning building', they didn't even report on floods and hurricanes. Everything was for one purpose only - Propaganda!

The Peace Talks had now moved a few miles south from Kaisung to Panmunjom and they seemed to be going reasonably well and I began to hope that we might all be home in a year or less. After lights out, Smudger, Bill and Ron took turns joining me listening to stateside music under the blanket while one of us always remained on the lookout for the Chinese. I insisted on maintaining control over the radio because I couldn't take the chance that one of the guys might try to change stations and accidentally let the volume blast out. I was sure that the Chinese wouldn't do anything so drastic as to have me shot at sunrise for listening to AFRS news, but I didn't know what lesser punishment they might decide to mete out. At worst, they could throw me into one of the Reactionary squads which were kept isolated from the other men and put me to work emptying latrines and digging holes. The next day the four of us went about our business with a smug feeling and itching to tell someone about it.

I managed to 'put-off' that poor, old Korean "Yobo" for a week before I decided that I had better 'fix' the radio and give it back. Keeping the radio too long could have made someone suspicious so I announced to Foongee that I thought I had finally fixed the radio one day. I showed her how it worked and tuned in several Korean and Chinese radio stations, which was all you could get anyway during the daytime.

The next day, my old Yobo showed up to collect his radio and was very pleased to hear it working. He asked me, through the interpreter, what I wanted for fixing it. I replied that, the only thing I could use would be a pair of glasses.

A few days later, the old gentleman showed up again and this time he had two more radios that need fixing but more importantly, he handed me a small dark blue glasses case. I opened it and inside was a pair of small round wire rimmed glasses of the type one would expect to see worn by an old maid 'school marm' or maybe by Ebenezer Scrooge. The lenses at first appeared to be perfectly flat, but when I put them on, I could see much better, in fact, I could actually read a newspaper and make out the wiring in the radios without taking them out into the sunlight.

I was delighted with the glasses and told the old man that I would try to fix as many radios as he wanted to bring me and I would not ask for anything further. It never occurred to me that the old guy might be getting a commission for getting peoples radios fixed, but I wouldn't have cared. I was just glad to finally be able to read.

In spare moments, I tinkered with the two radios. Both were similar to the first one. I soon found out that neither radio worked at all. The problem with one was obvious; one of the tubes did not light up. I noted that the second radio had one of the same type tubes, so I swapped them and once again I had a working radio. That evening we got the first update on the latest news in several days plus a few snatches of some more stateside music.

From time to time, Foongee or one of the non-English speaking Chinese would stick their head in our rooms to see what was going on. One seemed a little curious about out 'clothes line', so we made sure that we always had a pair of socks or something hanging up to dry. I also only worked on the radios during the middle of the day when it was impossible to receive any English language broadcasts from Japan, and I hoped they might be unaware that those little receivers could easily pick up Japan at night.

As Christmas approached, I managed to keep at least one radio in some sort of working condition most of the time. In the evenings when the visiting Peace Committee members gathered around our stove for their usual BS session, I now often retired to the sleeping room to catch the latest news. One or two others whom I thought I could trust were even allowed in on our little secret. They were cautioned to be very discrete when spreading the news they were given and asked to never even hint that it had come from a radio broadcast.

CHAPTER THIRTY-SEVEN

Christmas '51

I had been at Camp Headquarters for about a month and I concluded that I would have rather been back with my squad. I got along fine with the British POWs but the four of us at the Headquarters were just too isolated from the main camp activities. The only people I had to talk to were the three British guys and the Chinese interpreters except for two or three evenings per week when a few of the Peace Committee members came up for 'discussions.' Before the evening was over, the discussions always degenerated into bullshit sessions. But that was okay with me, I always liked to argue. If someone said; "the sun always sets in the West," I would jump in and point out that it wasn't true at the north and south poles. The 'bull' sessions were fun and helped pass the time of day, but I wasn't being exposed to a balanced point of view. Most of the guys who visited Headquarters were considered "Progressives" by the Chinese and in fact they had been picked for their positions for just that reason. One can't live in an environment like this for months and not be affected to some degree.

Thanksgiving arrived and the Chinese issued special rations for the occasion. This was in addition to the continued steady improvement in the chow we received each day. All this contributed to the general feeling many of us had, that something was up. Rumors were flying about the Peace Talks and I'm sure that I must have started some of them by discretely releasing news I had heard on AFRS.

By the end of November, they had finally agreed on a truce line at Panmunjom and then had begun discussing the prisoner exchange. When I heard this on AFRS one night, I could barely contain my joy. Ron, 'Smudger' and Bill agreed that the news looked very good. We thought we could be on our way home in a month or two, maybe even by Christmas. The news was too good to keep to ourselves, but we also didn't dare tell the guys in the companies exactly what we had heard because that would give away our secret. As a compromise, we only revealed general details, avoiding specific dates, and to some people we only hinted that we may have heard it from the Chinese.

Many guys also noticed that the Chinese, not just our interpreters, but guards and other camp personnel seemed to be much friendlier. One or two of the camp interpreters even dropped some very broad hints to me that we might just be going home sooner than expected. They obviously were hearing the same news from Panmunjom that I was getting surreptitiously, but of course they were getting the Communist version of the 'truth'.

The Peace Talks resumed in Panmunjom on Oct. 25, 1951 and things seemed to be moving rapidly. By Nov. 27, both sides had agreed to a Truce line and they then began to discuss prisoner exchanges. They had set a deadline of Dec. 27 for agreement on the remaining issues and this gave many people the false sense that maybe the war was rapidly coming to a close. This also probably had much to do with the rapid improvement in our chow and general conditions in the camp and accounted for the friendly smiles and good humor of the Chinese personnel.

Just as our captors had tried to use us to influence a decision on the 'Truce Line' issue, they now shamelessly told us to write letters home and denigrate the voluntary repatriation issue. At the time, most of us couldn't see any reason to prolong the Peace Talks and keep the men cooped up in prison camp while discussing whether or not POWs should be allowed the right to remain behind. If we had been allowed to hear all the facts from both sides of the issue and had learned that tens of thousands of UN POWs had been impressed into the North Korean army and forced to fight against their will, I'm sure most of us would have agreed with the UN position, even if it meant a long delay in our returning home.

On Dec. 18, 1951, the two sides exchanged lists of POWs and both sides were greatly upset by the results. The Communists contended that the UN list was short 44000 names. The UN had removed these men from an earlier list because they represented South Koreans who had been forced into the North Korean army and could not legitimately be considered POWs.

On the other hand, the North Koreans had previously bragged about the 65000 South Korean soldiers they had captured and now they claimed they only held 7000 ROKS and 4417 non-ROKs including 3198 Americans. The UN had estimated that there were about 11500 non-ROKs missing and captured and now they wondered what had happened to the other 7000. If they could have asked us, we would have told them - they were scattered in ditches and fields along the routes to the camps and in nameless graves behind the 'hospitals' of the various POW camps.

Our side continued to hide the fact that large numbers of UN POWs did not want to return home and when asked for numbers, we misled them by grossly underestimating the number at "only 16000" and hid our intentions by proposing only a "fair and equitable" exchange of POWs. Our chief negotiator, Admiral Turner Joy and some members of the Joint Chiefs of Staff did not agree with our position on "voluntary repatriation," but they were overruled by Truman. (**Blair**, *The Forgotten War*, pp. 960-965)

The three British POWs and I were not the sole POW occupants of Camp Headquarters. We had noticed that about 30 POWs were being housed in a row of rooms on the south side of the Headquarters compound about 200 yards from our rooms. Ron checked with our interpreter and was told that they were "reactionaries."

Anybody who strongly disagreed with the Chinese and interfered with their attempts to brainwash and propagandize was considered a trouble maker and labeled a reactionary. In the fall of 1951 the Chinese began to pull these men out of their respective companies and isolate them at Camp Headquarters. They seemed to be confined to their rooms when not on work details. Other POWs were not allowed to contact them and the four of us were specifically told not to talk to any of them.

The other POWs at Headquarters were the inmates of our little hospital occupying a row of rooms along the north side of the compound and perhaps 100 feet from us. In spite of the greatly improved food, we still had some men in the hospital who were very near death and every day or so, one would die. After listening to the encouraging news from AFRS, I couldn't stand to see some of these guys just lying there without any hope, so I would visit them several times per week in the evenings and try to cheer them up.

Several of them were really pitiful, they were so weak they could not even raise their own head, and they could only speak in a whisper. They were being tended by other POWs who had volunteered for the duty, feeding them chicken soup by hand like little infants and changing their soiled pants.

I would walk through the rooms and select the ones who looked most desperately ill, then kneel down beside them and ask how they were doing and if they were eating the food. Many of them seemed to have just given up, like Pfleegor and Tricomo had done only a few months earlier and as I had almost done. When no one could hear me, I would whisper that I was secretly monitoring AFRS and that the Peace Talks were going very well. I told them that the war could end in a month or two and it would be terrible to give up and die so close to going home. I also asked each of them not to tell anyone else what I had said, especially the Chinese. I don't know if any of this did any good because after January, I was not able to visit the hospital.

About a week before Christmas, the Chinese began conducting a census and inventory. As one can imagine, this created a tremendous flurry of rumors, almost all predicting an early release. The Chinese interpreters were going through the entire camp with a small half-sheet paper form titled; "Registration Card of POW's Personal Belongings." We were given ink pens and told to fill it out. At the top, under "Outfit" I wrote "R HQ" meaning that I was part of the camp "Regimental Headquarters." Under "Coy," "Plt'" and "Sqd," I left everything blank, but I did put down my name, rank, serial number and nationality as requested.

I then put down a complete list of all my personal belongings: One wallet, $17.70 in script, a money order for $40, one pencil and a ring. I also listed one wallet belonging to Bill Pfleegor with $23.10 in script. The bottom of the form stated that, "All Personal Belongings Must Be Kept In The Possession of The Owner. Exchanging and Trading Are Forbidden." I then signed the form and wrote the date, Dec.21, 1951.

It was a sad little form, and one of the few things which I brought back out with me when repatriated. Since the four of us were living apart in camp headquarters, we were some of the last to get inventoried. When the form was handed back to me it had "Number 1835" written on it. I assumed that this meant I was the 1835th prisoner to get counted in Camp #3. After the first of the year, the camp was re-designated Camp #1.

Christmas was coming up and the Chinese announced with their usual great fanfare and speeches of self-congratulation, that we would be having the greatest of feasts provided, of course, by the "lenient Chinese Peoples Volunteers." The day was awaited with quiet but happy expectancy. Food was still probably our primary interest in life.

On Christmas day the British POWs and I were temporarily sent back to the main camp for the big feast. I went back to Second Company which was my new 'adopted company' and there we all waited anxiously as evening approached. Some of the guys kept peeking in at the cook house to see what was being prepared and then they would hurry back to report that the menu earlier promised by the Chinese was really coming true.

Finally, the courses began arriving, delivered excitedly by the squad members we had selected to pick up chow that day. For a prison camp, it was a fabulous meal. We had dishes such as; turnips and beef, fried rice, boiled dumplings filled with meat and vegetables and other similar exotic (for us) fare. I sat in my room and carefully devoured each side-dish in, what might be called a state of subdued ecstasy as each new delicacy was carried in. The whole thing must have consisted of six or seven courses plus all the steamed rice and steamed bread you wanted. We also got a few cigarettes, a little wine, a handkerchief and a pair of socks. For the first time since capture I was sated, in fact, I was stuffed to the point that my stomach hurt. Almost as painful, was for the first time, having to turn down food that some of my squad members just could not finish. I also realized then that I had developed a compulsion for food which bordered on the psychotic. I crammed food down my gullet far beyond the needs of my body and then continued to eye each new dish and even my buddies left overs with covetous intent. Even today, 40 years later, that feeling has not totally vanished, and every day there is a little struggle within to tell myself that I really don't need to finish that bit of leftover potatoes or string beans or whatever.

That evening, I had time to quietly reflect on the past months and I could not help but remember Pfleegor, Tricomo and all the hundreds of other guys who could have used some of the excess chow we had just consumed. The entire situation had an air of surrealism about it.

Six months before I had watched five of my buddies die of starvation and dysentery just in my squad alone. In July, I had languished in our camp amid the stifling heat, hordes of flies, infestations of lice, the stench of urine and excrement and with the sight of death all around. The change in our condition had been almost unbelievable. If we had told someone about it, I'm sure that many would have suspected we were exaggerating the initial awful conditions. On the other hand, those who chose to believe the stories about the harsh conditions might have thought we had been brainwashed into giving undue credit to the Chinese for the great improvement later on.

We had all gone through more or less the same ordeal but that ordeal was almost never spoken of among ourselves and it was certainly, to my knowledge, never discussed with the Chinese. It was like one of those dirty little family secrets you sometimes read about, where the family has tried to hide their shame by not discussing it in the hope that maybe the whole thing will just fade away.

I'm sure some of the Chinese must have wished to erase the bad memories too but I also suspect that for other, more sinister Chinese, it may have all been part of the plan to degrade and humiliate us.

On our part, I think we avoided talking or even thinking about the initial months of captivity as a mechanism of denial. We didn't want to talk about those days because if we did, they might have returned. In the back of our minds we always knew that if the Chinese had done this to us once, they could easily do the same again. If the war had gone badly or if they had decided that we were no longer valuable as bargaining chips, then our whole situation could have collapsed back to its original sorry state.

I did, however, meet some nice Chinese. Foongee, for one, was a sweet and trusting young girl, whose only job was managing the public address system and interpreting for me. We got along fine and she, in turn, gave me a great deal of freedom to do as I pleased at Headquarters. Then I showed my gratitude by betraying her confidence in me when I began surreptitiously monitoring AFRS. In fact, she probably got in trouble with her superiors when my duplicity was discovered.

On January 12th, 1953, a B29 named Stardust Four Zero with 14 men on board was on a bombing mission over North Korea when it was shot down over Cholsan, North Korea, about 20 miles south of the Chinese border. Three men were killed in the crash and the remaining eleven were captured after bailing out. The Chinese collected all eleven and transported them under the utmost secrecy by truck and train deep into northern China where they were kept in solitary confinement in tiny frigid cells in the middle of winter.

They were also starved and threatened with death during months of grueling interrogation during which some of the men's weight dropped to as low as 110 to 120 pounds. They were deprived of all contact with their fellow captives and with the outside world and were continually told that they were criminals and would never see their home again.
After about a year, the food and treatment began to very slowly improve. Each year things got a little better, the food got better and increased in quantity, they got a little more freedom of movement within their cells and finally they were even allowed to join their buddies and receive mail from home. (**Brown**, 1961)

I have since read many similar stories of men who were imprisoned by the Communists. All of these accounts bore a strong resemblance to one another. They all began with severe starvation, humiliation, degradation and threat of death. Then there came gradual improvement in food and conditions as the 'carrot' to induce them to agree with the indoctrination. Finally, before release, they were usually feted with banquets and sometimes treated almost like comrades-in-arms.

In retrospect, I think the pattern of similarities is too close to be coincidental. The Chinese treatment of various types of prisoners betrayed the hand of a central guiding ideology. What we had, I think, was a cabal of old men under the iron willed leadership of Chairman Mao, who were absolutely certain that their way was the right way and the only way.

One of these days Communism will collapse in China just as it has in Russia, but until that happens, I doubt we'll ever know the truth about our treatment by the Chinese. Until then, I tend to believe that the Chinese knew exactly what they were doing, and that most of what happened followed a general plan for extracting the maximum usefulness out of a large bunch of "tools of the American Imperialists."

CHAPTER THIRTY-EIGHT

King George

Christmas was hardly over when the Chinese announced another gala feast, this time it was Chinese New Year. We had more of the same type of chow. I was almost getting blasé about the food and when I wrote letters home; I didn't have to lie about the food, at least the food at Christmas and New Year. In between holidays, the food wasn't bad either. Compared to six months previous, it was at least a thousand percent better.

The weather turned extremely cold after the first of the year. Some nights, the Chinese told us it got down to 30 below but there was very little snow on the ground. All day we huddled around the small stove in our 'living room'. Our pants, jackets, hats and mittens were all made of cloth stuffed with about an inch of cotton. Our shoes were oversized tennis shoes also stuffed with cotton. When we were really cold, we could also put on a cotton padded overcoat in addition.

It was too cold to do any work, too cold to write or type and too cold to work on radios. We just crouched next to our stove or walked around stamping our feet to keep our circulation going. The first night of extreme cold, I slept with all my clothes on, including the overcoat, and with the ear flaps on my hat pulled down over my ears and chin. My one thin blanket, I used to cover my face.

The next morning my feet were so cold I was afraid I had frostbite. After a couple of hours I was able to thaw out my feet by the stove and dry out my socks. The next night I tried something different; I took my damp socks and shoes off, put on dry socks, and slept with my blanket wrapped around my feet instead of my face. To protect my face, I tucked my overcoat over my face and nose. That night I managed to stay reasonably warm as long as I didn't move from one position.

I was born and raised in Minnesota and I thought I was used to cold weather, but that winter was without a doubt the coldest and most miserable of my life. All of the other 1800 POWs in the camp were living in relative comfort and that included the "reactionaries" staying in Headquarters. The under floor heating systems in everyone else's rooms were working as they were supposed to. Most houses had three rooms connected to a kitchen with a chimney at the far end of the three rooms. One only had to burn about three sticks of wood in the morning and another three in the evening to keep the floor toast warm all day and night. (See **Figure 23**)

The system wasn't perfect. The guys living in the end room always wanted a little more heat and the guys living in the room next to the kitchen usually complained that the floor was too hot to sit on. In fact, we frequently had small fires when the floor got so hot, next to the kitchen that the bamboo mats on the floor would begin to smoke and turn black. Some guys living down in the company area frequently had to open their doors, even in 30 below weather to cool the room off.

It wasn't 30 below all the time. Most days, it got up to somewhere around 0 degrees to 20 degrees F. At 20 degrees, you had to start unbuttoning your cotton padded jacket or risk getting damp from sweating. At times like these, we would sit out on our front porch and try to get some sun. One day at dusk I noticed a couple of Chinese soldiers coming my way with an American in the lead. As they got closer, I could see that they were bringing an American Air Force Officer in a flying suit into Headquarters. He walked right by me about 10 feet away and we looked at each other but said nothing before they took him someplace behind our house. The next day we saw others brought in and assumed that they were probably from one of the B29s we had seen flying over to bomb Supung dam about 15 miles to the northwest.

In the subsequent weeks we never heard any screams or other unusual noises from behind us so we guessed the interrogations must have been reasonably civilized. If the Chinese were keeping fliers in our camp, they were being very secretive about it because these were the only captured airmen anyone ever saw, besides the ones who spoke to us about Germ Warfare.

One day Ron came back from a tour of the company area and he was a little ticked-off. He had found out that the Chinese had started giving every man a meat ration of 5 pounds for each two weeks. This worked out to about a third of a pound per day per man. This included the weight of bone, gristle and other unusable parts, but this was still a lot of meat to us. The four of us staying at Headquarters were getting nothing other than the same food that the Chinese Headquarters personnel were getting. It was quite startling to discover that the Chinese were now feeding their prisoners better food than they themselves got.

Even the "reactionaries" next door were getting their meat ration. We were sure that this was another clue that maybe the war was coming to an end, but that didn't mean that we were going to let the guys down in the companies get more food than us. Ron had more guts than the rest of us, so he complained to the Chinese and lo and behold, they issued the four of us our own hunk of meat to cover the next month's ration. That night we got a little cooking oil and had our first fried pork for supper. Since we slept in a "meat locker," keeping the meat from spoiling was no problem.

Another night, we cut up a complete pig's heart and fried it on top of our tiny stove. Afterwards, we sliced up the steam bread buns we had received as part of our regular meal and toasted them on the stove top. It was delicious, but there wasn't near enough to satisfy me or the other guys so I decided to see if I couldn't scrounge up a little extra.

Late that night I quietly got up and sneaked out our front door. All seemed quiet. It was a dark, moonless, cold night as I carefully made my way south along the row of Chinese sleeping quarters to the cook house about a hundred yards away. The cook house was part of the group of rooms where the "reactionaries" were quartered and an armed guard always kept a watchful eye on them round the clock.

As I reached the door of the cook house, I saw the flashlight beam of the guard poking around the side of the building. I quickly ducked into the kitchen and hid behind some large earthenware pots just as the guard stuck his head in the opposite door. He shined his light around the kitchen but didn't spot me, and then he went on. Earlier reconnaissance in daylight had shown me that the big pots were full of leftover steamed bread, so I quickly stuffed as many as I could into my jacket, then waited for the guard to head back to his normal position before hurrying back to my room. The next day we all had toasted steam bread till our tummies hurt.

The guys winked, but they never asked where all the bread had come from. After time to think it over, I decided it had really been a dumb thing to do. The guard probably would not have shot me if he had caught me, but I surely would have been arrested and punished. The Chinese always took a dim view of stealing, and anybody caught at it, could expect to be digging latrines for a while.

One cold morning we got up and noticed a dead mule in the courtyard in front of Headquarters. He was lying partly on his back with two of his legs sticking up in the air and his belly appeared to have bloated up to about twice its normal size. The Chinese didn't have any opinion on the cause of death.

Later that morning, several POWs came by and carved the carcass up into smaller hunks, then hauled everything back to the companies. That night the guys had "fresh" mule meat, and once again, I missed-out.

On January 15, 1952, I received my first letter from home from my Aunt Florence, my mother's sister. I immediately wrote an answering letter. Our typist Bill had gone back to the British Company, so I had to do my own by the hunt and peck system.

> After returning home, I noticed that this letter had the return address torn off and about one third of the letter itself missing. I can't imagine what I said, but this just shows how touchy the Chinese could be.

All through most of November and the month of December and January, I was monitoring the news from Tokyo several times per week. As usually happens when one gets away with something for a while, he gets careless.

On February 6, 1952, I was listening to AFRS at about 8 P.M. when I heard that King George VI had died. As so happens, three British POWs were in the next room having a little discussion with Ron and Smudger, so I called them in to let them hear it directly. These particular 'blokes' had previously been discrete when we gave them information, so I felt that I could trust them again. But it was a mistake.

The next morning we heard that some of the British POWs were walking around the camp with black arm bands which they had quickly fashioned out of parts of some old uniforms. When the Chinese asked them why, they explained that they were in mourning for King George. Well, as it turned out, most of the Chinese had not yet heard the news, so it was immediately obvious that somebody was listening to a radio, and that guy had to be me.

That afternoon a couple of Chinese officers, who spoke no English, came around and looked in our rooms. They seemed to be interested in our 'clothes line', although I tried to make believe I didn't notice them. Later Foongee came by and said that from then on I would have to work on any radios in the PA room while she was there. That was the end of my 'radio days'. I finished the last radios, gave them back to the Old Korean, and after that I only worked on the amplifier or the lights. Foongee never accused me of anything and never mentioned the subject again. About a month later, I was sent back to Second Company.

CHAPTER THIRTY-NINE

Germ Warfare

After being caught with my 'hand in the cookie jar' on Feb.6, the Chinese didn't act right away. I was aware, however, that they seemed to be watching me more closely.

In the meantime, the Chinese were expanding their efforts to influence or indoctrinate us. They began by showing a Russian movie in the small theater which still remained standing at the south east side of our camp. The theater could only hold two or three hundred at a time so the POWs were brought in one company at a time. The movie wasn't bad, I think it was "Ivan the Terrible" produced by Serge Isenstein in Russia. Ivan was the tyrant Ivan the IV who ruled from 1530-1584. The technicolor screen was filled with the typical Russian scenes of tormented peasants and vast armies plodding across the snow-covered steppes. Just about everyone went. It sure beat staying home and picking lice out of your shirt. We also saw some black and white films of gallant Russian tractor drivers, both male and female, struggling against the elements and the odds to bring in another record harvest for Uncle Joe. A similar Chinese film showed hundreds of thousands of peasants digging, shoveling and hauling dirt, all by hand, to build a monstrous new dam on some river in China. It too was another triumph for the singing masses. They always seemed to be singing as they slaved away. I always thought they might get more done if they would just shut up and dig.

The next big production was a modern Chinese opera staged by a troupe brought in from China. It was titled "She Ur" or "The White

Haired Girl" and was straight out of the "Perils of Pauline" movies from the 1920's America. The plot was about this black haired peasant girl who was forced to flee from the unwanted advances of her wicked landlord. She had to hide in a cave for years until rescued by (you guessed it) the stalwart black-haired hero who had been her secret admirer. The only problem was that her hair had now turned white.

After getting strafed in October, the Chinese had finally put up a marker consisting of a platform made of wood about 20 feet square. The top was painted red with some words like POW CAMP in white. One night in March, we were jolted out of our sleep again by the sound of B26 engines and this time we also heard heavy machine gun fire. Next morning we confirmed that we had been strafed again. Charlie was probably after another truck on the road. Many of the houses in camp had fresh 50 caliber bullet holes and several had even stitched through the middle of our "POW" sign. Not one person was hit.

Every week it seemed that the Chinese were introducing some new propaganda ploy. One day, some lawyer by the name of Jack Gaster from an international association of lawyers came through camp supposedly investigating US war crimes. It was to be the beginning of their big campaign on Germ Warfare. I'm sure he never heard one word about all the hundreds of POWs who died of malnutrition and dysentery the preceding year.

Early in the war, the Chinese had captured AP photographer Frank Noel. We saw him for the first time that winter of '52. I guessed he was about 55 to 60 and he usually had a scraggly, grey two-week growth of beard. He certainly looked the part of the tough but good humored newspaperman who had been everyplace and seen everything. He had been given a Speed Graphic camera by his colleagues at Panmunjom and now he toured the POW camps taking propaganda photos for the Chinese. We were to see a lot more of Frank in the coming year and a half.

In February 1952, the Chinese started giving us lectures on Germ Warfare. They started off slow with a few talks by our camp or company commanders stating that the American Air Force was dropping disease infected insects, rodents, and fish, etc., in order to spread disease among their troops. They showed us bottles of flies which had supposedly been collected from around the POW camp in early March when the weather had been too cold for flies to hatch naturally. One of the POWs, when examining the flies, took one out, popped it into his mouth and swallowed it. The Chinese were horrified, but I'm sure they would have been delighted if he had then turned up his toes and died. Whoever he was, he was a gutsy guy and fortunately never got sick.

To reinforce their contention, and also probably to explain in the future why none of us got sick, the Chinese quickly gave the entire camp shots to ward off all these bad bugs the Air Force was spreading. In the year and a half following the alleged start of biological warfare, I was not aware of anyone who died due to any exotic diseases.

Sometime around the middle of March, I was abruptly told to pack up my things and move out of Regimental Headquarters. I was told that they expected me to attend "study" sessions in the company each week. I felt that I might, in a way, be on 'probation' from having been caught monitoring the radios. I was put into a squad in the middle of 2nd company right next to the central courtyard. The camp was integrated and blacks were scattered throughout the various squads. The squad I was assigned to had about eight guys, and a couple of blacks.

We now no longer had to sleep on the floor as before; instead, we built our own two level bunks from wooden posts and poles. In between the horizontal bed rails, we stretched whatever we could scrounge; rope, wire, braided rice straw or anything to provide a surface a little more flexible then the floor. Soft slats would then be stretched lengthwise between the ropes to give added support. All in all, they were a great improvement over sleeping on the hard floor plus each of us now had more room and we didn't disturb others when we had to get up.

As soon as I arrived in 2nd Company, the Chinese launched their "Germ Warfare" program in earnest. We had to fall out every morning for a lecture by the company commander on the evil deeds being perpetrated by our countrymen. No matter what the weather, we had to endure hours of alternating Chinese and broken English translations of lengthy papers read by the commander. All this time we sat perched on our little stools in blustery March rain, sleet and sometimes snow, often for two hours or more.

After a series of speeches, we were told that next we were going to be broken down to Platoon level and the reams of documents would be read to us by the designated POW platoon leader. The next day our platoon leader, whom we had elected because we liked him, began trying to read the material. He stuttered and stumbled through the heavy text at an unbearably slow pace. It took the entire morning before he had finished and by then, our butts were numb and our feet were frozen.

The next day we tried somebody else, but he was no better. The third day my squad asked me to read the papers because I had done a passable job of reading novels to the squad. We had a very small library in the camp stocked with the London Daily Worker, New York Daily Worker, Lenin's works and a very limited number of American and Russian novels in English. The only thing most people wanted to read, were the novels, so often, one guy would be asked to read the book to several others. Since I had done a creditable job of reading Balzac's Short Stories, I was selected to read the 'germ warfare' papers.

It was really tough reading. The text went into great detail about the various diseases and their bacterial and viral causes. It was filled with such words as; rickettsia, bacillus anthraces, epidemiology, etc. which I probably didn't pronounce correctly, but at least I got over them fast. This went on every day for two weeks during some of the worst March weather.

When I had finished, the Chinese still weren't through with us, they then brought out photographic exhibits for each company. All the POWs were lined up and made to walk past and view all the photos and read their captions. They looked very authentic. There were several different types of bombs; one type appeared to be made of fiberglass with small compartments for the bugs. The printing on the canisters was clearly readable and looked like the typical military jargon we used to see on shells, grenades and boxes of ammo. Some of the germ bombs were even shown lying on the ground with clumps of lethargic insects scattered around. A few guys thought it might all be a fake, but most of us were pretty much convinced of their authenticity.

As if this weren't enough, the Chinese followed up over the next several weeks with a whole series of talks by dozens of Air Force Pilots who spoke to the men in each company. They each introduced themselves as Major or Captain so and so, and then proceeded to describe the airplanes they had flown, the bases they had flown out of and their missions.

They all looked and sounded like real pilots and after their presentations, we were allowed to talk to them and ask questions. Each of them always had an English-speaking Chinese with them, but they didn't seem to be afraid of him and they didn't seem to be obviously controlled or manipulated by him. The pilots also had photographs of the various 'germ bombs' and explained once again how everything worked.

The pilots were the real clincher in the Chinese accusations concerning biological warfare in Korea. Most of us didn't want to believe it, but after all of those pilots confessed right in front of us, we reluctantly had to concede.

It was obvious that most, if not all, the Chinese around us really believed in 'germ bombs,' because they became paranoid about flies and insects. We were even ordered to kill a certain number of flies every day as the weather got warmer. One night we had another B29 raid on the nearby Supung Dam and the bombers dropped clouds of tinfoil strips to confuse the Chinese radar. Well, the next morning the entire camp was covered with little strips of aluminum foil and the Chinese went absolutely nuts. They ran around like chickens at a cricket farm, picking up each piece of foil with gloved hands as if it carried death itself.

Later that summer, the Chinese ordered camp-wide fly killing contests. Each of us was required to kill his quota of flies each day. Some days, when flies abounded, the quota might be as many as 250 flies per man. With the primitive fly swatter I had made, killing that many wily little flies a day sometimes became a real challenge. And, if we had any doubts about their sincerity, they were dispelled when the Chinese counted each and every fly.

After the Peace Talks got underway, the Chinese soon began using the POWs as a tool to influence public opinion. When the Truce Line became the primary issue in October 1951, the Chinese in control of our camp wasted no time in trying to seduce us into supporting their position, and to that end, we were deliberately misled about the facts.

Again on January 2nd, 1952, when the UN side surprised the Chinese by proposing that POWs be permitted to remain with their captors if they so choose, the Russians countered on February 2, with allegations that "germ warfare" was being employed by the Americans. The Chinese rapidly followed up these accusations in February and March with their very elaborate and detailed exhibition on biological warfare consisting of hundreds of pages of documentation and dozens of photographs followed up by the testimony of dozens of American Air Force officers. All this amounted to a propaganda blitzkrieg and the POWs found themselves right in the middle of it.

In Panmunjom, from January to April, the UN side had continued to mislead the Chinese into thinking that "only about 16000" Chinese and North Korean POWs might refuse repatriation so the Chinese finally agreed to allow independent screening of POWs to determine their preferences. Apparently screening of POWs had been going on in South Korea during the winter and spring, but I was certainly not aware of any screening of American POWs in our camp by the Chinese.

On April 19, 1952, the UN dropped its bombshell. When they turned in the lists of Chinese and North Korean POWs who wanted to refuse repatriation, there were 62000 names on the lists. The Chinese were hopping mad - they had been had, and they walked out of the negotiations, recessing the talks indefinitely on April 28. (**Blair**, *The Forgotten War*, p. 965)

In my experience, the Chinese Communists were masters of cunning and devious behavior. They seldom told the truth when a lie would do just as well and if a lie was more effective, and then one could count on the lie. I still, to this day, don't know whether the American Air Force used biological warfare agents in Korea. I have read that the US government has admitted to testing some type of flu or cold virus in San Francisco around the Korean War period. The object was to test airborne dispersal agents for viruses in preparation for use of those agents to disperse more deadly viruses in the event of a war.

In the final analysis, the US might have been testing "germ bombs" in Korea or they may have been fake devices to fool the Chinese into wasting a lot of manpower on collecting and neutralizing them. On the other hand, the Chinese could have easily faked all the devices with help from the Russians. If the American pilots were given the choice of either being shot or confessing falsely to germ warfare, I'm sure most of them would have gone along with it. I'm sure I would have.

In the end, it comes down to; whom do you want to believe? Since very few POWs died after the spring of 1952, and since there were no illnesses running rampant through the camp or the civilian population that I was aware of, I tend to think that the entire "Germ Warfare" episode was a hoax perpetrated by the Chinese and the Russians to retaliate for getting outfoxed on the POW repatriation issue.

PART FOUR

POW CAMP
The Last Year

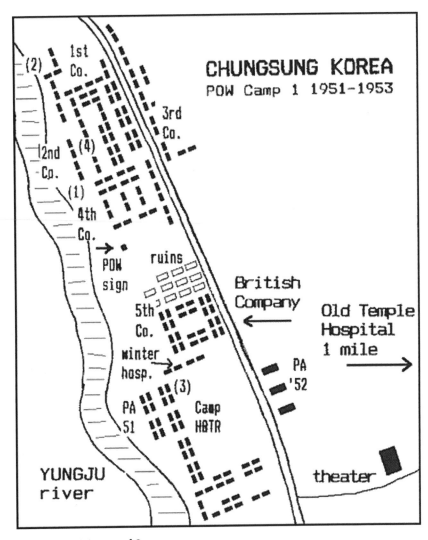

Figure 33: Main part of Camp

CHAPTER FORTY

Renewal

The detailed map of Camp 1 at the beginning of this chapter gives a rough idea of the size and lay out of the camp. The locations and numbers of buildings are approximate, since I am relying only on my memory. The numbers (1) through (4) in parentheses, show my successive residences during my stay there. The first location of the Public Address (PA) system is noted at "PA'51." The system was later moved to "PA'52." The "winter hospital," was only used during the colder months, while the "Old Temple" was used at all other times.

The "POW sign" was located in a clearing in the middle of camp. During one strafing run by a B26, it was hit by a few 50 caliber bullets.

By the coming of Spring 1952, I had made a remarkable recovery of my strength and health. I was not alone; most of the men were back to their normal weight. By "normal," I mean the proper weight for their size and bone structure. I had recovered to about 155 pounds which was about right for me, and in fact, I was beginning to develop a noticeable paunch due to stuffing myself with three or four bowls of rice at every meal. John Allen, one of the guys in our platoon, nicknamed me "The Gut." Even the Chinese in our company picked-up on it and started calling me "Fahntoong" which means "Rice Bucket" in Chinese. But, I didn't mind at all, because the memory of nearly starving to death less than 12 months before was still firmly etched in my subconscious.

Peter, who had joined Easy Company only a couple of weeks before we got captured had also been captured and was now in 2nd Company with us. Before capture, he had weighed at least 250 pounds. With all his excess fat, he had fared very well on the march and by the time he arrived in camp, he was down to a trim 150 pounds and almost unrecognizable. Peter had also started putting some weight on, but nowhere near his former self.

I still went on wood detail every chance I could. Getting away from camp and up into the woods was one of the few pleasures I had. But some of us now had found a new pleasure - running. We ran on the path along the river and up into the mountains just for the sheer pleasure of being able to run again. By midsummer, I was able to run for one to two miles before I would develop a crick in my side and have to stop. Running also got us up into the woods sooner with more time to enjoy the solitude before heading back.

Many of us now began competing with each other and with other companies to see who could haul the biggest log back. By late summer I, and many others, were often carrying logs weighing over 200 pounds. We had to set them down and rest every couple of hundred yards, and sometimes it took all afternoon, but it still felt good to haul in a "record" log. The Chinese cooks and other company workers also brought in their own wood for their kitchens. But I noticed that our Chinese interpreters and the other officers never touched a stick of wood. One more chink (pun intended) in the facade of the "classless society."

Wood detail wasn't the only detail; every morning we had to make up our bunks, straighten up the room and sweep-up the area around our houses. And the worst detail of all: every morning two guys had to empty the latrine. My turn came around every eight to 10 days. We had a large wooden bucket slung between two long wooden poles. This device, also known as a "honey bucket," would be set down next to the latrine pit and one of us then had to scoop up the soupy mess using an old GI helmet nailed to a long pole. When the bucket was full, we would hoist the carrying poles on our shoulders and stagger off down to the river, hoping we didn't trip. If the river was low, we would wade across and dump the contents on the Korean's fields. They were always very grateful for our especially high grade of fertilizer.

In winter time, the "honey bucket" detail wasn't quite as bad, because the cold weather seemed to suppress the noxious odors considerably; however, the detail now took on a new dimension.

During summer, everyone would urinate in one particular spot, next to the latrine and the urine would just soak into the soil, but in winter it would freeze almost immediately, and soon a large mound of yellow ice had built-up.

This, of course, had to be hauled away also and that job was always the least popular. It was accomplished by grasping the company ax firmly in both hands, raising it well above one's head, then bringing it smartly down on the center of the mound, while keeping one's eyes and mouth firmly shut! As you can imagine, the chips flew everywhere, and even inveterate New Yorkers soon learned to keep their mouths shut.

As the weather got hot in June and July, I made another discovery. About a quarter to one-half mile north of camp there were two pools formed by natural depressions in the river bed. The west bank of each pool consisted of a near vertical rock embankment dropping straight down to a depth of about 15 feet and forming a perfect diving platform. From the deepest part, the bottom sloped up gradually forming an oval pool about 150 feet long by 75 feet wide.

We had to pass these two crystal clear pools every day as we returned from wood detail, usually drenched in sweat. The temptation was too much and we would often drop our logs and jump in to cool off before heading back into camp.

I had always been terrified of deep water and had never learned to swim. I decided that it was time to get over my fear. My worst fear was getting my head under water, because I had to close my eyes, and then I couldn't see where I was or what was happening.

The first day I found that I could open my eyes under water after all, and although everything was blurred, I could see reasonably well. In the next days I practiced walking around under water carrying a large rock to keep me from floating to the surface, Soon I was jumping off the deep end carrying a big boulder. I would, of course, sink quickly to the bottom and then walk under water to the shallow end. I had no problem because I found it was easy to hold my breath for at least two minutes or more. From this, it was an easy step to swimming under water and I was soon going from one end of the pool to the other, all under water.

I now felt more comfortable under water than on the surface so I then began to learn to tread water or dog-paddle. The standard dog-paddle seemed to require lots of effort without much effect. While experimenting with various movements of my hands under water, I noticed that I could get considerable lift by sweeping my hand through the water horizontally. This led to my technique of sweeping my arms back and forth horizontally, much like a helicopter rotor, to keep myself afloat.

Next, I worked on swimming strokes. Most of the other guys used a standard overhand stroke while lying face down in the water. I always seemed to get a nose full of water when trying this so I settled for a kind of back stroke. This kept my nose out of the water, but I could only see where I had been and not where I was going.

By September when the annual monsoons came again, I felt very comfortable in the water, one could even say reckless. With the rain coming down in sheets, 24 hours a day for several days, our little knee-deep river soon became a raging torrent charging through the camp. The thick brown water was six to eight feet deep in spots and formed large waves as it swept over boulders and obstructions.

For something to do, some of us began jumping into the rapids and floating down stream. We would float on our backs, feet-first, so we could spot the big boulders and intercept them with our feet rather than our heads. It was great fun but dangerous. Still, no one ever got drowned, to my knowledge.

One of the men in our company from the Dakotas would occasionally drop to the ground and begin shaking uncontrollably. He also drooled and his eyes rolled up into their sockets. We all assumed they were epileptic "Fits" as we called them.

One day when the river was at its highest, he suddenly ran screaming down to the river bank and leaped into the water. As he floated down stream struggling face-down in the water, several men jumped in after him and pulled him out. It took six guys to hold him down as he thrashed around and babbled about devils being after him. In a few minutes he calmed down and then returned to his room. He said later that he was convinced that the men trying to help him were "devils." Until then, I was not aware that epileptic seizures ever took that form.

Another night during the monsoon, a POW from one of the companies decided he just had to have a girl. He leaped into the river in total blackness and somehow rode the torrent a couple of miles down the stream to where he saw the lights of a Korean house. There he climbed out, dripping wet and cold and went up to the door of one house and knocked. When the woman of the house answered, he propositioned her and her daughters. When she refused, he went to the next house. In the meantime, the first woman ran to get the Chinese.

As was usual in such cases, the Chinese locked him up then fell everybody out to give us another lecture as they criticized him for his evil deeds. Often the culprit was made to get up in front of his peers and criticize himself. We were finding out that self-criticism was very important for the Chinese Communists. They were required to criticize themselves for everything from the simplest social blunder to the most heinous crime.

Most of the men did not seem interested in making the half mile trek to the deep swimming pools north of camp, instead, they would just go down to the river bank and wade out into the knee-deep water for their daily bath. The population of the camp was over 1800 so on a typical hot afternoon there might be several hundred naked men splashing around in the river.

Most of the Korean men were either dead or they were away at the front. As a result, the field work was done almost exclusively by women. Korean fields stretched all along the western side of our river and we began to notice that the Korean girls working in the paddies were noticing us. Since they often were only a hundred yards away, we could hear them laughing and giggling. They seemed to be enjoying the sight and the exhibitionist nature of some of our guys also began to surface.

Our Korean girls also enjoyed a cool dip on a hot July afternoon but they were much more discrete about it. They would wade out into the river, all the while carefully pulling their dresses up as they crouched down into the water. In this manner, they could bath up to their waist without removing their clothes. This, of course, drove some of our guys up the wall. The thought of a half-naked woman only 100 yards away, even though she was under water, was almost too much. But there was nothing to do except endure the frustration, because one knew that somewhere across the river there probably was a Chinese guard who was keeping an eye on the situation.

If we couldn't touch, at least we could look and I discovered one day that the eyeglasses the old Korean had given me for fixing his radio could be used as binoculars. If one held the glasses out at arms-length and sighted through them, the lens in your eye combined with the convex lens in the glasses to give a magnified image. In my case, everything was magnified about four times like a pair of low power binoculars.

This didn't work for everyone though, but it seemed to work better for those who were farsighted. Some days we used to sit for hours on the bank watching the Korean girls and often there would be half a dozen guys lined up waiting to use my glasses for a better look. If I had been more entrepreneurial, I would have rented my glasses out for a fee, such as one teaspoon of sugar for 15 minutes of looking.

Another hot summer day we all started out on wood detail right after our noon meal. There must have been a column of about 1000 men, all walking single file, and winding up the rocky path along the small mountain stream. I, as usual, was near the head of the column in my eagerness to get up into the woods. Suddenly I heard the unmistakable sound of women's voices up ahead. As we rounded a bend, we came upon one of the many small natural pools formed by the stream where the water was trapped by large boulders. Three young Korean girls had been surprised in the midst of a midday dip. This time, we spied their clothes draped over rocks by the edge of the pool and knew that they were completely naked. As we marched by, they hunkered down low in the crystal clear water and giggled nervously. There were many broad smiles and a few wolf whistles, but otherwise, we were all almost perfect gentlemen.

As we moved into our second year as POWs, the entire character of the camp had changed. In some respects it was more like a boys scout camp than a POW camp. We had few duties or details and thus had much spare time to do whatever we wanted, within the confines of the camp and its regulations.

A very small number of the men in camp had been captured in fighting during the fall of 1951. These men had never been subjected to the mistreatment and deprivation that others had seen. For all the rest of us, we had not forgotten the near death camp conditions of the previous year, but we had pushed the memories far down below our conscious thoughts.

There are still 8100 men missing in Korea. I very seldom ever thought about my buddies (much less the thousands of others) who had died the previous years. Judging by conversations with others while in camp, I don't think any others did either. I don't think this was because we collectively didn't give a damn, but because we cared very much. We had survived and they were gone. What I think we did feel collectively was guilt, and suppression and denial are common mechanisms for dealing with such feelings.

So each day we all took advantage of whatever diversions were available and enjoyed ourselves with volleyball, swimming, cards, food and shooting-the-breeze. I never heard anyone challenge the Chinese and ask them why they had let so many die before and why now were they treating us so well. The subject almost never even came up among us.

As least, we finally felt more secure. Our government and our relatives knew we were alive and well. We were also made more secure by the fact that we had become bargaining chips at Panmunjom and we knew that the Chinese could not drastically change their policy without having to answer for it. All of this contributed to the remarkable changes in camp life.

Very few guards were ever in sight. There was always one guard on the main road (which ran right through the middle of camp) between the south end of camp and camp headquarters and another guard at the north end, again on the main road. Sometimes there would be guards on the east side where the camp bordered a Korean corn field, or on the west side which was bordered by the river with more Korean fields on the west side of the river. This meant that often the entire camp of 1800 men was only being guarded by two or at most four Chinese guards.

Even these guards were not really needed. The few who did escape were always brought back and made to confess and criticize themselves before us, after which, they were set to work digging turnip holes and emptying the Chinese latrines.

Each day as we headed out on wood detail the guard paid little attention as 1000 or more men "escaped." Also, on hot days groups of us would often take off for the swimming holes north of camp with no guard and no supervision. However no one ever wandered off into the Korean's fields or into the main town. We were never told not to; we just knew that we had no business in certain places.

The few times that men did escape, it seemed that the Chinese learned of it very quickly. We never had any roll calls and I was never aware of being counted by the Chinese but they must have been doing it.

Our Chinese platoon leader and his interpreter were the two we dealt with most directly and most often. They always lived in a group of houses in one corner of the company area and they obviously made it their business to know what was going on and keep tabs on each individual. Since they personally knew everyone in their platoon, anyone missing would be quickly noted.

The Chinese seemed to dote on organizations. They loved to set-up committees and organize sports competitions and games. Throughout 1952, the number of committees blossomed with members either elected by their fellow POWs or appointed by the Chinese. There were committees for Chow, Sanitation, Details, Camp Newspaper, Housing, Library, Sports, Discipline and lastly, the infamous Peace Committee.

Most of us just went along with all the activities. If the Chinese wanted to set-up committees, it was okay by us. Very few had any desire to make waves. When the Peace Committee drafted an "Open Letter to the Free Press of the World" in August 1952 (at the instigation of the Chinese) stating that we believed that the issue of voluntary repatriation was unfair, many POWs signed it. When we heard that the major issue holding up the Peace Talks in Panmunjom was Voluntary Repatriation, most of us thought it was just nit picking and not worth arguing about. But of course we were totally ignorant of vital facts.

At the time I, along with most of my fellow POWs, was young and naive and hadn't seen enough of the world to learn to be properly cynical. I gave the Chinese much more credit than they deserved. I thought everybody was right some of the time and that everybody's position deserved a fair consideration. What I didn't realize was that I just didn't have enough facts to reach a conclusion on many of these subjects.

Most of the Chinese we dealt with seemed like ordinary reasonable people who just happened to have a different opinion from us on many issues. Some of the non-English speaking platoon leaders were jerks and unreasonable disciplinarians, but they were the exception. But I didn't think any of us realized the extent to which we were being lied-to and deceived. In fact, I'm sure most Chinese, themselves, did not and still do not know how much they have been deceived.

> The Communist campaign (known as "Brainwashing") was astoundingly successful. Postwar studies were to show that only about 12% of American POWs "actively and consistently" resisted it. The great majority "cooperated in indoctrination and interrogation sessions in a passive sort of way, although there was a tendency to refuse to say anything obviously traitorous." Nonetheless, many UN POWs signed "peace petitions" and similar pro-Communist testimonials. (**Blair**, *The Forgotten War*, p. 966)

Figure 34: British and American POWs outside the theater

CHAPTER FORTY-ONE

Fun and Games

The men had become restless. Almost everyone was healthy and had his normal weight back. They wanted something to do. Some made makeshift softballs and tried knocking them around with a stick. The Chinese finally got the point and began to bring in softballs, basketballs, volleyballs and soccer balls.

Someone had carved a homemade bat out of a nice piece of hardwood and a good softball game was in progress in First Company. The outfielders had even made their own gloves out of the leather tops from old combat boots. Some of those guys must have played a lot of ball in civilian life because they were good. One of the POWs, in particular, could fire the ball about a hundred feet just like a rocket and when it hit the catcher's glove, you could hear the "whack" all over the field.

The pitcher, I'll call him 'Lem', was a tall, lanky hillbilly from Tennessee. It was a sultry, hot and humid Sunday afternoon in August and I was sweating profusely just watching the game.

The pitcher wound-up and threw a good ball right over the plate. The batter swung mightily and missed. The homemade bat did not have a knob on the end so the batter's sweaty hands could not hang onto the heavy bat, and it went flying straight at the pitcher.

He didn't duck in time and caught the full force of the end of the bat on his front teeth and his upper and lower front teeth were knocked out. As he was helped up, he spit blood and teeth all over the ground. He was then helped off to the hospital, while someone picked up the bat and took it off to the wood pile. Not long after that, the Chinese brought in a few real bats with proper handles.

Soon every company had organized teams for everything from soccer to baseball and they were beginning to play one another. One day the Chinese announced that there would be camp Olympic Games with the various companies competing and with prizes for the winners. We all knew that the primary reason for the entire affair was to score some propaganda points at Panmunjom but most of us just said "what the hell, it might be fun."

The whole thing soon snowballed and before we knew it, all the standard Olympic Games, from the 100 yard sprint and 10,000 meter run, to the shot put and javelin throw had been added. Even some nonstandard events were thrown in, such as: the caber toss, which is just a large log toss, added by the British and wood cutting, where the object was to see who could cut a one foot diameter log in two the fastest. Some of the camp Reactionaries were heard to state that they would like to get into the javelin team in hopes of spearing a few Chinese. I think they were about half serious.

The place was beginning to look more than ever like some type of boys scout or summer camp. The guys would be taking advantage of every spare moment to practice whatever sport they were going out for. Impromptu basketball or soccer games would often get started at most any time of the day. Even the Chinese cooks and interpreters often joined in as long as it wasn't a specific team practice.

I was healthy enough to engage in some of the athletic events, but I just wasn't interested. Sports never had been a big interest of mine. I was kept busy enough just hauling the PA system around to the various events to be used for announcing the play-by-play action. Johnny Ford had also completely regained his health and was now a reporter for the Camp Newspaper along with Richard Peterson, another friend of mine.

I didn't know if the entire spectacle was a propaganda success in the rest of the world, but it certainly was enjoyed by most of us. Even the camp Reactionaries begrudgingly acknowledged that they had enjoyed themselves. In fact, many of the winners were well-known reactionaries, or at least ones who hadn't yet got in enough trouble to get themselves pulled out of their company and placed in the "Reactionary Squad."

Apparently the Chinese must have thought that the games were a good thing for their cause because in the fall of 1952 they announced that next we were going to have an Inter-Camp Olympics. It opened with much fanfare on November 15, 1952 in Camp #5 at Pyoktong on the Yalu River.

This was even bigger than our Camp #1 games and they even published a rather slick brochure with lots of photographs. Only the athletes traveled to Camp #5, so the rest of us had to get our information from the Camp Newspaper and from the brochure printed after the games. The Chinese really played up the event. They even tried to copy all the usual Olympic pageantry with lots of flags and banners. I always thought it was rather strange that they chose to have the Olympics so late in the fall. The second week in November on the Manchurian border can be bitterly cold and usually is. It almost seemed as if the Chinese were in a hurry to have the games. Perhaps they thought they might not have another opportunity.

Just as the athletically inclined sought an outlet for their increasing vigor, those with musical talent were also seeking ways to express that ability. At first, all they could do was whistle or sing, and then a couple of guys in our company discovered that they could make something approaching music by blowing on combs covered with paper.

Rick Tenneson, another Minnesota POW, stated that he asked the Chinese to provide some musical instruments to give the guys something to do. At the time I didn't know whose idea it was, but at any rate, a few guitars did start to show up in camp in early 1952. A Mexican kid in 4th company was one of the first to get a guitar and I thought he was very good on it.

We also had a pianist in 4th Company. I'll call him 'Mark'. He said he had studied piano since he was about five years old. He had been studying music at the University of Texas when the Korean War broke-out. In a matter of days, he had first wrecked his car, and then his girl had left him. On the spur of the moment, and in anger, he quit school and joined the army. He was sent to Korea as an infantry soldier and was later captured in the winter of 1950-1951. On the march in the sub-freezing weather, he froze his feet and subsequently lost all his toes. Mark said he had been lucky; he could have lost his fingers. We were listening, one day, to the Mexican kid strumming chords on the guitar. About every-other chord would send Mark into rapture and he would sigh and say that they sounded just like piano chords. About a year later, the Chinese brought in a baby grand piano, and from then on, Mark was in heaven, relatively speaking.

Later in 1952, a few other instruments were brought in. The British POWs seemed to have the largest number of good musicians and they quickly formed a small band with a saxophone, clarinet, base, guitar and drums. We would occasionally put on variety shows at the small theater near the south end of camp. They weren't bad for a bunch of amateurs but then we were not in the mood to be critical, everything sounded good to us.

In the summer of 1952 we also discovered marijuana! I don't remember who first recognized its distinctive leaves and seed clusters, but soon virtually everyone in camp could spot a marijuana plant from 100 yards just as easily as I could pick-out a "fig" vine in the woods from a quarter mile away.

Marijuana, "Mary Jane," "grass," "weed," "the kind," or whatever one called it, soon became the number one passion for a few individuals and an occasional source of a "high" for many others. People who formerly had disdained wood detail, now could be seen 'chomping at the bit' in their impatience to get out in the woods.

Marijuana (MJ) seemed to be growing everywhere. The Korean farmers grew it openly in small patches near their houses, and it could also be found along the main roads and on the paths up into the hills, but the best seemed to grow in the semi-shade of the woods. There we often found plants that were six to eight feet tall, with large broad leaves and big clusters of seeds.

Some would just strip-off the leaves and bring them back tied up in large bundles with their shirts, but others would cut off the stalk and bring the entire plant. Back in camp, the men would usually just let the leaves dry in small packets stuffed under their bunks or in their extra clothes. The Chinese seemed to frown on the use of MJ, so most did not flaunt it by spreading the leaves out to dry in the sun.

In 1952, each man was receiving a regular tobacco ration plus paper for "rolling your own." With all the MJ floating around, some of the confirmed "hop heads" could be seen puffing on dark green cigarettes from morning till lights out. So naturally, a paper shortage developed. I even saw one "weed" addict, who carried a small pocket bible, carefully tear out pages of the 'Holy Scriptures', and then methodically roll himself a "joint." Others, instead of writing home to their worried folks, used their issue of writing paper to get high and forget where they were for a few moments.

The supply of MJ was often unpredictable. It depended mainly on the time of year, of course, but otherwise, on the number of wood details and whether or not some other company had gotten there first. Sometimes it seemed as if half the camp must be smoking it, and at other times, the few who seemed almost addicted to it, would trade almost anything for just 'one joint'.

When times got "tough," some of the squads composed of mostly hop heads, would gather in their room, close all the doors and seal all the cracks, then they would build a small fire in a hibachi with the dried stalks of the marijuana plant. I sat in on a few of these sessions, and I could easily understand how one could become attached to MJ.

A few hot coals in the hibachi (a small iron pot used to warm individual rooms) would keep things going, but the stalk was never allowed to burn, the object was to let it smolder in order to extract the maximum amount of smoke. Soon the room would be thick with the pungent and distinctive odor of marijuana and then one could begin to see its effects.

When the group was in a happy mood, the happiness would build until it often reached a hysterical pitch. We would be laughing and rolling on our backs and unable to stop, even though our sides were aching. Someone could say almost anything, such as "two plus two equals four," and everyone would then erupt into another round of uncontrollable laughter. Sometimes when the dried stalks ran out, we would begin tossing the dried seeds into the coals, where each would "snap, crackle and pop" in the heat. Every 'pop' or 'snap' would then bring forth renewed peals of mirth.

Just the opposite would happen when we were in a gloomy mood. As the cannabis began to take effect, someone would begin crying and before long, everyone in the room would be weeping like babies. We were inconsolable, nothing could reverse it, once started, until the last of the weed had burned and the room had aired-out.

Getting 'high' usually had very little appeal for me. It was true that your problems were forgotten for a few moments, but when you 'came around', your problems, whatever they might be, were always still there. I did think the effects of marijuana were interesting though, so I decided to do a somewhat scientific test.

I collected a small bag of choice leaves from some large plants I had found deep in the woods and brought them back to my room. After a couple of weeks I thought they were sufficiently dry, so I rolled about a dozen nice uniform joints each about one quarter of an inch in diameter. After supper that night, I lit-up one cigarette and smoked the entire thing, without sharing it with anyone. Usually, when one smoked MJ, you would share it with your buddies; but in this case, I told them I wanted to test the total effect on myself.

That first cigarette didn't have much effect. I thought I might have felt a little euphoric, but it was nothing like the times when we had sealed ourselves in our room. However, it did seem to diminish the pain of the slight toothache I had been having.

The second night, after supper, I smoked two of my joints, one after the other, and this time I began to feel a little weird, but neither happy nor depressed. The third night, I lit-up and smoked three cigarettes, one after the other.

This time, I noticed a very powerful effect. I had borrowed a friend's watch and had begun taking my own pulse and timing my breathing. After a few minutes, my pulse and breathing rate had slowed down (I thought) so much that I suddenly became terrified of dying. I stood up from my bunk, staggered outside and began walking unsteadily down the company street.

After several times around the block, I began to sober-up and also calm down. I never had the courage, or stupidity, to try four cigarettes in a row, and after that I never smoked another marijuana cigarette. However, I did keep the rest of my bag of 'grass' because it seemed to work quite well on tooth aches.

In the last year, the Chinese gave us a few lectures on why we shouldn't smoke marijuana, but it had little effect on those who really wanted to use it. They did ban it from the camp, but they never really cracked down, and MJ was usually available if you really wanted some.

One morning in the summer of 1952, I was summoned to Headquarters and when I arrived, I was told that I would be going to Camp 5 at Pyoktong for a day or so to fix their PA system. That's the way it usually was, no advance notice; they would just tell you that you're leaving. I couldn't even tell the guys in my squad that I would not be back for supper that night. But that was okay, maybe they would think I had escaped. That should provide everybody with a little excitement for a change.

A large open bed truck stopped and I climbed in the back. I guessed that they had told the driver where to drop me off. There were already five or six Chinese soldiers in the truck, sitting on the floor and leaning up against the sides and cab. They did not look at all friendly. I guessed that they had probably just came from the front and right at that moment they might just prefer to shoot me rather than shake my hand.

I sat down and leaned up against the slat sides of the truck as we started our bumpy ride north. None talked and they eyed me suspiciously as they fingered their rifles. A motorcycle was tied down in the middle of the truck bed so I began eyeing it for want of something better to do. I noticed that the nameplate had some Chinese characters as well as the name of a Chinese city printed in English.

To break the ice, I asked, with a slightly incredulous expression, if the cycle was made in China. This elicited a tirade from one of the soldiers and I guessed that the gist of his response was - "Do you think that only America can make motorcycles?" After that, one or two of them asked a few questions and I answered as best I could in my pidgin Chinese.

It was only about 15 or 20 miles to Pyoktong so we arrived well before noon. I was met by one of the camp interpreters and we went to have a look at their PA system. There wasn't anything much wrong with it that someone who was a little handy couldn't have fixed so I thought that the trip had been pretty much a waste of time. But then, what else did I have to do?

I spent the rest of the day looking over Camp 5 and meeting some of the guys there. Camp #5 was built right on the Yalu River or actually right on the Yalu reservoir. The Yalu, probably as big as the Columbia in Oregon or maybe even the Missouri river, had been dammed for hydroelectric power and the resultant reservoir stretched for probably 50 miles upstream.

I went down to the water's edge and looked down. The water was clear and clean and very deep. I couldn't see any bottom beyond about 3 feet from the shoreline. Having just barely learned to swim that summer, I got the creeps just thinking about swimming in the Yalu.

I didn't head back for Chungsung until mid-afternoon the next day. This time, they assigned me a guard for the return trip; I'll call him 'Lee'. He was a very young, and nervous looking kid carrying an old pre-WWII Japanese rifle, which with the bayonet fixed, appeared just as big as he. He eyed me warily as if I were the first American soldier he had ever seen close-up. I thought he might be wondering whether I might attack him if he turned his back on me. He was also carrying two large, awkward bundles of red-bound books destined for Camp 1: probably Mao Tse-Tung's collected thoughts or some-such.

Figure 35: Japanese Rifle

We both climbed onto the back of another open-bed truck and headed south. We hadn't gone more than a few miles, when we came to a Y in the road and the truck halted followed by some heated jabbering between the truck driver and my escort. Finally I got the drift; we were being dumped off in the middle of nowhere. Apparently the driver decided he wasn't going through Camp 1 after all and we would have to hitchhike or walk.

Lee, with his rifle slung over one shoulder, hoisted the two bundles over the other shoulder and we started walking. After a few minutes, I could see that he was struggling. Each bundle consisted of about a hundred books all tied together in one big, awkward rectangular stack which probably weighed at least 20 pounds. Whoever had tied up the bundles had sized them just right, so that you couldn't carry them in your hands, under your arms or even over your shoulders easily. But Lee had been entrusted with the job of seeing that the books reached

Camp 1 and he seemed determined to carry-out that duty without asking for help from anyone.

I finally took pity on the poor kid and offered to carry one of the bundles, he gratefully accepted. We both struggled on, taking a break every 10 or 15 minutes. Soon we discovered that our loads balanced better if we alternated carrying both bundles for 10 minutes apiece. I was feeling in a jocular mood as I handed the two bundles to Lee for his turn. I pointed to his rifle and offered to carry it while he lugged the books. He seemed somewhat startled by my offer and shook his head in a firm "no!" No sense of humor. In this manner we slowly trudged south along the deserted road as the sun fell behind the mountains. We had not seen one truck all afternoon.

The road wound through some very rugged terrain. Mountains to the east appeared to be over 5000 feet high and the surrounding hills were steep, rocky and tree-covered. As we approached a narrow defile where both the road and the river squeezed through a canyon, I noticed a long man-made wall stretching from the river bank up the steep hill sides. It looked just like the Great Wall of China only somewhat smaller. I estimated that it was only eight to 10 feet high and about the same width.

As we came abreast of the wall, I set my load down and pointed it out to Lee. He didn't seem at all impressed (I supposed he had seen the real thing back in China). I insisted on stopping for a few minutes to examine the wall in more detail. It appeared to be very old, constructed of dark grey weather-beaten rectangular blocks, covered with moss on the north side. I could see no end, as the wall snaked its way up the rocky mountain side and disappeared over a ridge.

We left my 'great' archeological discovery behind as we continued south. The sun had set behind the mountains to the west and the road was getting dark. Lee was getting more nervous. I didn't think he relished the thought of being alone on a dark mountain road with an American "barbarian," even if I was being relatively friendly and helpful with the books.

> Many warring kingdoms existed in the northern part of Korea between 400 BC and 57 BC when the entire area including large parts of Manchuria, were united under one leader as the Kingdom of Koguryo. I would thus guess that the wall was probably over two thousand years old. (*Travelers' Korea*, 1991)

We spied a light up-ahead in the deepening gloom. It was a lone Korean house nestled down close to the river. A Mamasan and a couple of younger children were busy in the front yard as we passed. I pointed to the house and gestured that maybe we could stay there overnight. Lee still had no sense of humor as he again shook his head vigorously.

We had walked about 10 miles and it had become quite dark when we heard the sound of an approaching truck. Lee set down his books and waved his arms frantically at the oncoming lights. The truck squealed to a halt and we climbed in back with our books. In 15 minutes we rounded a familiar bend and entered the northern end of Camp 1 at about nine in the evening.

They dropped us off at Headquarters with our loads and one of the camp interpreters, Chemeduh, asked how it went. Lee apparently explained everything and then thanked me, through the interpreter, for helping with the books. I, while still trying to kid-around, told Chemeduh that I had even offered to carry his rifle, but for some strange reason he refused. The other Chinese got a laugh out of that, but Lee still had no sense of humor.

When I got back to my squad, they all assumed that I had probably been living it up in Pyoktong, eating wonderful food and generally having a great time. I then informed them that the food in Camp 5 was just the same as Camp 1, and besides that, I had just had a 10-mile hike and then missed supper. It had been interesting, but then I wouldn't have called it a lark.

CHAPTER FORTY-TWO

Escape

I had finished the noon meal and quickly washed up my bowl to get an early start on wood detail. It was a beautiful day; the kind of day that made one want to just start hiking and keep on going.

To many men, wood detail was just a lot of work, something they had to do. These same guys would rather remain back in camp and take a nap, play cards or just shoot the breeze. But to me it was a total pleasure. It was an escape from prison camp, both figuratively and literally. It was a joy to slip the bounds of our little village with all its regimentation, intrigue and busy work, and plunge into the forest where each visit seemed to reveal something new and interesting. Each time we literally did escape. We did have two or three guards along, but they were merely a formality and usually just sat on a rock somewhere along the trail, smoked cigarettes and ignored the POWs.

As we hiked up the now familiar trail into the woods, I told myself, "to hell with wood cutting, today I'm going to do what I want to do." I was near the head of the column as we reached the edge of the clearing where we had been cutting the previous days and as everybody fanned out to start selecting trees, I just kept on going.

It was a very old wooded area with giant oaks, walnut and poplar extending up 80 to 100 feet above the forest floor. The sun was high overhead in some places, but down below there was perpetual twilight, broken occasionally here and there, by an intense shaft of sunlight slicing through the haze. The lush undergrowth consisted of dense bushes, immense ferns and hundreds of other plants that I couldn't begin to identify.

I scanned the area for some sort of path, but there was no sign that any human being had ever passed that way before. Ahead, the mountain side rose steeply in a jumble of immense angular granite blocks covered with moss and interspersed with bushes and ferns. I began climbing, watching carefully where I placed my hands and feet. Almost every time we came to these woods, we had encountered one or more copperheads and they seemed to especially like the crevasses in the rocks.

After climbing a few hundred feet, I began to notice a thinning of the trees and bushes as well as a change in the type of trees, with pine and poplar now predominating. The going became easier as I neared the top and I even found a few figs.

Finally after a couple of hours of fairly tough climbing, I reached what appeared to be the highest point for miles around. I searched the north and west for some sign of the Yalu River which was supposed to be only about 15 miles away, but there was nothing. There was also no sign of either Supung Dam on the Yalu or Sinuiju about 40 miles away. Everyplace I looked there were only rugged tree-covered mountains.

Continuing along a ridge line in a south easterly direction, I eventually came to a steep drop-off with the entire camp visible about 1000 feet below me. I sat down on a large boulder in the shade of a small pine tree and contemplated my home for the last year. From my vantage point it looked like any other Korean city. There was nothing to indicate that it was a POW camp. From over half a mile away, even the POW sign was not readable to me.

The woods around me were absolutely quiet, except for an occasional bird and only a gentle breeze fanned the perspiration as I rested in the shade. It was one of the best days of my life since I had been captured. I told myself that I would bring back some wood before dark, but otherwise, this day was all mine.

My reverie was suddenly interrupted by a very familiar but haunting sound. A Cuckoo bird had just called from someplace very close on my left. I had been trying to catch a glimpse of one of these illusive little devils ever since coming to Korea, but I had never heard one of them closer than a half mile away. I turned my head very slowly to the left, and there he was, perched on a pine bough about 50 feet away and about on my level. It was a very ordinary looking bird, about the size of a robin, uniform grey all over and with a long tail. I remained motionless for a minute as he repeated his call a couple of more times, and then flew off.

I gazed down at the camp again and memories of the previous summer came flooding back. I remembered that very early cloudy summer morning when I had heard the doleful sound of a cuckoo from somewhere up on this very mountain. It may well have been the same bird which I had credited with snapping me out of my decline, for from that morning on, I had resolved to fight and struggle until I got my health back.

I lingered on the mountain for almost an hour before finally heading back. I took a slight shortcut back down to the cutting area in the forest. On the way, I checked the numerous fallen dead trees and finally found a section of broken, dried pine tree about 6 inches in diameter and maybe 12 feet long. I hefted one end and estimated that it probably weighed between 150 and 200 pounds. I had carried that much before, so I placed my folded shirt on my shoulder as a pad and hoisted one end of the log until I could get underneath its balance point, then lowered it carefully to my shoulder. I then tipped the log back until I supported its entire weight. It was heavy, but I wanted to bring back a log worthy of such a fine day.

As I puffed and sweated down the rocky path toward camp, there was no one else in sight. Here I was bringing up the rear again, just like on the march north. The sun had just dipped below the mountain as I struggled into camp past the approving smile of the Chinese guard on the north end. Nobody questioned my being so late, because the size of the log was excuse enough. And, to top off a perfect day, I had made it just in time for supper.

Old Japanese topographic maps show one large mountain about 2 or 3 miles west of our camp. It is 2700 feet (897 meters) high and about 2500 feet above the valley floor. Before WWII, there was no large town at the present location of Chungsung, (also called "Changsung" or "Chang-ni") it was built during or after the war. From more modern maps, I have determined the location as: 40 27' N. Lat. and 125 12' E. Long. (see **Figure 36**)

The talks in Panmunjom were not going anyplace. All we knew about them was based on what we heard over Radio Peking or Radio Moscow and a few hints in letters from home. In the absence of any contradictory news, we tended to believe far too much of what we heard on the radio from Moscow and Peking. What I had heard convinced me that the war was probably going to drag-out for another two or three years at least.

The bad war news, combined with the return of my health, started me thinking of escape. The more I thought of it, the more feasible it began to appear. I had run across a book in our small library which showed a map of Asia. I was immediately struck by how close Alaska was to Korea and I began to kick around the idea of going north into Russia, then stealing a small boat and rowing across the Bering Strait to Alaska. One advantage, I thought, would be that in Russia I could more easily blend in with the population; whereas in Korea, an American stuck out like a duck in a henhouse.

An alternative plan was to go north to the Yalu, then drift with a large log down to the Yellow Sea and again steal a boat for the trip down the coast to South Korea. The third and final plan was to just head south sticking to the mountains. I didn't know how I was going to cross the war zone, given the intense concentration of troops and the mine fields.

I began discussing escape with two other men in our company. We all three became quite enthusiastic as we discussed the various alternatives, and finally settled on the third choice where we just headed straight south. We didn't know how we were going to get through the front lines, but we said we would just figure that out when we got there.

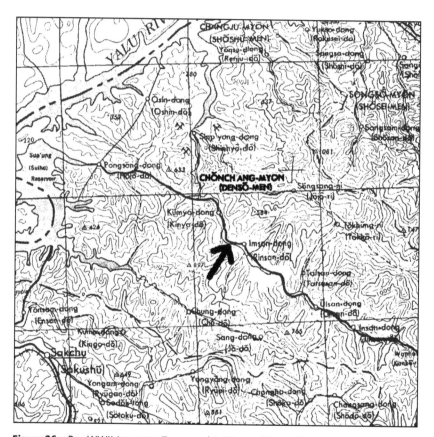

Figure 36: Pre-WWII Japanese Topographic Map , with 5 mile grid. Camp 1 was located at the arrow, 40 27' N. Lat, and 125 12' E. Long

To get in shape, we immediately began running all the way up to the mountains when going on wood detail. We also started saving a steamed bun every day from our meals. At the time we were getting steamed bread with one of our three meals each day. The buns dried in a few days without getting moldy and became hard as a brick but still edible. We also began saving up our sugar rations. We estimated that about 15 to 20 buns and 10 pounds of sugar per man might be enough.

As we collected everything we would need for the journey, we realized that we needed a compass. I said I could make one. At headquarters, the record player was the old-fashioned type common before WWII and used the old style replaceable straight needles. Each needle was made of hardened polished steel, about one inch long. After playing about 10 records they became dull and had to be discarded. I could get all the old needles I wanted.

I took a few old needles and placed them on the magnet inside one of the camp public address system speakers. After a couple of days I removed them and placed one on a small stick floating in a cup of water. It worked well, the small "boat" always quickly drifted around to point to north but it didn't seem to be very practical to have to always float the needle in water.

I then suspended a needle from a fine thread and it worked much better, provided the thread did not have any twist in it. While waiting for the most propitious time to depart, I decided to construct a little more sophisticated compass. I cut off a section of a tree branch about 2 inches in diameter and hollowed out the middle, and then I broke-up an old bottle for glass to make the bearings. A small piece of concave glass was then attached to the bottom of the wooden bowl I had hollowed-out and another piece formed the top bearing when attached to a small piece of wood which lay across the middle of the bowl.

One of my magnetic needles was then attached to a small rectangle of wood with two other un-magnetized needles forming the shaft which turned in the glass bearings. It must have taken me a week to make the first compass, which worked so well, that I then made another. We were now about set and our planned escape was only a week or two away.

All of this wouldn't have been possible without a knife. When we had first arrived in camp, the Chinese would sometimes have unscheduled searches or shakedown looking for weapons. Later they finally realized that we had been making the knives to use as tools, not as weapons. The best knives were made using the flexible steel shims from the soles of old combat boots.

At the time, I was in a squad located almost in the center of second company. Our room had one door opening to the west and another facing east. The south wall adjoined the central courtyard used for company lectures as well as basketball and volleyball. Company headquarters was located across the courtyard from our room.

There were eight men in our squad and two were blacks. When we were on the front line, none of the army units were integrated. The great majority of units, like our 23rd regiment, were all white, while many of the Field Artillery units were all black. When captured by the Chinese, all the enlisted men, black or white were thrown together. Officers were always culled out and sent to a separate camp, as were the noncommissioned officers in 1952. The reason, of course, was to prevent the officers from telling the men what to do and what not to do. Brainwashing would have probably failed completely if our officers had remained in charge of their men.

I remember our squad leader, one of the two blacks in our squad, his name was Rothwell Floyd and he was a big guy, about 6 feet, 2 inches. I got along well with the Negroes in our company and in fact, so did just about everyone else. There were a few red necks who occasionally grumbled about being integrated, but they were the exception. In one of the adjoining squads, the Chinese had placed one lone southern white kid from South Carolina in a squad with nine other blacks. The white kid was prim and well educated and had obviously been brought up in a genteel southern family. In spite of this, he got along very well with his sometimes ribald and uncouth squad members.

One afternoon, I was alone in my room working diligently on my first compass when I sensed that someone was watching me. As I quickly looked up, I met Floyd's eyes looking through the open door. He quickly turned away and I resumed my work. On a couple more occasions, in the next few days, I noticed that Floyd seemed to be surreptitiously observing me as I worked on the compasses

After finishing the second compass, I gave it to one of my buddies who planned to accompany us when we escaped. He was pleased with its operation and said that he was going to hide it away in a secure place until we were ready to go.

A few days later, I was called to Company Headquarters in the afternoon, expecting to have to work on the PA system. Instead, the company interpreter called me into his room and asked me to sit down. He then said quietly that he had heard that I had made a compass. I was too startled to speak for a moment but then I remembered the compass needle suspended from a thread which I had in my pocket. I said "Yes, I did have a simple compass of sorts," and I pulled out the needle and showed him how it indicated north when given enough time to settle down. He said we were not allowed to have such things in POW camp, so I gave it to him, after which I was dismissed. The Chinese never once mentioned the incident again during all my remaining months in POW camp.

I returned to my room and tried to figure out who had ratted on me. The prime suspect was Rothwell Floyd who was occasionally seen going into company headquarters. But then, I also was "seen occasionally going into company headquarters," but that didn't mean I went there to inform on somebody. Rationally, I could see how a very little circumstantial evidence could easily lead to falsely accusing someone, but still, in my gut, I felt that Floyd was the most likely culprit because of the way he seemed to be watching me.

That night, I told my other two accomplices what had happened and they got very nervous. At that point, the three of us unanimously agreed to call-off any escape plans. I said that I was going to get rid of my compass and they agreed, so we took them to the east side of the camp and threw them as far as we could out into the Korean's corn field.

For the next few days, I sliced-up my dried steamed buns and toasted them over the cook's chimney until they were all gone. That was the end of any serious plans, on my part, for escaping from Camp 1.

Over the subsequent weeks, I gave considerable thought to how the Chinese might have learned about my compass. I began to notice, as I sat in the shade of our 'porch' in the afternoon and daydreamed or just shot the breeze, that one could deduce much about what was going on in the company just by 'people watching.' When two people (who are up to no good) talk, they often telegraph their thoughts by the way they stand next to one another or by their furtive little glances over their shoulder.

The Chinese were not dumb. They also sat on their porches and observed the company activities and in addition they would often stroll around the area and strike-up conversations with the men as they walked. Each company had probably from eight to 10 unarmed Chinese living with us 24 hours a day. Not much would get past them if they were observant. They may have noticed us three conspirators talking frequently, and decided to keep a closer eye on me. The Chinese also strolled past my room on several occasions while I was working on the compass and they may just have put two and two together.

Not long after the incident with the compass, I was once more summoned to company headquarters to be then escorted to camp headquarters. As I walked up, our Company Commander said something to my escort in Chinese. It seemed obvious that he was talking about me. Four words were enunciated very clearly as if they had a special significance. They were, "*Hu Geah, Hu Way.*" A few days later I asked Shen what this meant, and he said it was an old Chinese proverb or saying. Such phrases had been popular for hundreds or even thousands of years. This one meant, "Tiger in Sheep's Clothing" which, he said, was equivalent to our, Wolf in Sheep's Clothing.

This little episode, made it clear to me, that all the Chinese probably now knew that I had been doing things behind their back. They never mentioned anything to my face, but I was sure that I was now on a list of POWs to be watched a little more closely.

Some men did escape, but no more than a handful the entire time we were in camp. They would always be discovered almost immediately. I don't ever remember the Chinese falling us out for a formal roll-call so they must have had other means for keeping track of each man. I always suspected that this was the job of the Chinese platoon leader, since he only had 40 or 50 men in his unit, he should have been able to know and recognize everybody personally. Whenever someone did escape, the Chinese would fall everybody out for a camp-wide lecture on the futility of escape. They would point out that Americans, with their "big noses," were very recognizable and every little Korean kid would be on the lockout for you. It was also mentioned that one could be killed by hostile Korean civilians who hated the Americans for bombing them. All of this was perfectly true, but some went anyway.

They were always eventually recaptured and brought back, where they would be placed in front of their fellow POWs and made to confess their wrong doing and criticize themselves. After this they would be put in permanent work details and made to work every day. There were no more leisurely afternoons or swimming in the river for them. The Chinese would often have them digging root cellars for the Korean civilians within sight of camp so that everyone could see what happened if you tried to escape. I also ran into a small work detail one day cleaning human excrement out of the Chinese latrines at Camp Headquarters.

There was one memorable escape in the summer of 1952, but not from our camp. It seems a British officer had escaped from the officer's camp by acquiring a complete set of Korean men's clothing. He was wearing a pair of typical baggy white pants and a white shirt along with a black hat, like that which many Korean peasants wore. He entered camp from the north and passed the Chinese guard there without incident. As he continued on through camp, he noticed a Y in the road about a mile ahead. Uncertain about which way to go, he quietly asked directions from a POW who happened to be walking on the road inside the camp in the same direction. Unfortunately, he was overheard by a little Korean boy who also happened to be walking a short distance behind.

Both the British and the Korean boy continued on past the Chinese guard at the south end of the camp and on past camp headquarters. It was here that the North Koreans had their own guard station where the little Korean kid told what he had heard. The British officer was then grabbed and beaten up by the North Koreans in full view of the British POWs at the south end of camp.

Of all the men captured by the North Koreans and Chinese in the Korean War, only one ever escaped and made his way back to the UN lines. (**Blair**, *Beyond Courage*, 1955)

CHAPTER FORTY-THREE

Raids

There was another source of 'entertainment' in camp; a source that was always unpredictable and sometimes a little dangerous. I'm referring to the almost daily and nightly raids by American aircraft. Seldom did a day go by when we did not see vapor trails, led by tiny glinting silver specks, approach from the south, and even on overcast days, we could hear the roar of jet engines high overhead. Camp 1 was directly below what was known to our pilots as "MIG Alley," and we truly had ringside seats at some marvelous dogfights when the Migs and Sabers tangled at 35000 feet.

Figure 37: F86 Sabre

Most days, there were only a few dozen aircraft overhead, but occasionally, battles of epic proportions raged high above us. I remember one clear, cloudless day when there must have been hundreds of Migs and Saber jets battling up above. The sky was actually filled with vapor trails from horizon to horizon and there was the almost constant sound of machine gun and cannon fire for many minutes.

The planes were usually too high for us to tell which was which, but we soon learned to tell the Americans and Chinese apart by the sound and the 'appearance' of their guns. When we saw a formation of vapor trails coming up from the south in the morning, we were usually quite sure that they were American. We would then continue to watch them closely and as they neared another formation approaching from the north, they would usually peel-off and split up into two or more groups. When the airplanes approaching from the south then fired their guns, we would usually see a marked and continuous thickening of their vapor trail which always coincided with the duration of the subsequent growl of 50 caliber machine guns about 20 to 40 seconds later. On the other hand, we knew that the Migs had 37mm cannons, which when fired, left a single puff of thicker vapor trail for each shell that was fired and then half a minute later, when the sound arrived, we would hear the distinctive "bump, bump, bump" of a heavy cannon.

One afternoon we noticed a Saber chasing a MIG, about 10 miles south of us, headed north precisely in our direction. The Saber was firing long bursts of his 50's in our direction, but it didn't occur to us that the spent bullets might drop near us. Suddenly I heard a staccato rattle sweep across the tile roofs of the houses in our company. It sounded much as if someone had thrown a handful of gravel across a greenhouse roof. Later we found a few spent 50 caliber slugs. Luckily no one was hit.

Figure 38: Chinese Mig 15

After that, we would duck inside if it looked like the firing was pointed our way. I also began to wonder what happened to all the 50 caliber cartridge cases which must have been spewed-out by the thousands. Then there were the 37mm cannon shells which contained an explosive charge, which must also have been dropping all over the place. But after a few months, we just ignored everything and enjoyed the show.

Some of the battles were almost spellbinding. We would sometimes stand for half an hour watching the action. Some of the POWs stood in the middle of the courtyard and hollered "*GIVE 'EM HELL!* ," and when they saw a MIG get hit and go down trailing black smoke, they would jump up and down and cheer for our side. If this bothered the Chinese, they gave no indication, and just seemed to ignore what was going on 'upstairs.'

A MIG got hit one afternoon almost directly overhead. We saw him trail smoke and then burst into flame. As it nosed over into an ever steepening dive, the pilot punched-out and his chute opened at about 20,000 feet. The MIG then entered a vertical dive and rolled slowly as it dropped like an arrow nose first toward the earth about a mile and a half east of camp.

It disappeared behind the hill and in a few seconds we heard the heavy "thump" as it hit the ground, followed a moment later by a rising column of black smoke. We watched the pilot's white chute slowly drift down and land somewhere in the vicinity of his wrecked MIG. Some of the guys in 3rd company, who lived right on the road, said they saw the pilot later that afternoon in a jeep headed north.

Figure 39: F9F Panther Jet

Another day, I saw four Saber jets headed north about 2 miles east of camp   at an unusually low altitude of about 10,000 feet. Simultaneously they all dropped their auxiliary fuel tanks in preparation for battle, and then they disappeared into the melee somewhere above. Many of the men watched as the aluminum tanks slowly spiraled down, reflecting the low afternoon sun like giant silver seed pods. Some guys standing near me began to wonder excitedly "Maybe they are dropping supplies to us," and "I'll bet parachutists will be next to rescue us."   I thought it was pitiful that, with the greatly improved conditions in camp, some of the men could still fantasize such irrational and childlike ideas. A year earlier, on the march and for the first months in camp, we all had been guilty of such behavior because we then so desperately wanted to survive.

We had been watching some tremendous dogfights one afternoon, with airplanes all over the sky, but most of the activity had seemed to concentrate a few miles to the north of us, which must have placed them right on the Chinese border.

A tiny silver speck was chasing an equally tiny black speck just a little north of camp and at about 20,000 feet. The black speck grew larger and began to trail smoke in his dive toward us, until we could recognize that it was a Navy F9F Panther jet (a carrier-based jet) and not a Saber. A bright orange flame erupted near the tail pipe as he pulled up steeply into a loop at about 10,000 feet. The Panther went inverted, and then came around and back down to complete the loop. He then did 3 or 4 more nice uniform loops, each time ending at a slightly lower altitude. On the last loop he seemed to get very slow when inverted at the top, then the Panther flipped over and entered a flat spin.

The jet continued its descent in a very slow, leisurely spin, the attitude almost perfectly level, and with bright orange flame, followed by intense black smoke, streaming straight up from the back of the shiny blue-black fuselage.

Hundreds of POWs watched intently, but no one saw the pilot leave the aircraft before it impacted about a mile north of Camp 1 with a rather distant "whump." One of the interpreters told us later that they had found the pilots dog tags, but that he had been cremated.

The Grumman F9F was one of the few confirmed American jets we saw get shot down; the great majority seemed to be MIGs, although it was often hard to tell the difference amidst all the vapor trails. We did see one MIG that apparently got away. At the height of a fierce battle overhead one day, I was outside Camp Headquarters watching the action, when a sudden tremendous roar, almost like a sonic boom, paralyzed me. Then I saw a MIG approaching a couple of hundred yards away, about 200 feet above ground, and at a very high rate of speed. He made a quick flip to the left, then to the right to get around the small hill north of camp, and then he disappeared up the narrow valley to the north and safety in China only a few miles away.

Since I had installed lights in the camp in the fall of 1951, there had been no interruptions of electric power, despite the frequent bombing of Supung Dam and its power station a few miles away.

One day in June I had been escorted to the small theater outside the camp to check its sound system and see if it could be used for an upcoming show the POWs were going to put on. It was a beautiful June day, with just the beginnings of fleecy white clouds that would later that afternoon turn into scattered thunderstorms. I was taken upstairs in the front where the movie projectors were installed and I was surprised to see that a Korean caretaker, his wife and teenage daughter lived in a small apartment there. They seemed very friendly, but as a POW, I felt like a fish out of water and afraid to say very much.

Before I had a chance to check anything, we heard the sound of heavy propeller driven aircraft engines and immediately rushed outside. The distant rumble had become a deep, throaty roar as half a dozen low wing, single engine, propeller driven bombers came into sight flying North West over the town and about a mile south of us at an altitude of about 1000 feet. I immediately recognized them as a type of small bomber used extensively in WWII against the Japanese in the Pacific.

As the first group disappeared behind the mountain to the west of camp, another group came into view, then still more until at least a couple of dozen planes had thundered past. Everyone, including the Chinese, was startled to see propeller airplanes this far north in broad daylight. There were no MIGs in sight anywhere so the bombers must have surprised the Chinese by taking off from a carrier off the west coast and sweeping in south of Supung Reservoir to attack the dam from the east.

Figure 40: Skyraider A.D. capable of carrying two 2000 lb. bombs

Shortly after the first bombers had passed, we heard a series of tremendous explosions from the direction of the dam and almost immediately, the lights went out in the theater. We soon discovered that the electricity was off everywhere and that night in camp, it was like old times, we had to stumble around in the dark until it was time to go to bed.

Sometime after the bombing, I noticed two or three very large flatbed trucks go through our camp headed south in the middle of the day. Each truck carried one immense diesel powered generator about the size of a semi-trailer and tractor. They were painted a light battleship grey, looked brand spanking new and were probably Russian. They had to be in a big hurry to get them someplace, to be traveling in broad daylight.

On June 23rd 1952, 35 Skyraiders (AD-2), each carrying two 2000 pound bombs attacked Suiho (Supung) dam on the Yalu River. **(Flintham, pp. 227,234)** All of North Korea was blacked out for two weeks.

It was a black, overcast night when I heard the distant sound of airplane engines. I wasn't sleepy, so I got up and went outside. If it was Bedcheck Charlie, I wanted to be ready to hit the ditch.   I heard him coming from the east, which was unusual; they usually flew north and south over the main road which ran through camp. I could just make out the black outlines of the surrounding mountains against the lighter sky, and then I spotted the silhouette of a B26 as it came in over the hill just east of camp. He was very low and I didn't understand how he could avoid the 2700 foot mountain to the north west of us. I didn't hit the ditch, because I could see that he was going to pass a couple of hundred yards to the north of me. Suddenly there was a bright red flash, followed almost immediately by a heavy concussion just like one of those big rockets one hears on the Fourth of July. Three more flashes followed in quick succession, all of them directly over the northern end of the POW camp.

The flashes were a deep red and thus didn't seem to affect my night vision very much, so I could still see the B26 as it pulled up sharply and banked toward the south. It was obvious that the US Air Force had just taken night infrared photos of Camp 1 and they had caught me just standing there looking up at them. Somewhere in the government files, if I knew where to look, maybe I could find my picture.

Some of the most spectacular shows were put on by the US Air Force B29s when they came over to bomb the Supung power plants, which were only about 15 miles west of us. Normally, the Chinese would have lights out at 9 P.M., but if we heard B29s coming over, many of us would get out of bed and stand out in our courtyard to watch the fun. This seemed to happen about every week or two and was well worth getting up for.

Usually we couldn't see the B29s, but we could hear the drone of their engines. As they approached the dam, the Chinese searchlights would begin snapping on until the sky to the west was filled with a dozen or more stabbing the night sky. As the planes got still closer, we would begin to see the tiny orange pin pricks of light flash momentarily here and there in the west as the big guns of the AAA (anti-aircraft Artillery) opened up. At our distance, it took the sound of the *"Ack-Ack!"* over a minute to reach us.

Figure 41: B29 Heavy Bomber

The search lights seldom caught an airplane in their beams and usually they just swept back and forth erratically throughout the raid. The guns were apparently radar controlled but they seemed equally ineffective because their shells would explode all over the sky and not just at one altitude. When the wind was right, the next morning we would sometimes find the ground littered with small strips of tin foil which had been dropped by the B29s to scatter the Chinese radar.

One particular night we had an exceptionally big raid which had been going on for several minutes when I saw one of the lights lock onto a B29. Soon there were half a dozen lights trained on the hapless craft and I could clearly make out the distinctive shape of a B29 glowing white in the brilliant beams and heading straight north at an estimated 10 to 20,000 feet. Almost immediately he was hit and something caught on fire. Moments later I saw the first tiny white speck of a parachute appear suddenly in the bright beams, then one after another, more chutes appeared. I lost count as the searchlights abandoned their prey and began looking for the next victim.

All I could see of the stricken B29 was the tiny streak of orange flame in the blackness of a moonless night. I watched as it slowly arced around and headed south, apparently the pilot was still at the controls and had turned it around to prevent its crashing on Chinese territory. I continued to watch the flame long after the sound of its engines had faded away. It was just a glimmer of light as it approached the horizon, possibly as much as 50 to 100 miles to the south, when it abruptly dropped vertically out of sight. If those guys had only stayed with their plane, I'm sure they could have gotten many miles out into the Yellow Sea, and could then have been possibly rescued by our ships.

There was a black guy named Roosevelt Lunn in our company living in one of the rooms on the east side of the courtyard. He had regained his health just as most everyone else had, but he still complained that his feet hurt and he would never go on wood detail or any other detail for that matter. Whenever he went down to the river to wash his bowl after supper or when he went to the latrine, he would always tiptoe across the rocky courtyard past our room as if the act of walking was quite painful, but most of the time he could be found in his room sleeping, playing cards or just gabbing. We all thought he was just another "goldbricker," which is the Army name for a "good-for-nothing lazy bum."

One dark night the B29s were having another try at the dam, so I, as usual, was outside watching the fireworks. The Chinese searchlights were lighting-up the western sky and also as a bonus, were illuminating our courtyard with about the same light as a half moon.

I suddenly heard what sounded like a freight train approaching from almost directly above. The sound rapidly increased to a screeching thunderous roar which seemed to be descending right on top of us, but there were no sounds of any aircraft engines. I immediately assumed that a B29 had been hit and was falling out of control toward the camp. I dropped to the ground, but continued to crane my neck for some sight of the object.

At that moment, a white wraith sprinted across the courtyard like a gazelle and flew into the nearby ditch. The sound reached a crescendo, and then quickly faded to the north. I listened for the expected crash, but there was nothing. The "ghost" arose from the ditch and asked; "What the hell was that?" It was our sprinter, Roosevelt Lunn, dressed only in a white shirt and not wearing any shoes. After that, Lunn was just as lazy as ever, but at least we had something to chide him with. We never did find out "what the hell" the noise was.

One summer we had another mystery which I later guessed had nothing to do with the war. Shortly after sunset about half the camp must have observed a large yellow ball appear in the north. It seemed to be about the apparent diameter of the moon as it rapidly and silently glided across the eastern sky and disappeared to the south. The whole sighting probably didn't last more than 10 seconds, but it was so bright that everybody outside saw it. Most assumed that it was a meteor and not some Russian or American weapon.

CHAPTER FORTY-FOUR

Strange People
(Or Boys Will Be Boys)

On remembering some of the following incidents there was some hesitation at including the more bizarre but my dictum to: "Tell it like it was" prevailed.

It was the summer of 1952 and most of us had now been POWs for over one year. A minority had been incarcerated for a year and a half and only a handful had survived now for close to two years. I only knew one man who had been captured in July 1950 by the North Koreans and he had somehow survived all that time, but he was in bad shape and spent all his time in the hospital.

With the return of our health, came the return of our normal sexual drives and some that possibly were not so normal. For most, this was manifested by the return of nocturnal emissions, more commonly known as "wet dreams." It became a common occurrence that summer for someone to announce triumphantly that he had a wet dream the night before. His buddies would then invariably question whether or not he had really been asleep.

One squad in our company even went so far as to celebrate their rediscovered abilities by having nightly contests to determine who could ejaculate the farthest or the first. For many, there was a great sense of relief to have regained their sexual as well as physical health after the previous years' starvation and weight loss.

Homosexuals also now began to come out of the woodwork. Two in our company became notorious throughout the camp. They made no attempt to hide their necking and petting in broad daylight, then at night they really got serious. I'll call them 'Bruce' and 'Bryan'.

To pass the time at night, especially after the bombing had knocked out the lights, some of the guys began "telling movies." To tell a movie, the listeners would gather in one room after dark and listen to one person take them verbally in detail through the entire plot of some movie that the 'teller' remembered from earlier years. The listeners could then close their eyes in the dark and mentally re-create the images of Bogart, Bacall and Betty Davis, or whoever else was in the cast of characters.

One night Bryan was telling a romantic 40's movie and Bruce was providing moral (or immoral) support. Somewhere in the darkness, part way through the movie, Bryan was interrupted in his telling by Bruce, who sounded like he had a mouthful of marbles, saying "hand me a towel." This naturally cracked-up the entire audience, who up until then hadn't been aware of Bruce's part in the movie.

This episode has now passed into the Roberts' family folklore, and even today, 40 years later, if I'm shaving and my wife steps out of the shower and asks, "Hand me a towel," we still have to laugh.

About this time, the blacks in 2nd company became openly envious of the whites with their Bruce and Bryan. They told of a black homosexual who had been in their Field Artillery unit and who had been captured with them and like so many others, had died in the winter of 1951. I heard more than one black say; "Why didn't we take better care of that little guy? Why did we ever let him die?"

We also had another POW in Third Company who was tall and slim with a very girlish figure, who I'll call 'Slim'. The Chinese had issued everyone white cotton underwear and Slim had cut his down to almost Bikini size and then dyed it pink by soaking it in water with some red cloth. Every day, Slim could be seen prancing around the company areas and everyone swore that he had the most beautiful long, tan legs they had ever seen.

Well, one night, some of the guys could take it no longer and Slim was raped by about half a dozen sex-starved POWs. He complained to the Chinese, and turned in all their names. The Chinese then had another one of their "trials," and all the culprits had to confess their sins in front of the whole company, after which, they all got hard labor.

In the early winter of 1952, the Chinese had started issuing a certain ration of meat per month for each man. Sides of beef and pork were brought in by truck and hung up in an unheated room next to our company headquarters. This was fine in the winter, but as the weather warmed-up in spring, the meat began to spoil.

I looked in the open door of the storage room one day and noticed two sides of beef, hanging from the rafters, covered with a green slime. The smell of rotten flesh filled the air. Nevertheless, our cooks scraped off as much of the slime as they could, and cooked it anyway. That night each squad had a side dish pan heaped with boiled beef, but despite loads of garlic and hot peppers, the smell and taste of rotten meat was pervasive. I ate some of it, but most guys wouldn't touch it, and most was thrown out.

To comply with the meat ration requirements, the Chinese brought in live cows, pigs and chickens. The chickens were turned loose within the companies to forage for bugs, etc. until the cooks had decided they wanted a couple for chicken soup. The pigs and cows were kept penned-up in a common area until their number came up.

I had been raised on a farm in Minnesota and thus was very familiar with the procedure for butchering a cow or pig. I watched a pig being butchered one day, and found that the Chinese method had some interesting differences. To start, they would cut the pig's throat and then catch the blood in a bucket, just as we used to do. Next, they would make a small slit in one leg and then shove a long steel rod up the leg, under the skin, until the rod had penetrated into the thoracic and peritoneal cavities. The Chinese butcher would then place his mouth on the slit in the leg and blow air into the internal cavities until the pig swelled up like a balloon.

The next step would be to pour boiling water over the pig and then shave all the hair off with a sharp knife, after which it was slit open and cut up in more or less the same way the Minnesota farmers used to do. However, the Chinese cooks would waste nothing. Even the intestines were taken down to the river and flushed out with water before they too were cut up and cooked.

The Chinese needed someone to feed and look after the penned-up cows and pigs, so one of the POWs, (let's call him 'Elmer'), who said he had been raised on a farm in the Midwest, volunteered. As it turned out, his motives may not have been entirely altruistic.

It was spring, and as Tennyson wrote, "In the Spring a young man's fancy lightly turns to thoughts of love." I suppose it was inevitable that someone would eventually notice that our bovine compatriots were similar in certain respects to the girls they had known back in the 'states. Well anyway, Elmer decided that he might just be able to pick-up a quick buck by a little moonlighting after a hard day's work tending his herds, although, the extracurricular work he had in mind was probably best done in the absence of moon light. So Elmer started selling the services of his "girls" for a fee, which back in the 'states, is sometimes called 'pimping.'

One night after dark, but just before lights out time, I heard a small commotion near the end of our house and some of us strolled out to see what was going on. In the very dim light spilling out of a few open doors, I could just make out the form of one of our cows with several guys standing around nearby and laughing. Then I made out what looked like someone standing up behind the cow.

At that moment, our Chinese platoon leader, "Horseface," showed up behind us and played the beam of his flashlight over the scene. Then we immediately knew exactly what had been going on.

Horseface began to sputter and curse in Chinese, the culprit climbed down from his stool with a sheepish, (or should I say Bovine) grin on his face and Elmer just stood there holding the cows rope and nervously wondering what to do next. The cow just kept on chewing her cud. Elmer and his 'John' were hauled off to headquarters by the Chinese to be disciplined. I would have given a week's sugar ration to have heard that interrogation. The cow was returned to her quarters, her honor still unsullied, I think.

The next day the Company Commander felled us out for another lecture. He was furious. He wanted to know what kind of animals these Americans were. Well, I think he had answered his own question, some of us were a 'little bullish.'

The Chinese, and Communists in general, were very prudish and I believe this incident truly shocked them. As for us, we just got a good laugh out of it and it also helped relieve some of the boredom for a few days.

A few weeks later, we arose one morning and discovered one of our chickens lying dead in the courtyard. Neither we, nor our cooks were going to waste what appeared to be a perfectly healthy chicken, so that night we had unscheduled chicken soup, or more correctly, chicken flavored side dish. We usually only got chicken about once per week.

The next morning, we found another dead chicken, and the morning after that, still another. This had turned into a first class mystery. The chickens were all found dead in pretty much the same area and all appeared to have been roughed-up somewhat; judging by the feathers scattered around. It wasn't a four-legged animal because there was no blood or damage to the body of the chicken.

We finally had to admit that the culprit must be one of us, but we could not imagine why anyone would kill a chicken and then just leave it lying there to spoil on a warm summer night.

Finally someone suggested that maybe one of the frustrated Bovine suitors had found a new love interest. At first, most of us were skeptical, but a little reflection on the relative size of a hen's egg versus the size of a man's penis, (we unanimously eliminated the blacks from suspicion), convinced us that it was at least feasible.

Most did not decry the violation of the hen's honor, but we could not abide the attendant foul murder of an innocent fowl, except of course, in the interest of chicken soup. But, from the perpetrators point of view, he would have had to throttle the hen, because no chicken would ever take such an affront sitting down, and without squawking to high heaven.

We had our suspicions who the rapist might be and everyone became more vigilant. Finally the prime suspect was told to quit messing with our food supply or else. No one told the Chinese, although they too must have had their suspicions, because the chickens were also moved out of the company areas not long after.

The stress of battle, getting captured and the subsequent starvation was traumatic for everyone, but for some it was too much. There was the POW, mentioned earlier, who had decided one night that he was going home, and who was shot and killed while crossing the river. Then there was Duckovich, who nine months earlier had chased a Chinese guard and taken his rifle away.

It was summer again and as usual Duckovich was still wearing his heavy coat and winter hat, only now he had adopted a new friend. Someplace he had acquired a pet magpie which often sat on his shoulder as he walked around camp or when he roosted in his favorite willow tree down by the river. I should emphasize that it was Duckovich who roosted in the tree, not the magpie.

One night after supper, Duckovich got up, walked across his room to one outside wall, and then just walked through the wall. He could do this, because the walls of Korean houses were only made of mud plastered over willow sticks and it didn't take very much to knock a hole in one.

Somehow the Chinese found out about the hole in the wall and how it got there and the next day they took Duckovich off to the hospital without a struggle. He spent the remainder of his time in camp locked up in a small group of one room cells behind the hospital with a few of the other nut cases. The only other borderline case in our company was a guy in one of the squads who seemed to delight in licking between the toes of people's dirty feet. His squad members either didn't think he was dangerous, or else they just liked clean feet, so he was never reported to the Chinese.

Mental aberrations took many forms. We had another POW in our company named Ernie Cormier, who was one of the horniest individuals I ever net. He seldom talked of anything but sex and his prowess with the women.

He said he had once heard of a man with a wart on his genitalia who was able to delight the ladies in ways that no one else could. He then decided that it was the perfect time to grow one so that by the time he got home, he too would be able to titillate the girls.

Ernie found someone who had a large wart on his finger and talked him into slicing it off with a knife. He then proceeded to scrape a small area on the head of his penis raw with a knife and when it was sufficiently bloody, he tied the wart to the area with a rag.

For the next week, Ernie waddled around camp with his private part, wrapped in a rag, hanging out of his pants. At the end of the week, he gingerly unwrapped (for a large audience) what was to be his pride and joy, to see if the wart had taken root. The wart not only hadn't attached itself, but it appeared that he had an infection, which wasn't surprising since he had not sterilized anything. So Ernie had to reluctantly give up on his prosthesis and be content with what he had.

By the summer of 1952, each POW was receiving a regular weekly ration of sugar, tobacco and cigarette paper (whether or not one smoked) and toilet paper (which most everyone used). Some of the guys in 3rd company, just north of us, decided to try making a cake. They pooled their sugar rations and scrounged some flour from the kitchen, and then they mixed the two together with a little water to a creamy consistency. They didn't say if they added any yeast from the kitchen.

The mixture, in a side dish pan, was baked in one of the unused rice pots in the kitchen. As the cake was removed from their "oven," and while waiting for it to cool, their Chinese platoon leader, "Ratface," walked in. Since they had taken the flour from the kitchen without authorization, Ratface promptly confiscated their cake, then took it back to Company Headquarters and shared it with his Chinese buddies.

Most of the Chinese were given nicknames by the POWs, and in this case "Ratface" fit both his looks and his personality. The guys were furious. They really shouldn't have stolen the flour, but then it wasn't very much and none of us were concerned about it. The guys vowed to get even.

About a week later, they again stole enough flour for another cake, and then got some more sugar. After mixing everything in the side-dish pan, about half a dozen of the conspirators ejaculated into the cake, then mixed it up thoroughly and put it in their makeshift oven once again to bake.

This time, they made sure that they were very obvious about it, and sure enough, Old Ratface caught them again, and again he confiscated their "cake." They watched as the cake was taken to Headquarters where they knew that Ratface and his friends would dispatch the cake in the same way as its predecessor.

The next day, there were no repercussions from any of the Chinese, much less Ratface. The only conclusion was that they had eaten the cake without noticing anything untoward. That day, there was considerable debate over whether or not to tell Ratface what ingredients had been in the cake. The guys were in a quandary; if they told the Chinese, then they knew they would be punished in some way, but on the other hand, you can't very well insult someone when he is totally unaware of having been insulted. As far as I knew, Ratface never did find out what he had eaten.

Hypnotism was another diversion that surfaced sometime in 1952. One of the hypnotists was located in my company, and I believe there may have been one or two others in camp. What started out as something to pass the time later became more complicated.

I watched one of the earliest demonstrations in our company, when Davis, who had helped me install the PA system, was hypnotized in front of a crowd of at least 30 POWs. Davis appeared to be one of the best subjects in camp. After only a few seconds, he would be "under," and then they would test him by sticking needles in his arm. The needles were not sterilized, so I could never understand why he let them do it.

When they were sure that he was in a trance, the hypnotist might tell Davis that he was a baby, where upon, he would begin sucking his thumb or crying. Another time, he was told he was a rabbit, after which, he began hopping around the court yard.

Quite a few of the POWs allowed themselves to become subjects and it eventually got to be a fairly popular pastime. To entice one to become a subject, the hypnotist always told the person that one would never do anything under hypnosis that he wouldn't do when conscious.

I never did trust them though, and one day that mistrust was justified when I noticed a crowd gathered around the open doorway of one of the squad rooms. On investigation, I was told that one man who had been hypnotized was engaging in a sex act with another POW who was not hypnotized.

The one who had been hypnotized did not impress me at all, as the type of person who would do such a thing, so from then on I have discounted that oft repeated claim made by all hypnotists. I suppose it's always possible that the particular individual was predisposed to such behavior and possibly he wasn't even under hypnosis, but I seriously doubt it.

Eventually, the hypnotism game degenerated into little more than public séances where the hypnotist would quiz the subject as to the precise date when the war would end and we would all be allowed to go home. The subjects would always be forthcoming with a date, but it was never the same date as that given by the previous subjects, and also usually didn't match whatever date they themselves may have given earlier. But the hypnotists continued to put on their little shows and the men continued to gather around to find out when the war was going to end.

It was perhaps fortunate that the Chinese didn't adopt hypnotism. Who knows what might have happened? On second thought, I couldn't really say that the Chinese had not tried it, for if they had, I'm sure no one would have known about it, least of all, the guy who was hypnotized; as in the book, The Manchurian Candidate.

I met many people in the Army, but I didn't really get to know them until POW Camp. Most of the guys were likable, ordinary and easy to get along with, but it seems that I met more strange, unusual or downright weird people only in the camp. Maybe this was because of the unusual stress in our situation, but on the other hand it could be that the men in camp were a representative cross section of society that one could observe anywhere if you just took the time.

CHAPTER FORTY-FIVE

Propaganda

In the fall of 1952, most of us were entering our second winter as POWs. By then, there were no more big surprises; we all knew pretty much where we stood with the Chinese. Life had become more boring, to be sure, but boring also meant security, of sorts.

By late October, we had a plentiful supply of wood for the winter, we had brand-new cotton padded uniforms and the food, if anything, seemed to improve even more each month. I had resigned myself to another winter and most likely another year or two in camp but not without getting depressed every time I thought of it.

We were settling into the routine of another winter, when as Christmas approached, some of us were asked if we wanted to record a Christmas message to our folks for broadcast over Radio Peking. Why not?

I was taken to a house at Camp Headquarters, across the street from where I tended the PA system, and was ushered into a small room with only a table, a chair and an old wire recorder, (the predecessor of the present day tape recorder). I was greeted by Chemiduh, an older woman, who spoke quite good English and who I dealt with often when working on the PA system. She seemed to be some sort of political 'wheel' at Camp Headquarters and directly supervised Foongee, who was in charge of the PA system.

She suggested some things I could say about the "good treatment and good food being provided by the lenient Chinese Peoples Volunteers." I then spoke into the mike and told my mother that I was well and being very well treated and that the food was excellent, or something to that effect. I knew it was 50% propaganda, but then I also believed much of it to be true. After a year and a half as a POW, the food had improved more than I would have ever believed possible a year earlier.

I was then faced with a mild quandary as I spoke into the recorder; how to truthfully describe the improved conditions without providing undeserved propaganda benefits and also without seeming ungrateful. I later learned that my message was broadcast over Radio Peking on December 27, 1952 and picked up by a Ham Radio operator in New Zealand, who in turn, notified my mother.

Each holiday, the Chinese acted as if they had to top the food and festivities of the previous holiday. From Thanksgiving to Chinese New Year in January, it seemed like we were having a feast almost every week. I was now in good physical shape with only a remnant of last summers "gut" which provided the source for my camp nickname. I was also becoming more rational in my attitude toward food and I was now actually able to refuse some leftover food although I still felt a powerful twinge of discomfort when I saw food thrown out.

Christmas cards were the latest propaganda gimmick, that Christmas in Korea. We were each given several small cards printed in color and depicting scenes typical of cards one might see in the United States. I mailed cards to all my relatives and was surprised a few weeks later as I began receiving Christmas cards by the dozen. Soon I was inundated in Christmas cards.

What had happened was that Rick Tenneson's mother, back in Minnesota, had put a notice in the paper suggesting that people should write to all the Minnesota POWs. As a result, the two dozen or so, Minnesota POWs each got stacks of Christmas cards and letters while all the rest of the guys could only look on enviously.

One night in January we had a heavy snow storm, and then in the morning, the weather had turned clear and bitterly cold. After breakfast, our company fell out for exercise with two feet of fresh snow on the ground. There were no clouds in the sky and not a breath of wind. From the way our boots squeaked on the freshly packed snow, I guessed the temperature must have been somewhere between 10 and 20 below Fahrenheit.

It felt good to be away from camp as we stepped briskly out on the main road and headed north. Our lone Chinese guard started counting cadence in Chinese just as we had done in the US Army. We would go "*Yee!*" and take four steps, then shout "*ARR!*" and take another four steps. In similar fashion we counted "*San*" and "*Suh.*" In the next sequence we would take two steps in between counting "*One, Two, Three* and *Four,*" and then finally we counted "*One, Two, Three* and *Four,*" in Chinese of course, with one count per step. If someone from US Intelligence had been listening, he probably would have thought, "There goes about 100 American POWs who have all converted to Communism." But, he would have been dead wrong, we just felt good to be getting some exercise.

As we marched, we approached a small, lone thatched-roof farm house located about 100 feet off the right side of the road. It was completely surrounded by fields buried in pristine sparkling white snow from the previous night's storm, but there was life inside, because a thin streamer of smoke curled up from the chimney.

At that moment, the front door opened a crack, and a tiny figure shot out into the snow. It was a small boy, maybe only six or eight years old, without a stitch on, running as if the devil himself were after him. About 75 feet from the house, he squatted down and did his job, and then without bothering to wipe, he raced back to the house just as quickly as he had left it. The door opened briefly, and he disappeared inside, once again. We all got a good laugh, including our guard.

The morning hikes were only for the winter months. In summer, wood details gave us all the exercise we needed. It wasn't always cold on winter hikes, some days we would get a warm moist wind from the south west and on those days we would have to unbutton our padded coats to keep from overheating. On such days, the Korean kids used to sometimes stand by the road and watch us as we passed.

I remember one morning, as we passed a group of little Korean kids, one of our guys with false teeth, bent down, looked one of them right in the eye, and then pulled out his dentures. The kids were absolutely flabbergasted? They screamed with delight and a little fear, as if they weren't quite sure if this funny looking, big-nosed person was really human. The story must have gotten around, because after that, there would always be a group of kids waiting by the side of the road to see the "ogre who could take his teeth out."

Talking to men who survived the winter of '50-'51, I wasn't surprised to hear that baths were just about the farthest thing from their minds. During the winter of '51-'52, the four of us sleeping in an unheated room had no place to take a real bath; all we could do was heat a little water once a week and wash our hands and face.

Most of the men living in the main camp area had much better sleeping quarters, but there were still no provisions for bathing. A very few, very fastidious individuals were occasionally seen to run down to the river, on unusually warm days, chop a hole in the ice, and then take a quick and perfunctory bath. A few other less dedicated ones, might borrow a bucket of hot water from the kitchen, and give themselves a quick once-over, but the great majority of men went from November to February without washing anything besides their hands and face. One or two guys wouldn't even wash their faces all winter, and soon they began to look as if they had rubbed their faces with charcoal. Some of the cooks became especially black in this way due to the soot from the fires.

When most of us didn't bath for three or four months, one would think that the smell would be overpowering, and we wouldn't be able to stand ourselves, let alone the others around us. But surprisingly, we hardly ever noticed, even in a hot stuffy room full of guys' playing cards or shooting the bull. I think the answer lies in man's sensory systems. When ones sense of touch is constantly bombarded by the same stimulus, the body soon learns to ignore the feeling. The sense of smell is the same, as can be verified when one eats garlic. Afterwards, the only ones who smell the garlic are the ones who ate none of it.

The odors in camp were undoubtedly fended off by our senses in the same way. There were dozens of open latrines in camp, two thousand smelly, sweaty bodies and hundreds of us eating garlic by the bulb. The truth was, our senses just adapted to it all until we hardly noticed.

In the winter on '52-'53, things had improved a little. About midwinter, the Chinese announced that we were all going to have hot baths. We were marched into town in small groups of less than 50 at a time. The "bath house" turned out to be an old Japanese bath probably built before WWII. It was a small well-built house with a large electrical transformer outside and heavy wires leading inside.

As we came through the entrance, we were met by a wall of steam and found ourselves in a large room with benches lining the walls. They told us to leave our clothes on the benches and go into the next room, where I saw two large sunken concrete tubs about eight by 6 feet and four or 5 feet deep.

The water in the tubs had been heated steaming hot by immense electrical coils immersed in the water; but of course, the electricity was disconnected before anyone got into the water. Our guard told us to get into the first tub for a preliminary soak and then after a few minutes, we could transfer to the second for a final rinse. I soaped up and then climbed into the first bath. It was heaven? I climbed out after five minutes, and got into the second tub, however no soap was allowed there. The second bath was even hotter than the first and I managed to stretch it out for maybe 10 minutes.

After drying-off, we had to climb back into our cruddy cotton padded uniforms and head back to camp as the next group marched up for their turn. I only had one bath that winter, but it was a memorable occasion. In the ensuing days, I was reminded that the Chinese had always appeared clean and neat in their uniforms when compared to the average POW. For the first time, I began to wonder how they managed such a feat in the middle of winter. Possibly they had been using the bath house all along but had kept it secret from us.

We were all healthy now and the food was not only adequate, but sometimes it even tasted good. We were about 2000 men full of vim and vigor and with not enough to do. During daylight, if the weather was warm, most would be outside, playing basketball and volley ball or just talking and getting some sunshine. Those inside would play cards or chess and talk, talk, talk. Talking, arguing, shooting the breeze or just plain bull sessions, were probably the primary means of passing the time, but no matter what you did, the time passed slowly.

Of course, the Chinese were always stirring the pot. They would fall us out maybe once per week for a lecture on something or other. One week it might be on sanitation and the next week we would hear someone scolded for alleged reactionary behavior. No matter what the subject, they always managed to inject a little socialist or communist philosophy into the talk.

The many committees set up by the Chinese, also helped some pass the time. There was Rick Petersen and his Sanitation Committee (they sure had their work cut out for them), the Chow Committee, Sports and Recreations and on and on. The Committees were really just another way for the Chinese to infiltrate and control the camp, although none of us fully realized it at the time.

In the midst of all this, the Chinese began doling out little rewards for various good deeds. Johnny Ford wrote a series of articles for the camp newspaper on sports, and was paid some thousands of Yuan, (if I remember correctly). He was then able to take his chit for the amount down to the Chinese PX near camp headquarters and exchange the chit for a pound of hard candy. Rick Petersen wrote an article on Sanitation for the company bulletin board and also got a pound of candy.

I wrote a series of articles on the Theory of Radio for the bulletin board, for which I also received a paper chit with some Chinese characters on it. I didn't even ask what it said, but just took it to the PX and handed it to a rather sullen Chinese behind the counter. He picked up a small bag of hard candy and slammed it down on the counter in front of me with obvious displeasure. I took the bag and returned to my squad, where I divided the candy equally among my squad members.

In the summer of 1951, the Chinese had tried to force us to study and discuss Communism, and when that didn't work they tried other methods. Candy was now being handed out for almost any excuse to anyone they thought they might be able to influence. I suppose the candy was part of the "carrot" approach as opposed to the "stick" tried earlier.

The "study session" was still another device used by our captors to try to influence us. When I had been summarily removed from Camp Headquarters in March of 1952, I was told to attend the study session held in 2nd Company. The Chinese were displeased with me, and they knew that I knew it. Their methods could be quite subtle at times. But I didn't really mind very much, I had grown to look forward to sitting-in on the bull sessions held by the Camp Peace Committee in our little room at Headquarters.

The Study Sessions held in the Company, turned out to be little different from the meetings at Camp Headquarters, in other words, just more BS. In the Company, however, Chen one of the interpreters was always present and he might kick things off by stating; "Tonight let's discuss the class struggle in America." His position was always that the workers produced all the goods with their labor, but that the Capitalist who owned the factory reaped all the benefits. We had to admit that he had a point, but I thought that his position was greatly oversimplified.

Our interpreter's theses were always very simple, and stated so that even the least educated could understand them. For example, they continually brought up the fact that there are many poor people in America but that most of the wealth is held by a few very rich. We found this hard to refute, but we would always emphasize that most of the people are neither poor nor rich, but somewhere in the middle. At that point, Chen would often ask many detailed questions about life in America; who among us had cars, what kind of houses we lived in, our jobs, food, family relationships, etc.

At such opportunities, I liked to then ask Chen similar questions about China and his upbringing. Whether it was Chen, or some other interpreter, they always described a pretty rough life and, although we didn't rub it in, we all realized that we had a comparatively soft life.

One or two guys in our Study Session seemed to really eat it up. To them, all the Chinese statements seemed obviously valid and they were apparently totally converted. The rest of us had to acknowledge that they had some good points, but no one stood up and pounded the table while arguing the converse. In fact, there was usually very little or no dissent. If we had opinions to the contrary, we kept them to ourselves. Although the Chinese may have made a couple of converts through their Study Sessions, the great majority of us felt they were dull and repetitious, and soon found other things to do.

Each company had its own small library, if one were generous with the term- 'library'. In our case, it was one small room with a table on which one could find four to eight-week-old copies of the New York and London Daily Worker, a Chinese English language newspaper and a few Russian magazines. No one read the Daily Worker, but many did skim it to look at the ads for restaurants, cars, theaters and such, just to assure ourselves that such things still existed. I liked to read the Russian picture magazines which reminded me of Life and Look. The articles ran the gamut from immense dam projects on the Volga River to pictures of a smiling, young Uzbek girl picking apples. I didn't know which was most appealing, the apples or the girls.

There were a few hard cover books available, such as Das Kapital and other less well known works by Marx, Engles and Lenin or Mao.

One day, bored and desperate for something to read, I tackled a tome on Dialectical Materialism. After about ten pages, I found it so unutterably dull, that I had to put it down. The other books by Marx, Lenin and Mao were equally dreary. It was enough to make one wonder how the millions of Russian and Chinese could be converted if they all had to read and understand such leaden prose.

Besides the political books, we had a handful of novels by Jack London, Howard Fast and some obscure Russian writers. One of the most popular books, a group of lascivious short stories by Balzac, was in such demand that it could only be lent out to one squad at a time, to be read by one designated person in that squad. In our squad, I was the designated reader. In his time, Balzac was hot stuff, but then in the age of Henry Miller, he was really quite droll.

In the months since we had been in Camp 1, three basic types of POWs had emerged; (1) the "Reactionaries" or "Trouble makers" as the Chinese called them, (2) the "Progressives," those who agreed with them and (3) the remaining 80% or 90% of the men who just tried to get along without making any waves.

First of all, a "reactionary" would be someone who had listened to a Chinese lecture and then said, "*it's all bullshit, and anyone who believes any of it is a Commie or at least a Pinko.*" One or two in our company were typical red-necked southerners who knew what they didn't like, but couldn't tell you why in words of more than three syllables. Another by the name of Grey, from Iowa, had two years of college and was quite articulate.

Speaking your mind openly in opposition to the Chinese in camp didn't necessarily mean you were in trouble, but you could be sure that it got your name added to a list of people to be watched. But anyone who threatened or beat up a progressive (or anyone else for that matter), destroyed property, incited others to rebel or formed any secret organization could count on a visit by the Chinese some evening. They would then summarily be told to pick up their belongings and follow the guard, after which, they would seldom be seen again.

We assumed that they had not been taken out and shot, because we saw some of them being housed in a separate area near Camp Headquarters. But others just disappeared and everyone speculated that a separate camp had been established just for "trouble makers."

The continuous weeding out process thus eliminated some of the most violent anti-communist POWs, but many others remained while keeping a low profile. One small group in our company formed a secret order, calling themselves the "KKK," and apparently planned to raise cane, wherever they could. There were rumors of mysterious fires, of trucks passing through camp at night having flat tires and frequently books and magazines would disappear from the library. The most serious incident, however, occurred when a pistol belonging to the Company Commander in an adjoining company was stolen out of his room. I think that caper had the Chinese worried. As far as I know, the pistol was never found.

Now, a "progressive" was at the other end of the scale. Someone who bought the entire communist propaganda package would certainly be called "progressive" by the Chinese and by everyone else in camp. But "progressive" was also used as a complementary term by the Chinese. Someone who was beginning to agree with them or come around to their way of thinking was said to be "progressing." To some reactionaries, anybody who didn't openly denounce the Chinese was a 'progressive,' or at least soft headed. Others were a little more liberal and limited their use of the 'word' to people who signed petitions, attended study sessions or seemed overly friendly with the Chinese.

Most of the men in prison camp were between 18 and 21 years of age, not even old enough to walk into a bar and buy a drink in many states, but more importantly, we were naive. I was probably as naive as any. While in High School during WWII, I remembered Hitler, Mussolini and Tojo as the ultimate bad guys, while Roosevelt,

Churchill and Stalin were the great leaders in the fight against Fascism. Stalin was usually called "Uncle Joe" in the papers and was portrayed as a tough guy, but I didn't ever remember anyone even hinting at the mass crimes he was later shown to have committed. In school, I thought Roosevelt and Churchill were great men and as for Stalin, I thought he must be ok; otherwise we wouldn't be helping him. When Roosevelt died in 1945, I still remember my mother saying; "Well, that's one down and two more to go." She thought that all politicians were crooks and when one died, that was just good riddance.

That winter of 1952-1953 I was still emotionally immature and unsophisticated, but I had also become unctuous and argumentative. I was becoming what was then called a "smart-alec,", now generally referred to as a "wise-ass." I had lots of time on my hands and not enough to do, so I would deliberately provoke arguments, especially with people whom I didn't like or who didn't like me. I had never been a good physical fighter, but I had now discovered that I could challenge anybody verbally, and usually win.

The subject was usually religion. Everything I had seen since entering the Army had only confirmed my previous beliefs, and it irked the hell out of me to hear guys giving God credit for saving their lives, but then saying nothing about all those other guys who had died in camp. At best, I thought they were stupid, and at worst, self-centered and hypocritical, and I told them so. Needless to say, this didn't make many friends for me.

My contentious attitude, along with weekly trips to Headquarters to work on the PA and the fact that I had attended some Study Sessions, soon had me tagged as a progressive by some of the reactionaries. But I was just ornery enough to think that I ought to be able to say and do what I damn well thought as long as I didn't hurt anyone else.

One day, I was down at the river washing-up when someone heaved a small rock at me from behind. It bounced off harmlessly but that made no difference, I was furious. I found a club and began looking for the culprit, without any luck. A couple of days later, I was called into company headquarters. The interpreter said he had heard about someone throwing a stone at me, and wanted to know who it was. I said I had no idea and that I would handle it myself.

I didn't know who told the Chinese about the incident, but I assumed that one of the progressives in the camp had heard the rumor and passed it on. In the camp, as in the Army, one did not rat to the authorities when you got into a fight, instead you settled it yourself. Later I was glad that I hadn't seen the guy throw the rock that day, because for a few minutes, I was mad enough to kill him.

Occasionally, the subject got around to politics or the war. In hindsight, I realize now that I was beginning to believe some of the things the Chinese were telling us. The evidence for our use of germ warfare seemed overwhelming and I thought it was a terrible thing to do to innocent civilians in Korea, not to mention our POWs. I should have been a little more skeptical, but at the time, I thought I had enough information to make a judgment, especially after hearing our own pilots confessing in front of us.

When our interpreters described how bad things had been in China before WWII and how millions had sometimes starved to death, I had to acknowledge that apparently the Communists were an improvement over the previous feudal warlords. However, I didn't see how their situation had any bearing on the United States.

I also got into numerous arguments over the conduct of the Peace Talks in Panmunjom. I just could not understand why our side was being so adamant about not forcing the repatriation of POWs. I thought that everyone should be returned to their home country, whether they wanted to or not, and if they didn't like their government, that was their problem, not mine.

In many cases, the Communist's influence on our minds was insidious. I found out much later, when back in the 'States, that I had come to accept certain things without subjecting them to critical analysis. For example, we were often told in lectures that Capitalism needed war to prosper. I had remembered how quickly the US economy had rebounded with the start of WWII after the depression of 1929, so their statement seemed to be reasonable. After returning home in 1953, I found myself waiting for the depression that never came, and only then did I realize that this was just one more example of the many little things they had programmed into our minds.

Still another example of Communist influence would be Lysenko's theories on genetics. He believed that training of the parent would carry over and be inherited by the child. This was supposedly Science, so it captured a little more of my interest than most of the other things they said. The Communist leaders wanted to believe that they could teach or force people to be altruistic. They thought that if they could eliminate greed and sloth in one generation, then the next generations would all be selfless, tireless workers for the common good. In camp, I only heard the arguments for Lysenko, but later in college, I was exposed to the other view point, and immediately saw that Lysenko was a fraud.

I think we were all influenced or "brain washed" to some degree in the camps, even the reactionaries were probably affected in some ways. If nothing else, they learned that a Communist could be a dedicated and determined foe, and that clever and organized deceit by a government could create a populace of fanatics who are certain of the righteousness of their cause (as in North Korea). In the end though, all the effort expended by the Chinese was for naught, because a couple of years back in the 'states exposed to a free press, radio and television was sufficient to make clear where the truth lay.

If I had been kept in China for 10 or 20 years, I suppose it's always possible that I could have been converted to Communism, but I think it's very unlikely. In prison camp, most of us did not ask critical questions of the Chinese because we were always very much aware that we were the captives and they were the captors. But if I had to live in that society, I would have eventually begun asking all the questions that I didn't dare ask in camp.

I think it's very significant that twenty-one Americans and one British POW decided to remain behind in China, but that few of them could stand the mind-numbing oppression more than a few years. After 12 years, only three of the original 21 were left. (**Wills**, p. 155)

I personally knew only a couple of them, but from them and others, I understood that they all had quite similar motives; generally they were young, impressionable and very idealistic. They accepted the idealistic frosting on the Communist cake and ignored all of the many negative aspects, but they soon discovered that a few pretty phrases do not a paradise make.

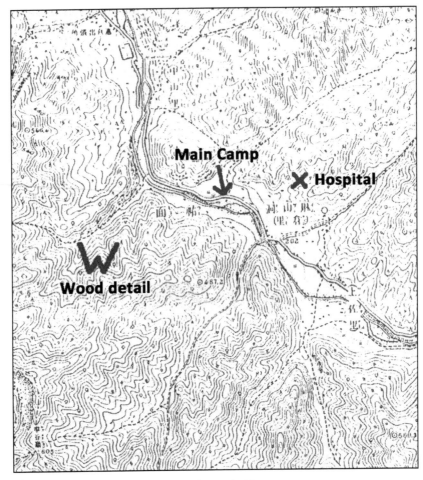

Figure 42: WWII Japanese map at 2 miles each side

CHAPTER FORTY-SIX

Hospital

March 1953 began as always with cold, rain, sleet and snow. The weather was miserable and I also began to feel miserable. I felt weak and my legs and joints hurt. I was still wearing the same winter cotton padded uniform that I had first put on the previous November. I had lived and slept in this same pair of pants and jacket for four months and it had only been removed for one bath and for the monthly change of underwear.

Upon pulling up the pant leg, I noticed large lumps or nodules on my ankle. Further examination revealed similar lumps all over both legs. Someone decided that I needed to go to the hospital, so I grabbed my bowl, spoon and a few other things and followed the guard south on the main road. The trip through camp and up the hill was slow and painful.

The hospital was located in an old Buddhist temple, which we always called Confucian, just south east of the main camp and some ways up the hill behind the theater. It is located at the "X" on **Figure 42**. The arrow points to the main camp. The "W" is the location of our wood details.

The path narrowed and steepened as we climbed among the sparse pines. After a few hundred yards, we came to a steep stone staircase on our left which led up to a tile-roofed wooden temple perched on a massive stone promontory.

The tile roof was very ornate, with hideous looking gargoyles glaring out from all the cornices. The massive roof was supported on heavy, round wooden columns and wood plank walls. All the wood visible under the eaves and in the wall had once been elaborately decorated with vividly colored symbols, which were now fading after years of neglect.

Halfway up the staircase, I paused at a large wooden gateway which was the only opening through an eight-foot stone wall which completely surrounded the upper temple grounds. In the middle of the grounds, a stone promontory or hillock with near vertical walls shaped somewhat like a large ship had been built, and the temple itself was perched on top, like the superstructure of an ancient vessel approximately 100 feet long by 60 feet wide.

I climbed the remaining steps up to the temple and was led into a small ward with a dozen or so other POWs. I was given a bunk in the corner with some blankets and made myself comfortable.

Later, our doctor, a Chinese woman in her 40's wearing a half-length white coat with a stethoscope projecting from its pocket, came around to examine me. She prodded and poked my legs and asked (in excellent English) about the lumps, then she listened carefully with the stethoscope to my heart. After no more than five minutes, she announced that I had rheumatic fever, and would have to remain in bed and avoid exertion for the next two weeks. She prescribed some medicine and when I asked what it was, she only said that it was Russian.

While I was in the hospital, on March 5th, we were told that Stalin had died. Most of the Chinese looked genuinely sad and I saw one Chinese girl actually cry. I felt about the same as the day I heard Churchill had died. They were both famous world leaders, but I didn't have any strong feelings one way or the other. If I had known what I know today, I would have cheered for joy and probably gotten myself in a lot of trouble.

Our woman doctor had a couple of male Chinese assistants, but the majority of the nursing duties were handled by POWs. The nurse in our ward was a British POW. I'll call him 'Benny', and he really seemed to enjoy his work. He bustled around all day humming old English ditties to himself as he changed bedpans, cleaned-up dirty bed clothes, spoon-fed patients and handed-out medicine, all the while, with a cigarette in one hand.

The patient next to me had been constipated for some time, so I watched one morning as Benny gave him an enema. The patient was lying on his stomach with a small tube inserted in his rectum. The tube was connected to a large bottle filled with warm water, which Benny held aloft with his left hand as he continued to hold his cigarette with his right hand. A bedpan stood at the ready.

Nothing happened immediately, then it broke loose and a creamy brown geyser erupted and gushed all over the bed. Benny grabbed the bedpan with his right hand, while still holding the bottle in his left, and made a valiant attempt to catch the stream in the bedpan without even dropping his cigarette.

He was only fifty-percent successful, and now the patient, the bed covers and Benny's right arm from wrist to elbow were coated with a soupy brown mixture. But it didn't faze Benny one bit, he continued to hum and crack jokes as he raised his right hand and took a few puffs on his cigarette, while waiting for the discharge to subside. I'll never understand how some people can handle such a job, but I'm glad that there are such people.

Another patient, (I'll call him 'Joe') in a bunk near mine, was in really bad shape. He wasn't a big guy to start with, but now he looked unusually small and emaciated. He was only a bag of bones, weighing less than 100 pounds, and even in worse shape than I had been two years earlier.

I found out that he had been captured in July 1950, only a couple of weeks after the start of the war, and he was one of the very few who had survived capture by the North Koreans. I had heard that there were a few others captured in the summer of 1950 still alive in camp, but that was the first one I had ever met.

Benny said that Joe was severely constipated and had resisted all efforts to unblock him using enemas. Joe said that he himself had been constipated for at least a year. I found that hard to believe. It just didn't seem possible for a human being to survive that long without a normal bowel movement.

Joe was well taken care of though, two or three times a day Benny would bring in orange juice and chicken soup or some other type of soft nourishing food. The only trouble was, Joe often couldn't keep it down, and whenever he vomited, he would throw-up his own excrement. At Operation Little Switch in April, I was told that Joe was one of those released and I was glad to hear that he had made it that far.

We were having our noon meal one day, and I was discussing something with another patient who was sitting near the foot of my bed. Suddenly he complained of a tickling sensation in his throat and began to cough. At that moment, I pointed out that something red was dangling from the corner of his mouth, whereupon, he reached up and pulled out a twelve-inch round, reddish worm. At that time in my life, it had no effect on my appetite, and I just kept on eating my soup, but I made a mental note to make sure that I got myself checked for worms when released.

Life wasn't always grim and morbid in our hospital. After a couple of weeks, I was moved to a large open ward with maybe thirty patients scattered throughout. The floors were quite smooth painted planks and the POW orderlies kept everything very clean. I was now feeling much better and began to be my old contentious self again.

One of the men in the ward had some sort of rash on his scrotum and around the groin. It was apparently so painful, that he couldn't stand to have any clothing come in contact with the area, so he spent the day lying or gingerly sitting up without any pants on. One afternoon, the Chinese woman doctor came in to apply some sort of ointment to the affected region. When she began to paint his scrotum, he began to moan with pain and jumped each time she touched him.

To get better access, she then suggested that he get down on his hands and knees so that the testicles would hang down and allow her to paint both the front and back.

That arrangement apparently worked much better for the doctor, but was no less painful for our patient who now began to crawl across the floor, still on his hands and knees, in his attempt to avoid the doctor's swab. But the doctor was also determined to get the job done, so she too got down on hands and knees, and began following behind, swabbing as she went.

By this time, everyone in the place was watching the show, and some began laughing, until the entire ward was in an uproar. Even our doctor managed to join in with a smile as she got up from the floor.

After more than two weeks, I was getting restless, and began to move around the ward and take short walks outside the hospital. On warm days I would sit in back and watch some of the healthier patients play volley ball with the Chinese cooks and assistants.

One day I walked along a narrow path through the pines to see where the cemetery was. I could see where many small wooden crosses had been pounded into the ground in a flattened area a little further up the hill. I guessed that Bill Pfleegor was buried somewhere up there, but I was still weak, so I didn't investigate further.

I returned to 2nd Company after three weeks in the hospital and my platoon leader was told that I should not engage in any heavy exercise, such as wood detail, for the next two months. I had been in the process of overhauling the PA system when I got sick, so I continued with that project. I was replacing the old speakers, which were really only intended for indoor use, with all metal, horn type speakers. Davis and a British POW did the hard work climbing the poles and I just supervised. When we got done, I went around to all the companies and checked the sound. It was a big improvement.

One evening as I was finishing up changing the connection of the new speakers to the amplifier, Chemeeduh was in the room tuning over the band on the short wave radio. I assumed that she was searching for some Chinese language broadcast. As usual, the bands were filled with at least ten Morse code stations for every voice modulated station. Most code stations broadcast in what is called CW or continuous wave and they can't be heard easily on a simple short wave radio that doesn't have a BFO, whose purpose is to beat with the station and make it audible as a chirping or beeping tone. But a very few stations broadcast a tone modulated signal which is easy for anyone to hear with any simple receiver.

For a moment, I heard her tune past a tone modulated station with very nice, precise Morse code being sent at about 20 words per minute. I asked her to stop, and I began copying the code just to see if I still remembered it. I was barely able to keep up and I got maybe 90% of it.

After a couple of minutes, I gave up and put my pencil down, then went back to see what I had copied. All the letters of the English alphabet were there, but the words sounded like Japanese. When we sounded them out phonetically, Chemeeduh said she understood some of it, but couldn't understand how I could copy Japanese without understanding what I was copying and she also hadn't realized that I knew code.

She wasn't technically very sophisticated and from the way she looked at me, I got the impression that she was suddenly a little suspicious of me. I thought that maybe she was beginning to suspect that I might be a spy, and a spy who had been in their midst all along. The Chinese could be very paranoid, and I decided that I certainly didn't want to stir up any doubts like that so I explained it to Shen, who spoke much better English, and I think he was able to make her understand.

A few months earlier, I had also had a language problem with Foongee who directly supervised the PA system. Her English was terrible and sometimes, to make ourselves mutually understood, we would end up talking a mixture of Pidgin English and pidgin Chinese.

Foongee was a very sweet, innocent young girl, only about 18 or 20 years of age. By then I had been working with her for over a year and a half and found her very attractive. I was beginning to understand how one of those rats in some of the animal psychology experiments must feel when they are offered cheese, but then receive a very painful shock if they try to eat it.

I was strongly attracted to her, but I was frightened of what might happen if I made a pass at her. One day I had tested the speakers hooked up in a certain way, and then I had disconnected them while intending to try a different combination. Without thinking, I turned up the volume to maximum and spoke "one, two, three, test" into the mike.

All I heard was a snapping sound and immediately realized what I had done. One never turns up the volume on one of those older amplifiers when there are no speakers attached because it will usually burn up the output transformer. I was instantly furious with myself for my stupidity and forgetting that Foongee was present, I blurted out - "Oh Fuck It!"

Well someplace, sweet little Foongee had heard of that word, but she wasn't exactly sure of its meaning. She knew it was a swear word, but she wasn't sure if I was swearing at her or at the amplifier, so to clarify that, she asked in her timid little-girl voice - "You fuck me?"

For a fraction of a second, I thought my dreams had been answered, but then I came back to reality and realized that she was only trying to ask if I were directing that swear word at her. Recovering my composure, I quickly explained what I had done and said that I was only cursing at myself.

Fearing that the Chinese might think I had sabotaged their amplifier, I began dismantling the transformer, something that a technician normally never does. I was fortunate enough to find the area inside where the insulation had been burned by the high voltage arcing across and was then able to repair it. The next day, everything was working fine, and I felt that I had given myself a reprieve.

On March 25th, I wrote a letter to my sisters Barb and Ethel. In it, I was a little discouraged and said that I expected the war to last another two to four years. Operation Little Switch, for the return of the sick and wounded POWs, was going to start in less than a month and none of us had any inkling, despite listening carefully to Radios Moscow and Peking every day. This showed again how well the Chinese could control news when they wanted to.

In a previous letter, my sister Barb had enclosed a black and white negative as a joke. But I managed to turn the tables on her by asking Shen, the camp interpreter, to make a print for me, which I then sent back to her.

I first met Shen when I moved to Camp Headquarters in the fall of 1951, where he often interpreted for me in matters relating to the PA system. As I got to know him a little better, he told a little about his life back in China. He said that his father had been the president of the Bank of Shanghai and they had been very wealthy. As a youth he had his own car and when not partying, he liked to play the rice market, which was similar to our Commodities Market.

As I listened to Shen, I sometimes got the impression that he was more than a little nostalgic for the old days, but he was always quick to correct such impressions by saying that the people were now much better off under Communism than they had been under the old system. He said it, but I didn't think there was a lot of conviction in his voice.

Not long after I met him, I saw Shen walking near my room at headquarters eating an orange. He had then broken off a section and threw it about 50 feet through the air in my direction. I caught it, but it would have made no difference to me if it had hit the ground, I would have eaten it anyway. I thought his action had been a little insolent and a little patronizing, but I wasn't going to refuse a piece of an orange, in the winter of 1952, in a POW camp in North Korea of all places. I never saw anyone else, Chinese or POW, eating oranges, or any other type of fresh fruit during the first years in camp. Shen obviously had some connections.

Shen was also one of the few Chinese with his own camera, which looked like a Leica. In addition, he had a darkroom somewhere at Headquarters where he developed the film and made enlarged prints. We would often see him around camp taking pictures of POWs or Chinese friends of his, especially at sporting events.

One day as he walked by my squad room in 2nd Company, he stopped and stuck his head in the door to ask how things were going. Then out of the blue, he said he had a puzzle for me, which went as follows: You have 12 coins but one is counterfeit and will be either heavier or lighter than the others. With only three tries of a balance scale, determine which coin is false and also whether it is heavy or light. He said if I could figure that out, he would give me a pound of candy. This was the winter of 1953 when the Chinese were throwing candy around right and left, but I was still intrigued.

I accepted the challenge, and went off in a corner with paper and pencil, and after a few hours I had it solved. It turned out to be a fairly difficult problem, so when I gave Shen the solution, he seemed a little surprised, but he gave me the bag of candy. As with all the previous times I had received candy from the Chinese, I took it back to the company and shared it with my squad. They hadn't earned any of it, but I wanted to make damn sure they didn't think I was exploiting my acquaintance with the camp interpreter.

I often wondered why Shen gave me that challenge. It was almost as if he were testing me, but for what? I always knew Shen was sharp, but I was a little surprised to learn later that he hadn't been a playboy all his life, but had taught Physics at Peking University.

Shortly after I got out of the hospital in March, The Chinese gave the whole camp more shots. We had been given shots the previous year when their Germ Warfare program started and now we were getting some boosters. At the same time, the Chinese issued each of us a shot record which looked very much like the ones we had received from the Army. The shot record supposedly listed all the different shots we had received since becoming a POW, but I couldn't tell when each shot had been given.

The shots were of three types; a Vaccine Vari Alae, Tetra Vaccine and Plague! The last shot, for Plague, was especially interesting. It meant that either the Chinese really believed that the US was engaged in germ warfare, or else they just gave us the shots as part of the game they were playing.

The Chinese doctors also performed a limited number of medical experiments on a few POWs. I talked to a POW one day who told us that a Chinese doctor had asked him if they could perform a minor operation to insert "monkey glands" or "goat glands" in his side. The doctor assured him that these glands would do wonderful things for him and the operation would not be painful.

The POW said he and several other men had willingly agreed to the operations and he even lifted his shirt to show a group of us his fresh stitches covering a slightly raised inflamed area on his lower right side. When I talked to him a few weeks later, he said that he had developed an infection which subsequently had cleared-up, but that he had noticed no difference due to the gland, whatever it was.

Figure 43: Buddhist Temple similar to the hospital in POW camp

CHAPTER FORTY-SEVEN

Suspense

With no warning, in mid-April, the Chinese announced that there would be a prisoner exchange for the sick and wounded. There was an immediate atmosphere of anticipation. Could this be the end finally? Over the years we had often over reacted with foolish joy at rumors which later turned out to be false or over blown. Now that we had a bonafide indication that the end was near, many men became more subdued and introspective as if afraid that an expression of elation might jeopardize the moment.

As the first news of returnees began to circulate, we were generally in agreement, but some of the men selected did not seem that sick. One man had lost both feet due to frostbite, others were crippled due to their wounds and one man in particular deserved to be released early, he was the one I had met in the hospital a month earlier, near death with severe constipation.

But there were a few others who most believed should not have been released ahead of some we knew to be very sick. One man in my squad was very ill with active tuberculosis and apparently wasn't sent to the hospital because they couldn't do anything for him. He was gaunt and still losing weight and everyone in the company thought he should have been sent back.

A couple of the guys released at Little Switch, who did not appear to be really ill, were thought to be progressives, and may have been cynically selected by the Chinese so their favorable reports might partially counteract some of the unfavorable stories they knew the other POWs would be telling.

Operation "Little Switch" for repatriation of the sick and wounded began on April 20, 1953, and was completed on May 3rd. A total of 149 American, 32 British and others were turned over at Panmunjom. (**Blair**, *The Forgotten War*, pp 972).

After the short-lived euphoria of Little Switch, things rapidly deteriorated. What little news we got from the radio sounded like both sides had returned to a stalemated situation again. Still we remained optimistic for an agreement maybe within a year as opposed my pessimistic guess at two to four years, made only a month earlier.

Earlier in the spring, our captors had resumed the yearly series of the athletic events that would culminate in another camp-wide set of Olympic Games. As usual, I had no interest in participating, but I was required to handle all the electrical and public address wiring. Everything was very primitive and I had to make do with whatever materials were at hand.

I remember that for one event, they wanted some lights out on the edge of a field. I had wire, hammer, nails and wooden posts, but no insulators; so I just nailed the wire to the fresh cut, green pine posts. When I hooked it up, nothing worked and in addition, the wire and post started to smoke. I was surprised that green wood could conduct electricity so well.

In another case, I was faced with the touchy problem of getting 110 volt AC power from one side of the busy highway to the PA system on the other. In order to clear the tops of the large trucks, I had to string the wire over a bunch of telephone wires but below the high voltage distribution wires, which I guessed carried somewhere between 12,000 and 30,000 volts.

Then I did one of the dumbest things I have ever done in my entire life. I tied a rock on one end of my wire and tried to flip it just over the telephone wires while remaining well below the high voltage. After several frustrating attempts, I saw my next try heading right for the high tension wires and immediately let go of the wire.

There was a big flash as my wire contacted the 30,000 volts and conducted the current back down to the surface of the road, where the wire continued to dance and writhe while emitting tremendous sparks. At that moment, a POW standing nearby, whom I did not know, shouted that he was an electrician and would help as he ran toward the dangling wire and reached for it with his bare hands. I literally screamed at him to not touch the wire. I told him he would be instantly electrocuted. He then looked surprised and frightened. I really think he knew nothing about electricity, and had only been trying to be helpful.

I wondered what to do for a moment, and then I told someone to get me some heavy, dry planks to stand on, while I guarded the wire. When they came back with several old, dry boards, I placed them on top of each other next to the still arcing wire and stepped on top. I then grasped my pliers carefully by its insulated handle and flicked the pliers across the hot wire. I felt nothing, so I guessed that it was probably okay. I then reached up as high as I could and cut the dangling wire so that it would be more difficult for someone to contact it.

After that, I asked the Chinese to call the Koreans and have them remove the wire before somebody got killed. After a while, a North Korean linesman came by and removed my wire after turning the power off. We then strung our wire on a couple of poles over the road in the proper way.

The news from Panmunjom was usually depressing, but yet conditions kept improving in camp as if our captors knew of something they weren't telling us. We were now getting issued regular rations of sugar, tea, candy, soap, tailor-made cigarettes, tooth paste and toilet paper and we had also been issued handkerchiefs, socks, extra underwear and more blankets. One morning we were given bowls of warm bean milk and then the cooks brought out large tubs of long deep-fried twists; which tasted just like stretched-out doughnuts. There was a near riot, as each man fought to get his share. After that, we got the "doughnuts" once a week. The Chinese were clearly piling on the goodies in order to try to make a belatedly good impression, which only reinforced our suspicions that something was up.

The rations were usually delivered by our Chinese platoon interpreter, "Buttercup." Buttercup was a male, but his walk was very effeminate, and used to drive one or two of our sex-starved fellow inmates to distraction; hence the name, "Buttercup." One day while doling out some new socks and underwear, he made the surprising statement that it originally had only cost the Chinese three cents in American per month to support each POW. This seemed incredible at first, but then we remembered that all we ever got back in 1951 was sorghum, beans, and a few turnips, while hundreds of guys died.

As the big second annual Olympic Games got underway that summer, my squad leader Shepard began winning right and left. He won the shot put, log toss, decathlon, hundred meter dash, and several others which I have forgotten. In keeping with the new atmosphere of affluence in camp, the Chinese were outdoing themselves in the prizes they were giving.

Shepard had won several beautiful silk pillow cases, a set of printed silk pictures, an ivory fan and a leather wallet, among other things. I immediately began dickering with him for as many of the above prizes as I could.

Now one should know that Shepard was not only one of the biggest and toughest guys in camp, he was also one of the most ardent reactionaries. The two of us used to argue, but he was just too easy-going and likable to get mad or violent, so we got along fine.

Well anyway, all I had to trade was my sugar, tea and cigarette rations, but both Shepard and I knew that we might not be POWs much longer, so there probably wouldn't be enough rations for the duration of our stay to pay for the prizes I wanted at the going rate. I, in turn, knew that Shepard (the good reactionary that he was) wouldn't be caught dead going through Panmunjom with any of those prizes.

So, after a little bargaining, we settled on one pair of socks, one month's sugar, two months cigarettes and two candy rations for the set of prints and one pillow case. By the end of the Olympics, Shepard had won a couple of more pillow cases and a fan which I wanted very much. Since the Peace Talks at that moment, seemed to be looking up, I took a gamble and traded all my cigarette rations for the rest of my time as a POW, and he accepted.

Things were now getting more relaxed in camp, and the Chinese seemed to be more cheerful. Someone even said they thought they had seen our old nemesis Horse Face smile. However, the Chinese were being very cagey about the news from Panmunjom. Many days, we would not get to hear Radio Moscow or Peking over the PA system.

Since the Chinese wouldn't tell us anything, we all began to monitor the sky very closely, and if no one saw any vapor trails overhead one day, then the rumors would start to fly, but then the following day the jets would always return.

For over a year, I had been trying to learn Chinese on my own. Whenever I learned a new word, I would write it down in a small notebook that I always carried with me. I would also listen carefully when they talked and then practice repeating the words and phrases later. The Chinese said that there were hundreds of different dialects in China and that many Chinese were unable to understand one another in their native dialects, so they were trying to standardize on the "Peking dialect." Whenever I learned a word, I tried to make sure that I was hearing and speaking only the Peking dialect.

One night, I had to return to camp headquarters to work on the PA, so after supper, instead of asking the interpreter to escort me there, I decided to try it on my own. It was a very black night as I approached the guard at the south end of camp, outside the British company. As expected, the guard called out, "*Sha Ahh!*" which means "who's there?" I answered, in Chinese, "Me, from 2nd Company," at which, the guard became very peeved and replied, again in Chinese, something to the effect, "What the hell do you mean, Me from 2nd Company?"

I knew that the guard had a flashlight, but I also knew that they hated to waste the batteries, so I continued my bluff with the response, "I'm from 2nd company and going to headquarters." At that, the guard grumbled, "Haw," which means okay and continued grumbling what sounded like some choice Chinese cuss words at a much lower level of voice.

I continued on down the road until I saw the light at Headquarters. As I walked in, Chemeeduh greeted me and asked how I had gotten there. I told the truth, that I had just walked past the guard after telling him where I was from and where I was going. She said no more about it and when I was done, I returned to my company the same way, only this time when the guard asked, "Who's there?" I only answered, "Me," and continued on.

After getting past the guard at night, I thought I might try it in daylight. So one morning I headed out and when I came to the guard I told him that I was from 2nd Company and was going to headquarters to repair the radio. I only knew the word for 'radio' so that's what I said and the guard just shrugged his shoulders as I walked past. I probably only got away with it because the guard, also had been hearing the news from Panmunjom, and by then he could care less.

Something was up, I could feel it! Planes had come over that day, but the mood of the Chinese seemed to have changed. It was near the end of July.

Lights out was at 9 P.M., but as usual, everybody in the squad was awake. We often lay in our bunks, telling stories until 10 or 11 P.M., unless a guard came by and told us to be quiet. It was probably around 10 P.M., when someone came hurrying through the company shouting something in Chinese. This in itself was very unusual, so I listened carefully and picked up enough to understand that, "the war is over and the POWs are going home." I heard the same thing being repeated in the adjoining companies.

I leaped out of bed and stuck my head out the door so see what was going on, but saw only a couple of flashlights bobbing in the darkness. I told the squad what I had heard, or thought I had heard. They all wanted to believe me, but they weren't going to start leaping up and down until they had heard it themselves in English from the Chinese.

I didn't sleep much that night, and the next morning at the first chance, I asked our platoon interpreter, "Buttercup," but he just smiled and gave me a non-answer. I then made an excuse to go to Headquarters and asked Shen but he was even more coy than Buttercup.

That day, no planes came over. I cornered one of our Chinese cooks, who spoke no English, and asked him if the war was over. He nodded his head "yes." With that, I began going all over; first the company, and then the camp telling everyone I knew. I was getting a lot of guys excited, but most just didn't know if they should believe me.

A few more days went by. There were no more planes in the sky, and at night we hadn't heard any B29s. Now I was sure that there had at least been an armistice. I guessed that the Chinese hadn't told us anything because they were afraid that we might riot. I continued to bug Shen until he as much as admitted that I was right, but he said I shouldn't spread it around. So, I returned to my squad and continued spreading it around.

Finally, our Company Commander fell us out and announced that an Armistice had been signed and that we would all be going home in a few days. A quiet murmur rolled through the assembled men, and then there was absolute silence as everyone listened attentively for further details.

We were dismissed, and I headed back to my room. One or two guys let out a whoop or a rebel yell and ran, full tilt, down to the river and jumped in, clothes and all. Most however, just gathered in small knots and quietly talked or returned to their rooms, lost in their own thoughts. We had waited so long for this day, and now that it had arrived, we didn't quite know what to do.

That night, the Chinese issued each man a small bottle of wine. I still owed Shepard my sugar, cigarette and candy rations, so I gave him my wine in partial compensation. I didn't really mind, because I just was in no mood that evening to get drunk; there were too many things to think about. However, quite a few guys did get drunk that night, but they were very quiet and subdued drunks. I think the Chinese were pleasantly surprised, since they probably expected all hell to break loose.

The next day we were all ready to go, despite the hangovers, and the camp began to bustle with impatience. Another assembly was called, and the Commander announced that there would be a delay, because we couldn't leave until the Red Cross had delivered packages to us. Now there *were* some ominous rumblings. We saw no need for Red Cross packages and many men were getting angry at the thought of keeping us in camp a few more days for such a frivolous reason.

One of the lesser known reactionary POWs in our company came by the room late one evening and said he wanted to talk to me outside, down by the river. I couldn't imagine what he wanted with me, so I was a little apprehensive. It was after 10 P.M. and pitch -black as I slowly made my way down past the latrine. I made out a form and then called his name. We'll call him 'Archie'.

Archie then verified whom he was talking to and came right to the point. He said he had been told by the Chinese that he and certain other reactionaries, who had committed crimes, had been sentenced to prison and would be kept in China at hard labor until their time was up.

Archie's voice was quivering as he then admitted that he was the one who had thrown a rock at me about a year earlier. He said he was sorry and asked me to forgive him and then he asked if I would go to the Chinese and put in a good word for him.

My immediate reaction was anger; not because of the stone throwing incident, but anger that he would think that I had such influence. What the hell did he think I was? a stooge or puppet for the Chinese? In addition, he seemed to think I was the one who had ratted on him.

I struggled to control my anger as I told him that (one), "I did not have that kind of influence with the Chinese" and (two), "I had never ratted on him or anybody else." And besides, if I had known it was him at the time, I would never have let the Chinese rob me of the satisfaction of beating the hell out of him. And furthermore, I said, trying to intercede on his behalf would be a form of collaboration and not much different from someone trying to influence the Chinese against him. After a few moments I simmered down a little and told Archie that the rock hadn't hurt anything but my feelings and that I wasn't the least bit mad anymore.

In the following days, the Chinese made it official that certain reactionaries had been given prison terms and they implied that they might not be released with all the other POWs. I didn't think that was right at all because most of them hadn't done anything but shoot off their mouths, and I had done a little of that myself.

Then another bombshell was dropped. One of the progressives told me that he had heard that some of the American POWs were going to refuse repatriation. My first thought was a fear that this was going to become another monkey wrench in the works down at Panmunjom and possibly delay our release. Then I couldn't imagine how anyone could not want to return home, even if you couldn't get along with your family, one could always go somewhere else. But more important, China was an alien culture and an alien ideology.

Even if they thought they agreed with the ideology at the moment, it should have been clear that they would not be able to disagree later. The clues were everywhere. It's true, we were POWs, but in listening to the Chinese themselves, and the Russians and by reading their magazines and newspapers, it was obvious to me that no one ever disagreed with the "party line." Another clue was the adulation heaped on Mao and Stalin. If one were to believe their newspapers, you would think that neither one of them ever made a mistake or were ever anything less than the perfect role models for their people.

I remembered one article in a Russian magazine which asserted that Stalin was a genius in Science, Engineering, Agriculture, Philosophy, Military Tactics, etc., etc. No human being is that perfect. In over two years as a POW, I had never heard the slightest hint, or the faintest breath of criticism of Mao, Stalin or the Communist system. Nothing in this world or any other world is that perfect.

Our Red Cross packages finally came. We received American-made cigarettes, tooth paste and brushes, razors, towels and DIAL soap. Some of the men were ticked-off. They had kept us POWs while we waited for DIAL soap, as if they were afraid we were going to smell bad when arriving at Panmunjom. Some guys said, "To hell with it, just let us go home!"

CHAPTER FORTY-EIGHT

Release

The next day, after our Red Cross parcels had arrived, the trucks began to arrive. Men began climbing on the trucks carrying the small Chinese Army issue khaki shoulder bags stuffed with whatever they wanted to take home. In most cases they were taking only a towel, shaving kit, tooth brush and the DIAL soap which we had all waited so long for.

There seemed to be no order to the departures. As trucks arrived, POWs would be loaded on, and they would depart in a cloud of dust. The Chinese didn't even appear to be counting noses. They probably figured that no one needed any urging in this case.

Our company interpreter called me to headquarters in the morning and asked which truck I wanted to go on. He said they were trying to separate people who didn't get along so that there wouldn't be any fights on the way down. I said I didn't care; it could just as well be the last truck as long they made sure I got there on time. Then he said we should just go back to our squads and wait until they came to get us.

The trucks kept coming and going intermittently all day long. I went down by the road and watched them loading-up. As each truck took off heading south, I could see hundreds of Korean civilians, mostly kids, lining the road waving and hollering. As each truck passed a group of kids, I saw why they were giving us such a joyous send-off. The men in the trucks were throwing cigarettes, candy, clothing, shoes, towels; everything that they didn't want. They were even throwing the DIAL soap.

I returned to my squad to wait. As night fell, we had our last supper in camp. Throughout the night, the Chinese kept coming by with lists of names, (they knew exactly which squad each person was in), and quietly calling the next ones to go. They were better organized than I had thought earlier.

Very few were sleeping that night but finally I thought I would just take a little cat nap. When I woke up, it was daylight and it was very quiet. I jumped up and went outside. The camp was almost deserted, and Davis, the POW who had helped me set-up the PA system, seemed to be the only other one in our company.

I then checked some of the other companies, and they too, were almost deserted. There had been almost 2000 men in our camp and apparently the Chinese didn't have quite enough trucks to take everyone the first day and night. The few of us who remained in camp would now have to wait for one of the first trucks out to make it back. I was beginning to get a bit nervous, but there was nothing to do but wait.

Back at my old squad room, I sat down on my bunk and glanced around the room I had called home for over a year, now deserted. I got up and began walking through the other empty rooms in my company. Everywhere, the floors and bunks were littered with all the things we had once prized, such as; an old GI field jacket, a prized pair of lace-up paratrooper boots, porcelain chow bowls, a homemade chess set, sugar rations, carefully crafted homemade knives and one of the most treasured, a stainless steel GI spoon. When we had first been captured, many of us had to eat using our bare hands to scoop food out of the bowl or tin can, and those who had a GI spoon, received many an envious glance.

Late in the afternoon, an interpreter came to the company and escorted Davis and I to Camp Headquarters. As we followed him, I glanced around the now deserted camp for the last time. There had been some good times, but somehow only visions of the bad times filled my consciousness.

When we arrived at Headquarters, Johnny Ford along with eight to 10 other guys who I didn't know, were waiting next to a medium sized open bed truck with wooden side railings. Everyone piled on eagerly along with a young Chinese guard carrying a rifle, with bayonet fixed as usual. Our interpreter climbed in next to the driver and we started off as the sun was setting.

There was still a small band of dedicated Korean kids lining the road so I fished in my bag and began tossing candy, cigarettes and extra clothing as we passed. I finally reached in and withdrew my one unused bar of DIAL soap, and then I selected a smiling urchin who looked like he could use the DIAL more than I, and carefully tossed it into his waiting hands. He looked very appreciative.

I glanced back one last time at Chungsung, Korea and at the hospital on the hill, and the hundreds of men we were leaving behind. At such a moment, I should have been deliriously happy, yet instead, I was perilously close to crying.

We traveled all night, without stopping, over bone-jarring, dusty, washboard roads. Our driver drove much faster than I would have. Much of the road was narrow and mountainous, with numerous switchbacks and no guard rails anyplace. Often the beams of our headlights would stab out into a black void with no visible bottom. No doubt, our driver had crawled over these same roads many nights during the war when headlights were not allowed, and now that he had the luxury of lights, I felt that he had abandoned caution altogether.

At first we all stood up clutching the side rails and swaying with each curve, but soon our legs became so tired, that we were forced to sit down on the hard floor. We soon found that sitting was even worse than standing so we then tried crouching. After a couple of hours, the ride became shear torture. If at that moment, I had been given the option of walking to Panmunjom, even if it took a month, I would have jumped at it.

Just when I didn't think I could take it anymore, the driver stopped for a short break, and then it was back to the same bone-jarring torture. We kept it up all night with only short breaks every two or three hours. It was a black night, but occasionally we could catch glimpses in our headlights of the wreckage of war; bomb craters, pieces of trucks and shells of houses.

After sunrise, the road dropped down into a broad valley and we saw that we were passing through the ruins of a large city. It was Pyongyang, the capital of North Korea. Everything was flattened for miles in all directions. The streets had been cleared of rubble, but there were no houses visible anywhere. On the eastern side of this desolated valley, I could see a large building, like a school, still standing on the hill. It seemed relatively undamaged and I wondered why our B29s had spared it, but nothing else.

About midmorning we finally pulled off the main road and drove a hundred yards up a side road to a small isolated building. We were going to get a welcome long break and a breakfast of cold steamed bread and cold canned beef. A month earlier this would have been a treat, but now we knew that we would soon be getting much better food.

When finished with breakfast, our interpreter, who had a camera, decided to line us up for a group picture with the small house in the background. After a couple of snapshots, Ford, who could never stay serious for long, asked the guard to get in the picture with us. For a final picture, Johnny then asked to borrow the guard's rifle. I can still picture Johnny Ford standing there with a big silly grin on his face, and holding this Jap rifle with fixed bayonet next to a slightly uncertain Chinese soldier. We knew then, that the war was over.

We only got about an hour break and then it was back to our torture chamber on wheels. The roads south of Pyongyang were not as mountainous as earlier, but this only allowed the driver to increase his speed and if anything, the bouncing and jarring got worse.

Toward evening we arrived in Kaesong, a small village just north of Panmunjom, where we were allowed to clean up and shave, and then we were given fresh blue uniforms and a good meal. Many of the POWs from Camp 1 were still there along with many others from other camps, waiting to be repatriated. We appeared to be the last to arrive from the north.

One group who came down the day before said they had been lucky. Their truck ran off a mountain road and then a couple hundred feet down a very steep embankment into a river. Some of the guys were able to bail out, but most rode the truck all the way down. They were calling their driver a hero, because he stayed with the truck and steered it straight down the slope, otherwise it probably would have rolled over and some of them might have been killed. For his efforts, the driver got all his front teeth knocked out.

The next day, August 13, 1953, I got up, washed, shaved and had breakfast; I then climbed into a Chinese truck for the short ride to Panmunjom. There we transferred to small Red Cross ambulances for another very short ride across "Freedom Bridge," and we were then dropped off at nearby tents.

The area was literally crawling with officers, from "Bird Colonels" on down to ordinary lieutenants. The reception was bewildering, and I seemed to have almost lost the ability to speak. Everything began to blur together, then I was ushered into a large quiet olive drab tent, and I could begin to get ahold of myself.

First, we were given brand-new fatigues, underwear, socks and shoes; we then carried everything into another tent where we stripped down and got rid of our POW garb. After the delicious hot showers, we put on our new fatigues and began to feel like Americans again.

Next, the Red Cross took my picture, and allowed me to send a telegram to my mother with a short message and immediately after that, we were led into another tent for chow. And what chow! There was a line of cooks preparing just about anything one could want, and if you had a special request, they usually could rustle it up for you.

Figure 44: American Red Cross photo at release

I ordered a big thick T Bone steak, mashed potatoes, brown gravy with vegetables and then for dessert I had apple pie a-la-mode plus vanilla ice cream smothered in crushed strawberries. And I ate every bit of it, and washed it all down with a big glass of cold milk.

Following the meal, we were taken into a small tent, two or three at a time where soldiers went through all our belongings. When they encountered the five silk pillow cases, silk prints and Chinese Fan, I saw a few raised eyebrows. I quickly pointed out that I had not received them from the Chinese, but instead I had gotten them from fellow POWs by trading cigarettes and sugar rations. They still looked skeptical.

That summer, I had saved a few dozen seeds from the vines we called "figs," and had packed them away in my bag, hoping to take them home to start my own fig orchard. When the soldier found them, he confiscated them as illegal plant material. He also confiscated the medicine I had been taking for rheumatic fever and a small notebook. The notebook was empty, so I didn't know why he took it. They gave me a piece of paper which said that I was "bailing" these things to the Army, but I never saw them again. They let me keep another notebook in which I had been phonetically writing down a few Chinese words.

I threw my few souvenirs along with some letters and photos I had received in camp into a duffle bag and shipped them home. They didn't do a body search on any of us, so they missed the homemade knife I was carrying in my pocket. Most of the men had made their own knives in camp, not intending them to be used as weapons, but just for cutting bread, whittling wood or whatever.

By now, they were moving us along very rapidly. All the previous procedures probably hadn't taken over two or three hours. We were next put on a large Sikorsky helicopter, flown to Inchon, and billeted in a big enclosed compound with several hundred other former POWs. After getting settled with a bunk, I got a cash advance and bought a Canon Camera in the small PX located within the compound, and immediately began taking pictures of all the guys I had recently been incarcerated with.

The following day we were taken to Inchon Harbor and then by a small Navy craft out to the General Hase, a typical, large Army transport of the type I had been on at least three times previously. Before, they had always packed us down in the hold like a bunch of cattle, but this time we were placed in large, bright, cheery rooms on the upper decks with large windows and a view of the ocean. I guessed there were about 100 guys in each room.

As we pulled out of the harbor, debriefing and interrogation began almost immediately. I would get called into a small stateroom and typically there would be one or two officers present. They asked me questions by the hour about activities in camp, and who did what. They wanted to know who the "progressives" were and what they had done.

Then they began on me. They said some of my fellow POWs had accused me of collaborating with the enemy, of being overly friendly with the Chinese and of signing petitions. I explained all about my installing and maintaining the PA system and how I had also helped wire the camp for electricity. I said I didn't consider that collaboration and I would do it all over again if I had to.

And as for being overly friendly, I was only friendly to those who were friendly to me. A few of the most ardent reactionaries had seemed to go out of their way to be unfriendly and discourteous and all they got for it was a lot of trouble and misery. We all knew that the Chinese were trying to brainwash, or at least influence us, so it was not surprising that they would select camp personnel, who were friendly and outgoing. The great majority of us had tried to be friendly and civil when we were treated with civility. And we were, after all, prisoners of war. If these reactionaries wanted to be such heroes, why hadn't they gone down in a hail of lead; or if out of ammunition, they could have always fixed bayonet and died as they charged the enemy one last time.

Instead, when they were forced by an ultimatum to die or drop their guns, they "chickened out" just as I had done. I often felt that some of these "latter day heroes" were really feeling subconscious guilt pangs because they had surrendered, and now they were trying to make up for it.

And as for the petitions, by then most of us had enough of war, so when the camp was strafed and bombed twice by B26s, it didn't seem such a bad idea to sign a petition against "Indiscriminate Bombing of POW Camps." If you had any doubts, the Chinese helped you make up your mind by lining us up to sign them. And it couldn't hurt to at least let those B26 jockeys know that maybe they ought to sharpen up their bombsights a bit. We didn't mind if they dropped bombs, we just didn't think they helped the war effort by dropping them on us.

The Army continued to question me during the return voyage for several days. One day, the interrogator would be a "nice guy" and then maybe that afternoon, I would get a "mean guy." Somewhere I had read about this "trick," and I soon caught on. All in all, I thought the questioning was interesting but thorough, and I was glad to have the chance to explain my side of the story. In between interrogation, I was also given various psychological tests and an IQ test. After the IQ test, one of the "nice guys" told me that I had scored extremely high, but he didn't say how high that was.

About one week out of Inchon, we began to hit some very rough weather. It was a black overcast night and I was getting some air by the railing when Ford came by and said he had heard a rumor that there were three "reactionaries" on board who were looking for a progressive, (any progressive would do) to throw overboard. Johnny mentioned their names, and said he thought they were from Camp 5 at Pyoktong. He mentioned three names, but I didn't know them and they couldn't have known me.

As I returned to my room, three men there confronted me and said they were "going to get me." At that point, I pulled out my knife as I backed into a corner next to my bunk. One came toward me as a second tried to flank me by crawling over the bunk.

I was scared, but then suddenly something within me just flipped like a switch. One of them stood in front of me. I wanted to kill him! Every muscle and nerve in my body seemed to vibrate from the tension. At that moment I wanted nothing more in this world than to plunge my knife into his gut and twist it in his entrails until the warm blood gushed out over my fist. There was no conscience, like some small voice telling me it was wrong, there was only a powerful, insistent urge telling me to do it!

It was pure rage, but rage tempered by my minds tactical evaluation of the situation. If I had lunged forward, I would have left my back open to attack by the two to my left and right. He had halted in front of me and began to slowly back up. I taunted him. I now had become aware of the room. It was absolutely quiet and everyone else had backed well away from us. No one seemed to be trying to help them or help me.

Suddenly an officer appeared in the doorway and in a loud commanding voice told us to "knock it off." My three assailants slunk off to the side and the officer strode toward me without the slightest hesitation. He asked for my knife and I gave it to him. Then he told me to pick up my gear and come with him.

I followed him to the ship's dispensary where I was assigned a bunk for the night. For the next few days I slept and got all my meals in one small room in the dispensary. There were only four bunks and two other "patients." The other two patients appeared very healthy and one said he had been a POW in Camp 5. We started to shoot the breeze and after a few minutes, it became obvious that neither of my cell mates had ever been POWs.

Maybe they thought I was nuts. Maybe I was. After I had calmed down, I had time to think about what had happened. It was very sobering to realize that a vicious animal lurked within me, only waiting for the right trigger to release him. I realized that I could easily kill another human being; the only requirement was that I had to hate that person. In fact, if I had been taught to hate the Chinese while I was on the front line, maybe even I could have been a "good soldier."

Apparently they finally realized that I wasn't a danger to anyone, at least now that they had my knife, so I was allowed out on deck and the run of the ship. But evenings, I still had to return to my "cell" to sleep.

About midday on August 29th, 1953, I sighted land. We slowed outside the Golden Gate Bridge and picked up a pilot. There was much cheering and a lot of guys wiping their eyes as we slid under the bridge and docked at Fort Mason near downtown San Francisco.

Everybody was topside as the lines were thrown out, then we heard a band amid all the tumult and someone said that Marilyn Monroe was going to sing. All 5000 men immediately rushed to the rail on the dock side and the ship heeled over noticeably. I estimated that 5000 men must have weighed about a million pounds.

I craned my neck and could just make out a cute, little blond in a red dress singing some song that was just audible above the din. I later found out that it wasn't Marilyn after all.

For once, the Army didn't keep us waiting; we were going to be the first off. I grabbed my camera and duffle bag and headed down the gang plank. I was back on US soil again.

Figure 45: Me and Macmillan, Mid-Pacific on Way Home

Figure 46: Left and Center Images: the author and sisters in Minnesota, in January 1951 before going to Korea; Right image: the author's mother in 1970.

Bibliography

Blair, Clay. *Beyond Courage.* Random House Publishing Group, 1983.

Blair, Clay. *The Forgotten War: America in Korea 1950-1953.* Doubleday, 1987.

Brown, Wallace L. *The Endless Hours: My Two and a Half Years as a Prisoner of the Chinese Communists.* W.W. Norton Co. 1961

Fehrenbach, T. R. *This Kind of War.* Bantam Books 1991.

Flintham, Victor. *Air Wars and Aircraft.* 1990.

Goulden, Joseph C. *Korea: The Untold Story of The War.* McGraw-Hill, 1982.

Knox, Donald. *The Korean War: Uncertain Victory.* Harcourt Brace Jovanovich, 1988.

Lech, Raymond B. *Broken Soldiers,* University of Illinois Press.

Munroe, Lt.Clark.C. *The Second United States Infantry Division in Korea.* Tappan Printing Co. Ltd. Tokyo, Japan.

Rowley, Arden A. *U.S. Prisoners of War in the Korean War.* Turner Publishing Co..

Travelers Korea, Korea National Tourism Corp. 1991.

Wills, Morris R., *Turncoat, the Story of Morris R. Wills.* Pocket Books.

References: Figures
(Maps, Photos and Drawings)

Figure	Description	Source
1	Korea and Route to POW Camp (map modified by author)	Munroe, Lt.Clark.C. *The Second United States Infantry Division in Korea.* Tappan Printing Co. Ltd. Tokyo, Japan
2	M1 Carbine .30 Cal	Wikimedia Commons from Swedish Army Museum through the Digital Museum (http://www.digitaltmuseum.se)
3	M101 105 mm Howitzer	Wikimedia Commons in public domain from US Government.
4	M1 Garand 30.06	Wikimedia Commons from Swedish Army Museum through the Digital Museum (http://www.digitaltmuseum.se)

5	Area of 2nd Infantry April & May '51 (map modified by author)	Munroe, Lt.Clark.C. *The Second United States Infantry Division in Korea.* Tappan Printing Co. Ltd. Tokyo, Japan
6	Truck, GMC Short Wheelbase Cargo w/o Winch, 2 1/2 Ton, 6x6	Wikimedia Commons in public domain from US Government.
7	Browning Automatic Rifle	Wikimedia Commons in public domain from US Government.
8	A M-20 75 mm recoilless rifle being fired during the Korean War	Wikimedia Commons in public domain from US Government.
9	WWII era 60mm U.S. M2 Mortar	Wikimedia Commons from Curiosandrelics; http://commons.wikimedia.org/wiki/File:M2-Mortar.jpg
10	Sherman Tank	Wikimedia Commons in public domain from US Government. US Army Photo by PFC Gray in the National Archive

11	Eastern Front, Late April	Ebb And Flow, November 1950 - July 1951 - The United States Army in the Korean War, Center of Military History, United States Army, Washington, D.C., 1990. Scanned by the Korean War Project in 1995 for the Center of Military History; http://www.koreanwar2.org/kwp2/cmh/ebb_and_flow.pdf
12	Russian 76mm Howitzer	Wikimedia Commons in the public domain from S. Filatov; http://en.wikipedia.org/wiki/File:ZiS3_nn.jpg.
13	2nd Division on May 16-18, 1951	Ebb And Flow, November 1950 - July 1951 - The United States Army in the Korean War, Center of Military History, United States Army, Washington, D.C., 1990. Scanned by the Korean War Project in 1995 for the Center of Military History; http://www.koreanwar2.org/kwp2/cmh/ebb_and_flow.pdf

14	Below Soyang, May 1951	Ebb And Flow, November 1950 - July 1951 - The United States Army in the Korean War, Center of Military History, United States Army, Washington, D.C., 1990. Scanned by the Korean War Project in 1995 for the Center of Military History; http://www.koreanwar2.org/kwp2/cmh/ebb_and_flow.pdf
15	Vought F4U Corsair	Wikimedia Commons licensed under Creative Commons to Gerry Metzler; http://www.flickr.com/photos/flyguy71/7427977930/sizes/l/in/photostream/
16	Soviet army ppsh 41 (Chinese Burp Gun)	Wikimedia Commons from Lposka http://en.wikipedia.org/wiki/File:PPSh-41_from_soviet.jpg
17	Missing telegram	Author
18	Letter returned	Author
19	May 18 ambush when recaptured on May 23rd	US Army Photo by Cpl R.T. Turner in the National Archives.

20	North American advanced AT-6 Texan advanced trainer	Wikimedia Commons in public domain from US Government.
21	A-26 (B-26) Invader Light Bomber	Wikimedia Commons in public domain from US Government.
22	Hwachon Dam (map modified by author)	Ebb And Flow, November 1950 - July 1951 - The United States Army in the Korean War, Center of Military History, United States Army, Washington, D.C., 1990. Scanned by the Korean War Project in 1995 for the Center of Military History; http://www.koreanwar2.org/kwp2/cmh/ebb_and_flow.pdf
23	Typical Korean House Heating System	Author
24	A U.S. Air Force Lockheed P-80A-1-LO Shooting Star	Wikimedia Commons in public domain from US Government.

25	Eighth Army - Spring and Summer '51	Ebb And Flow, November 1950 - July 1951 - The United States Army in the Korean War, Center of Military History, United States Army, Washington, D.C., 1990. Scanned by the Korean War Project in 1995 for the Center of Military History; http://www.koreanwar2.org/kwp2/cmh/ebb_and_flow.pdf
26	37-mm automatic anti-aircraft gun 61-K in Saint Petersburg Artillery museum	Wikimedia Commons from One half 3544; http://en.wikipedia.org/wiki/File:61-K.jpg
27	P-51D-5NA Mustang 44-13357	Wikimedia Commons in public domain from US Government.
28	C119 Flying Boxcar	Wikimedia Commons in public domain from US Government.
29	Camp 1 and Immediate Surroundings	Author
30	First letter home	Author

31	Typical letter home with propaganda address	Author
32	Davis, Mac, Pete and me and the amplifier	Author, from Chinese camp interpreter Shen.
33	Main part of Camp	Author
34	British and American POWs outside the theater	Author, from Chinese camp interpreter Shen.
35	Japanese Rifle	Wikimedia Commons in public domain from US Government.
36	Pre-WWII Japanese Topographic Map	Author courtesy of Seoul Korea University Library.
37	F86 Sabre	Wikimedia Creative Commons under Document License to Paul Maritz. http://commons.wikimedia.org/wiki/File:North_American_F86-01.JPG

38	Chinese Mig 15	Wikimedia Commons in public domain from US Government.
39	F9F Panther Jet	Wikimedia Commons in public domain from US Government.
40	A U.S. Navy Douglas AD-1Q Skyraider	Wikimedia Commons in public domain from US Government.
41	B-29 in flight	Wikimedia Commons in public domain from US Government.
42	WWII Japanese map	Author, courtesy of Seoul Korea University Library.
43	A Buddhist Temple in South Korea	Jimmy McIntyre - Editor HDR One Magazine, http://strange-lands.com [CC-BY-SA-2.0 (http://creativecommons.org/licenses/by-sa/2.0)], via Wikimedia Commons; http://www.flickr.com/photos/73064996@N08/6805469269/

44	American Red Cross photo at release	Author, from American Red Cross
45	Author and Macmillan, Mid-Pacific on Way Home	Author
46	Author and sisters; mother	Author
47	Portrait of the Author (2013)	Chris Epting

Acknowledgements

I want to thank my good friend **Ralph Ricks** for his enthusiastic support and for encouraging me to publish this story which I would not have done if it weren't for him.

I am forever grateful to my late wife and love of my life **Dorothy** for all her love and patience and support throughout our 51 years of marriage; I thank her also for her enormous hard work typing the numerous first drafts of this book on a manual typewriter some 20 years ago, before the days of word processing programs and computers.

Thanks to my daughter **Susan** for copyediting, proofreading, designing and assembling this first published edition of the book; and I thank my other children, **Doreen** and **Jim**, for their love and support.

Many thanks also go to **Mike Farrar** of the **Veterans History Project of the American Red Cross** and to **Lisa Taylor** of the **Library of Congress Veterans History Project** for their interest and help in preserving my Korean War POW story by adding this book, along with an Oral History Interview, to the collection of the **Veterans History Project of the American Folklife Center of the Library of Congress.**

ABOUT THE AUTHOR

Figure 47 Photo of the Author by Chris Epting (2013)

After returning from Korea in Aug '53, the author met his wife to be and enrolled at the University of Minnesota studying Physics. He graduated in '62 with a BS in Physics and accepted a job in southern California at Douglas Aircraft in Flight Guidance Systems Engineering retiring in 1990. He has four children, two boys and two girls.